FOCUS ON

First Certificate

SUE O'CONNELL

Nelson

Thomas Nelson and Sons Ltd
Nelson House   Mayfield Road
Walton-on-Thames   Surrey
KT12 5PL   UK

51 York Place
Edinburgh
EH1 3JD   UK

Thomas Nelson (Hong Kong) Ltd
Toppan Building 10/F
22A Westlands Road
Quarry Bay   Hong Kong

© Sue O'Connell 1987
First published by HarperCollins Publishers 1987
Reprinted 1987, 1988 (twice), 1989 (twice), 1990 (twice), 1991
ISBN 0-00-370051-8
This edition first published by Thomas Nelson and Sons Ltd 1993
ISBN 0-17-556613-5
NPN 9 8 7 6 5 4 3 2 1

Acknowledgements

*The publishers are grateful to the following for permission to reproduce
copyright material:*

The Sunday Express Magazine: page 2; Danny Danziger, pages 15,
19; Robin Cousins, page 184; page 191
The Times: Frank Barrett, page 3; pages 75, 76, 134; Ronald Faux,
pages 178/9
The Sunday Times: Tim Rayment, page 23; John Barnes, page 47;
Peter Watson, pages 52, 53, 56
The Sunday Times Magazine: Maureen Walker, page 24; Rosalind
Plowright, Bill Sirs, Geoff Capes, Sally Oppenheim, page 32
Octopus Publishing Group: *Cooking Step by Step* by Elizabeth
Pomeroy, page 36
The Sunday Telegraph Magazine: Tim Heald, page 39
Private Eye: cartoons on pages 41, 103, 149
Redwood Publishing: *Intercity* by Mike Lancaster, page 42
Central Office of Information: pages 50, 155
The Daily Mirror: page 54; Marjorie Proops, page 165
Wayland (Publishers) Ltd: *Project Earth – Waste Age Man* by
Jonathan Holliman, page 60
Tim Hunkin in the Observer Magazine; pages 64, 152
Friends of the Earth: page 66
The Countryside Commission: pages 68, 69, 70
The New Internationalist: illustrations redrawn by David Mostyn
from an original by Peter Wingham, pages 71, 215
Tomy UK Ltd: page 73
Usborne Publishing Ltd: *Usborne Introduction to the New
Technology*, page 77
The Carphone Company: page 79
Random House UK: *Slow Boats to China* by Gavin Young, published
by Hutchinson, pages 89, 95
The Sunday Express: Mark Elsdon Dew, page 89; David
Hemplemann Adams, page 89; page 134

The Observer: Trisha Greenhalgh, page 91
Good Housekeeping: Edwina Conner, page 105
Mail on Sunday Magazine: page 108
Living Magazine: pages 109, 110
Aberaeron Sea-Life Aquarium: page 115
Association of Welsh Tourist Attractions: page 115
Talyllyn Railway: page 115
Felin Geri Ltd: page 115
Harper and Row Ltd: *The Good Health Guide*, pages 118, 121, 130
The Health Education Council: pages 120, 127; *Minor Illnesses*,
page 185
Bristol Journal: page 134
Transworld Publishers Ltd: *The Book of Narrow Escapes* by Peter
Mason, page 135
Salamander Books Ltd: *Into the Heart of Borneo* by Redmond
O'Hanlon, page 141
HarperCollins Publishers: *Graded English Puzzles No 6* by Lewis
Jones, published by Collins, page 144
BBC Books: *Beat the Teacher* by Clive Doig, page 144
Woman Magazine: Wendy James, page 154; Mervyn Edgecombe,
page 166
The Consumers Association: pages 155, 157
Caliban Books: *The Pools Winners* by Peter Razzell & Stephen
Smith, page 163
Sunday Magazine: Simon Kinnersley, pages 170, 172
The Macmillan Press Ltd: *Family Life* by Olivia Bennett, page 182
The Guardian: Richard Sleight, page 187
Bristol Zoo: page 207

Every effort has been made to trace owners of copyright, but if any
omissions can be rectified, the publishers will be pleased to make
the necessary arrangements.

Photographs

Barnaby's Picture Library: pages 162 (C), 196, 198
Bubbles Picture Library: page 162 (A)
Stuart Boreham Photography: page 57
Camera Press Picture Library: Page 170
Capital Press: page 76
J. Allan Cash Photo Library: pages 87 (D), 104 (right), 109, 121,
147, 162 (B), 202, 204, 206 (right)
Chester Zoo: pages 142, 177
Good Housekeeping: page 105
Hutchison Library: page 77
Image Bank: pages 39, 110, 158 (top), 197 (left & right), 206 (left)
London Express News: page 87 (A & C)
The Military Picture Library: page 66
Network Photographers Jordan: page 197 (centre); Lewis: pages
104 (left), 150, 162 (D); Sparham: page 173
The Observer: page 87 (B)
Arthur Pollock: page 200
Popperfoto: page 119
Rex Features: pages 19, 135, 158 (bottom)
Chris Ridgers Photography: pages 28, 60, 121
Times Newspapers: page 24
Zefa Picture Library: page 121

Illustrations

Angela Barnes: pages 12, 51, 59, 100 (bottom)
Joan Corlass: pages 1, 9, 31 (bottom), 46, 86, 130, 131, 151, 167,
203, 212, 216
Teri Gower: pages 27, 36, 94, 138
David Mostyn: pages 8, 15, 18, 31 (top), 44, 50, 71, 78, 100 (top),
215, 218, 219
Ian West: pages 30, 33, 41, 102, 118, 164

Other artwork by Gina Smart and Mike Strudwick

For my parents

Contents

UNIT 1A Taking a break

▶ Lead-in

What sort of holiday would you choose as a break from studying or working?

1 Look at the pictures below and think about the kind of holidays they represent. Choose **two** that you would prefer and think about the reasons why you would enjoy them. Think also of **one** thing about each holiday which you are not so keen on!

2 Work with a partner. Ask each other about your choices and say what you like about them, and what you are not so fond of. Use the following exchange as an example.

   A Which of the holidays would you enjoy most?
   B Well, I'd prefer . . .

   A What do you like especially about . . .
   B I really enjoy . . .

   A Is there anything you don't like about . . .
   B Well, I don't like . . . very much

3 Now check the Functions Bank on page 208. How many of the expressions did you use or hear? Make a note of the ones you didn't use and try to include them next time.

4 Change partners and discuss your choices again.

5 Report back to the class what your second partner told you.

▶ Text 1   Read the article.

I CAN'T TRAVEL WITHOUT . . .

What are the things you can't do without when you go away?

Patrick Lichfield, the photographer, never goes far without the Olympus Pearlcorder dictating machine which lets him catch up with his correspondence wherever he is. The tiny tapes are either posted to his secretary, Felicity, or he gives them to someone to bring back. The quality is very good but there are often some interesting background noises.

Mel Calman, the cartoonist, jokes about filling his suitcase with tranquillisers and three different kinds of toothbrushes after recent, expensive dental treatment, but it is his diary and sketch-book that are always with him when he is on the move. "I don't keep a diary except when I'm away. I start a new one each trip now since I lost irreplaceable notes on two previous trips on a bus in the States."

Richard Branson, who recently launched Virgin Atlantic Airways, believes in travelling light. "Sun-tan lotion for my nose and my notebooks which are my lifeline. But I will always sling in a pack of cards. I love a game of cards, particularly bridge, canasta or spades, but I'm not a gambler."

Barry Norman, the film critic, who never travels anywhere without his credit card. "The days of anyone being stranded abroad are now over. I remember once, before credit cards were common, the *Daily Mail* sent me to Italy at a moment's notice. It was a bank holiday, I had no money and the banks were shut. There I was in Milan on a beautiful sunny day sitting in my hotel because it was the only place I could eat or drink because I could sign for it."

Frank Muir, the TV scriptwriter, and humorist, never sets off on a journey without packing his Swiss army penknife. "It does everything," he says. "It has about 140 things that come out. It opens bottles, gets things out of horses hooves, it has scissors, screwdrivers, tweezers. I never go anywhere without it and I have never used it."

From Sunday Express Magazine

Answer the following questions:

a Who likes to take as little luggage as possible?
b Who likes to keep a record of his travels?
c Who takes something he hasn't tested?
d Which two people seem to take their work with them when they travel?
e Which two people take something to avoid bad experiences they've had in the past?
f Who takes the strangest thing, in your opinion?
g Who takes the most useful thing, in your opinion?

▶ Communication activity 1

Work in pairs   Think of one thing **you** always take with you when you travel, but don't tell your partner what it is.

Try to find out what your partner always takes by asking questions like:
   Is it useful?   Can you carry it in your pocket?   Does it cost a lot of money?

▶ **Text 2**

1 Look at the headline below and say what you think the article is going to be about.

2 Read through the article fairly quickly to find out if you are right. In particular, look for answers to these two questions:

    a Where did the story about the cows happen?
    b What is the story an example of?

Dear travel agent, please stop the cows staring at me . . .

For the next few weeks, tour operators will be sorting through the annual deluge of complaints. Ron Wheal, head of customer relations for Britain's biggest holiday company which took more than a million abroad this summer, says, "Holidaymakers are complaining about petty, silly little things." Such as? "The fact that their hotel is next to a road. How do they expect to get to their hotel if it's not next to a road?"

Perhaps one of the most common complaints is that the holiday fails to live up to the brochure promises. A family from Berkshire with two young children were attracted by a two-week package in a three-star hotel that was described as "friendly" and "particularly suitable for families with children". It offered "cots, baby minding, high chairs and early suppers". When they arrived, the hotel was not up to three star standard, the staff were rude and the promised facilities for children were practically non-existent.

An initial complaint which had been sent to the holiday company by the family was answered with an "ex-gratia" payment of £30. With the help of a consumer magazine, the family issued a summons claiming £500 – which the holiday company eventually met in full.

One of the big travel successes of recent years has been the "gite" holiday; a gite is self-catering accommodation in France, often on a farm. The director of the Gite de France's London office recently received a telephone call from one client furious about the cows that passed in front of her gite. Was she complaining about the mess? "No, she was angry because the cows used to stop and look in at her as they went past the window."

Britain's biggest seller of long-distance holidays says that the majority of its complaints come from people who have chosen the wrong sort of holiday. People who fail to do their research could find themselves in the Caribbean during the hurricane season.

Mr Wheal says that if someone really wants action over a spoilt holiday, "they should try to sort it out with a holiday company representative there and then." Those who complain to the tour operator on their return and are unhappy with the response, can take their case to the Association of British Travel Agents (ABTA) which will provide conciliation facilities free of charge.

From an article by Frank Barrett in The Times

3 Now read the article again and mark the following statements as either **true** or **false**. Underline the word or phrase which gives you your answer.

    a Ron Wheal thinks that most of the complaints his company receives are reasonable.
    b The most frequent complaint is that a holiday is of a lower standard than expected.
    c The family from Berkshire expected that someone would be available to look after their young children.
    d The first thing they did was to write a letter of complaint to the company.
    e The company paid £500 as soon as they received the letter.
    f If you stay at a gite, you have to prepare your own meals.
    g The gite client complained because she was afraid of cows.
    h The long-distance holiday company suggests that holidaymakers should find out about the area they intend to visit.
    i Mr Wheal advises people to deal with problems as soon as they occur.
    j He suggests that people with complaints should contact ABTA as soon as they return home.

When you have finished, check your answers with another student's.

Vocabulary matching

4 Find the word or phrase in the text which means the same as the following:

a large quantity (usually of water) (paragraph 1) ....
b unimportant (1) ....
c holiday including travel and accommodation (2) ....
d beds for small children (2) ....
e almost unavailable (2) ....
f sent out an order to appear in court (3) ....
g paid completely (3) ....
h very angry (4) ....
i storm with strong wind (5) ....
j a service which helps to bring agreement between two people or groups of people (6) ....

Discussion points

5 Work with another student and find out if they:

a have ever had a journey or holiday when something went wrong. If so, what?
b have ever complained to a travel agent, tour company or hotel. If so, why?
c have ever complained in a restaurant. If so, why?
d have ever wanted to complain but felt too embarrassed. If so, when?
e would prefer to complain in person, by telephone or in writing, and why.

6 Report back any interesting stories you have heard, and discuss these questions:

a What can a customer hope to achieve by complaining?
b Is the customer always right to complain if they are dissatisfied with service?

Language check: prepositions

7 Complete the following sentences with the correct prepositions.
Ten of the fourteen prepositions come from Text 1.

(If you need some help, choose answers from the list at the bottom of the page. Each preposition should be used **once** only.)

a He was described .... a tall man .... dark hair and a bushy beard.
b The insurance company has agreed to meet our claim .... full.
c The shop repaired the clock free .... charge, as it was still ....
guarantee.
d The model TX200 is said to be suitable .... use as a home computer.
e .... his return to England, he was arrested and put in jail.
f We didn't think the television pictures were .... to standard so we asked to
have the set replaced.
g .... return for my first payment .... £50, I received four volumes of the
encyclopedia.
h I managed to find my way .... the path in the dark, ... the help of a
torch.
i In certain cities, such .... London and Manchester, household insurance
premiums are higher than elsewhere.
j I've tried complaining to the neighbours .... the noise they make but they
don't seem very co-operative.

on	as	of	with	up	along	in
for	as	of	with	under	about	in

STUDY BOX 1

Phrasal verb **Catch.**   . . . a machine "which lets him **catch up with** his
correspondence" (*Text 1*)

catch on – become popular.   I think our new song will really **catch on**.
catch on – understand.   I explained it to him but he didn't seem to **catch on**.
catch up with – succeed in reaching.   Hurry or you'll never **catch up with** the rest.
catch up with – bring up to date.   I've got a lot of work to **catch up with**.

4

► Focus on grammar 1 · Relative clauses

Look at these two examples from Text 2:

a People who fail to do their research could find themselves in the Caribbean during the hurricane season.

b Ron Wheal works for Britain's biggest holiday company, which took more than a million abroad this summer.

In sentence *a*, the relative clause in red is essential to the meaning of the sentence. Not everybody would have the problem. The relative clause tells us **which** people could go to the Caribbean at the wrong time. This is an example of a **defining relative clause**.

In sentence *b*, the relative clause in red is not essential to the meaning of the sentence. We know which holiday company Ron Wheal works for (the biggest). The relative clause gives us some **additional information** about the company. This is an example of a **non-defining relative clause**.

There are differences of grammar and punctuation between the two types of clause.

Exercise 1 Say whether the following are **defining** or **non-defining** relative clauses.

a The majority of complaints are from people who have chosen the wrong sort of holiday.
b We stayed in our usual hotel, which had just been redecorated.
c My mother, who is 60 today, has just come back from Australia.
d The letter that I've been waiting for has just arrived.

DEFINING RELATIVE CLAUSES

Main points
● Commas are not used to separate the relative clause from the rest of the sentence. (See sentences *a* and *d* in Exercise 1 above).

● **That** is often used instead of **who** or **which**, especially in speech. *For example:*
One client was furious about the cows that passed in front of her gite.

● If the relative pronoun is the object of the clause, it can be omitted.
Compare: That's the bus which goes to the station. (subject–pronoun cannot be omitted)
The bus which I caught didn't go to the station.
= The bus I caught didn't go to the station. } (object–pronoun can be omitted)

The woman I told you about lives in that house.
= The woman that I told you about lives in that house.

Summary

	People	Things
Subject	who, that	which, that
Object	who, that, whom	which, that
Possessive	whose	

Other points
● **That** is usually used after superlatives (the biggest, the best, etc) and also after all, only, any(thing), every(thing), some(thing), no(thing), none, little, few, much, many. *For example:*
There's something that I ought to tell you.
1976 was the hottest summer that we have ever had.
If it is the object of the relative clause, 'that' can be omitted.

● **Whose** is the possessive relative pronoun. It can be used for people and things. *For example:*
My neighbour is a man whose hobby is playing the drums.
That's the car whose engine blew up.

● **Whom** is grammatically correct as the object of a relative clause (people only), but it is very formal and is not often used in modern English.
Compare: (Formal) He's a man for whom I have the greatest admiration.
(Less formal) He's a man (who/that) I have the greatest admiration for.

Exercise 2 Column A opposite has the first half of ten sentences. Column B contains the second half, but they are not in the correct order. Match the two halves and then link them with relative pronouns **who**, **which**, **that** or **whose** to make complete sentences. *For example:*
1 All the people who/that have met him say he's awful. (*f*)

	A			B
1	All the people	....	a	sits next to me is always cheating in tests.
2	Can you take the suit	....	b	you lent me has some very good articles in it.
3	She's the best friend	....	c	we had never been to before.
4	The boy	....	d	wife works in the library?
5	What's the name of the man	....	e	is hanging in the cupboard to the cleaners?
6	I've lost the new pen	....	f	have met him say he's awful.
7	Don't tell anybody	....	g	anybody could ever have.
8	We decided to go to a restaurant	....	h	car you scratched is walking this way.
9	The man	....	i	I bought this morning
10	The magazine	....	j	you meet where I am!

When you have finished, check your answers with another student.
In which sentences can the relative pronoun be omitted? (See 3rd main point)

Exercise 3 Join the pairs of sentences below, using a relative pronoun where necessary. Begin the new sentence with the part which is in red. (You may need to change **a** to **the** in some cases.) *For example:*

I'm reading a book. It has two pages missing.
The book (that) I'm reading has two pages missing.

a We used to live in a house. It's just been sold.
b An old lady lives across the road. She's got eight cats.
c You were looking for a friend. He's just come in.
d My grandmother left me an old chair in her will. It's worth a fortune!
e I bought my watch at a local shop. I can't remember its name
f The writer lives in New York. His latest book was published on Tuesday.
g A neighbour has been to Sao Paulo. He says he's never seen anything like it.
h I gave Helena blouse for her birthday. It's worn out already.
i The student has gone to university. He came top in maths at school.
j Several people went to Paris this spring. None of them complained about the hotel.

NON-DEFINING RELATIVE CLAUSES

Main points
● Commas are usually used to separate the relative clause from the rest of the sentence.
● **That** cannot be used instead of **who** or **which**.
● **Who** or **which** cannot be omitted.

Exercise 4 Give some additional information with a relative clause beginning **who**, **which** or **whose** in the following sentences.

a Wimbledon, ..., is in south London.

b He's hoping to be chosen for the next Olympic Games, ...

c The Prime Minister, ..., will face an election soon.

d Every schoolchild has heard of Columbus, ...

e Mount Everest, ..., is the highest mountain in the world.

Exercise 5 Put commas in the following sentences where necessary.
In which of the sentences could the relative pronoun be omitted?

a A corkscrew is a device which removes corks from bottles.
b I've just read his third novel which is his best.
c The person who I spoke to yesterday was very rude.
d They gave their car which was very old to their son.
e Take the road which is signposted to York.
f The book which I recommended to you is out of print.
g I met your friend Jane who wants to be a pop singer.
h The man who was supposed to meet me didn't turn up.

STUDY BOX 2

Phrasal verb **Live.** "... the holiday fails to **live up** to the brochure promises"
(Text 2)

live on – have as food or income.   I don't know how he manages to **live on** the salary he gets.

live through – survive despite difficulty.   He's **lived through** two major wars.
live up to – reach the expected standard.   See example above.

▶ Communication activity 2

1 Vocabulary and definitions:

a Look at these ways of defining things and describing their use:

It's a thing	
an instrument	**that . . .**
a tool	**that you use for + ing**
a device	**to + inf**
	for + ing
They're things	

Now look at the pictures on page 8. *For example:*

In square 1C there's a picture of a spade.
A spade is a tool that you use for digging in the garden.

In square 1E there's an alarm clock.
An alarm clock is a device that wakes you up in the morning.

In square IB there's a bucket.
A bucket is a thing for carrying water (in).

b Now practise naming and defining the other objects in the top two rows (lines 1 and 2). If you're not sure of a word, ask your teacher.

c Work in pairs using the objects in the remaining rows (lines 3–8). Choose an object and define it, without telling your partner what it is. Then let your partner guess the object. Continue, taking it in turns to define and guess.

2 Game: you need to work in groups of 3–5. Sit round a table if possible.

Preparation (for each group)

A *Equipment:* You will need 3 sets of slips of paper:
First set: 5 slips of paper with the letters A–E written on them.
Second set: 8 slips of paper with numbers 1–8 written on them.
Third set: 8 slips with the names of the types of holiday from page 1 written on them.

B *Language*: Before you begin, turn to the Functions Bank (page 211) and look at the Language for Expressing Need and Use.
Refer to it again during the game, if you like, but don't read from the page. Feel free to express your ideas in other ways too!

How to play

A 1 Lay the slips of paper with the types of holidays on them, face down.
2 Each player takes one. This represents his/her holiday for the game.

B 1 Lay the two sets of papers with numbers and letters on them face down.
2 The first player selects first the letter, and then a number from the two piles. He/she then finds the picture which matches. *For example:* C7 is a camera.
3 The first player must say why the object will be useful on his/her holiday.
4 The rest of the group can accept or challenge the suggested use. If they are satisfied, the player has won a point. If they are not satisfied, no point is won.
5 The player returns the letter and number to the piles, and mixes them. A second player chooses and the game continues.

The winner in each group is the player with the most points.

A   B   C   D   E

▶ Focus on listening 1

You are going to hear a conversation in a travel agent's shop. The customer is interested in going to the Greek island of Crete.

Four hotels are discussed. These are:

The Concord   **The Royal**   **The Atlantic**   **The Plaza**

For questions 1–4, write the name of the hotel next to the picture which matches the description you hear.

The Hotel

For questions 5–8, fill in the missing information about flights to Crete in the spaces.

The Flight **5 Days:**   Fridays and ....

6 Time: Third week in ....

7 Price: From £159 to ....

8 Insurance: The most expensive: ......£14:25......
The cheapest: ....

STUDY BOX 3   Adjectives + prepositions

furious about the cows (*Text 2*)	furious, angry, annoyed, upset **about** something / **with** someone **for** doing something
unhappy with the response (*Text 2*)	happy, unhappy, pleased, delighted, bored, fed up **with** something

interested **in**, fond **of**, keen **on**, excited **about**, surprised **at/by**, attracted **by**

► Focus on grammar 2 · Review of the present tenses

The **present continuous** tense refers to **temporary** situations, and actions **that are happening now**.

The **present simple** tense refers to **more permanent** situations, and actions **that are repeated**.

Look at the examples below, and discuss with a partner why the present simple is used in two of the sentences and the present continuous in the others.

> Be quiet! I'm listening to the news.
> He has the kind of voice that everybody listens to.
>
> Do you wear jeans when you go to work?
> Why are you wearing that awful hat?

Exercise 1 Choose the correct form of the verb to complete the following sentences:

a The kettle ....:..... Please switch it off.
Water .... at 100 degrees centigrade.   **boil**

b I .... with friends until I can find a flat of my own.
I .... in a small village about 5 miles from here.   **live**

c He .... tennis three days a week.
John isn't here. He .... football.   **play**

d Look, it .... You'd better take your umbrella.
People say it .... more in Manchester than anywhere else.   **rain**

e We usually .... the children at bedtime.
Oh no! The children .... the cat!   **bath**

THE PRESENT SIMPLE

Form

I speak	
She speaks	Italian
They speak	

Negative: I don't speak Italian very well.

Question: Do you speak Italian at all?

Use The present simple is used in: (Complete the examples in your own words)

1*a* habitual or repeated actions and situations. *For example:*

> He often runs in races but rarely ....

b situations that never change. For example, scientific facts. *For example:*

> Hot air rises while cool air ....

2 future plans with particular reference to journeys and timetables. *For example:*

> The train .... at every station on the way to London.

3 time clauses introduced by **when**, **as soon as**, **after**, **if** etc. *For example:*

> I'll phone you as soon as I arrive.

THE PRESENT CONTINUOUS

Form

I am	
She is	listening
They are	

Negative: You aren't listening!

Question: Are you listening?

Use The present continuous is used to talk about: (Complete the examples in your own words)

1*a* actions and situations happening at the moment of speaking. *For example:*

> The telephone .... Please answer it.

b temporary situations. *For example:*

> I .... in an ice cream factory to pay my college fees.

2 future plans. An expression of future plans is usually needed to avoid confusion. *For example:*

> We're taking the boat to Calais but .... the rest of the way by train.

3 annoying habits (with **always**, **continually**, **constantly** etc.) *For example:*

> You are always criticising the way I speak.

Verbs not usually used in the continuous form

Some verbs are not usually used in the continuous form. The most common are:

wish	believe	hear	seem	mean
want	feel	see	understand	belong
like	suppose	smell	consist of	remember
hate	know	notice	contain	

Some other verbs which are also normally used in the simple form, may be used in the continuous form, but with a change of meaning. *For example:*

> I expect you are hungry. (= I am sure)
> I'm expecting a visit from the doctor. (= I am waiting for)

The most common ones apart from 'expect' are:

think	see	look	hold	have

Exercise 2 Complete these 10 sentences using each of the 5 verbs in the list above twice, once in the continuous form and once in the simple form of the present tense. Notice the change in meaning.

a I .... for the contact lens that I dropped on the floor.

b He's a real animal-lover and he .... two cats, a tortoise and some goldfish.

c Don't disturb him! He ....

d This jug .... exactly one litre of liquid

e You .... like your father in this photograph.

f I .... how to do it now. Thanks for showing me.

g Tell me what you .... of your new teacher.

h Who .... you .... at the club tonight?

i My parents .... a wonderful time in America, I hear.

j Who .... the baby in that photograph?

Exercise 3 Complete the sentences below by putting the verb in brackets into the most suitable form of the present simple or present continuous.

a 'What .... you .... (do) this summer?' 'We .... (spend) a week with friends in Greece'.

b Oil and water .... (not, mix). Oil .... (float) on top of water.

c Why .... you .... (cook) those carrots? You .... (know) Helen .... (eat) only raw vegetables.

d I .... (not, understand) what he .... (say). .... he .... (speak) English or German?

e I .... (normally, go) to a keep-fit class on Wednesday evenings but tomorrow I can't because I .... (work) late.

f I .... (know) what you .... (mean) but I .... (not, agree) with you.

g We have a system in this house. I .... (do) the housework, he .... (cook) the meals, and we both .... (give) the orders!

▶ Focus on listening 2

Vocabulary check 1 The pictures on page 12 (in the margin) show things to do with fastening or carrying. Write the correct names underneath. The first letter and the number of letters are given to help you. If you don't know them all, see if your neighbour can help.

L _ _ _ _

L _ _ _ _

H _ _ _ _ _

C _ _ _ _ _

B _ _ _ _

Z _ _ _

S _ _ _ _ _

P _ _ _ _ _ _

2 You are going to hear a short radio programme which gives information about suitcases. Before you listen, look at the four questions below very carefully. Then, while you listen, fill in the missing information.

1 The main disadvantages of leather suitcases are that they are both .... and ....

2 Modern materials used in making suitcases combine lightness and ....

3 Four-wheeled suitcases have the disadvantage that they are more likely .... than two-wheeled suitcases.

4 Complete the table below:

	Riviera	Windsor	Tornado	Mayfair
a Length	67cm	68cm	75cm	
b Material *(see below)				aluminium
c Fastening/Security	zip+padlock			2 locks
d Number of wheels		2		
e Strap or Handle for pushing/pulling		strap		
f Price			£109.50	
g Tester's verdict	good value for money			

Note Choose from the following materials: SOFT – vinyl, nylon, PVC   RIGID – polypropylene, ABS, aluminium

▶ Focus on writing · Directed writing

Writing Bank: page 234

It's becoming increasingly common for people in Britain to spend Christmas or New Year away from home, and nowadays many hotels offer special arrangements at that time of year.

1 Scan the advertisements on the next page to find answers to the following questions.

 a Which of the advertisements refer(s) to Scotland? ....
 b Which don't mention price? ....
 c Which say they are by the sea? ....
 d Which mention(s) the beauty of the surrounding scenery? ....
 e Which mention(s) a discount for children? ....
 f Which mention(s) good cooking? ....
 g To which could you take a dog? ....

A

Christmas in the Highlands at McConnell's Hotel

Scotland's for me!

Enjoy a truly memorable Christmas at McConnell's, Scotland's highland retreat.
Traditional Scottish hospitality at its best – a champagne welcome, candlelit dinner, carols, and a full programme of entertainment over three days. Plus full use of the Country Club, including a Jacuzzi, pool and sauna.
Write or phone for full details of McConnell's Christmas or New Year Breaks. Please quote reference 2g.

McConnell's Hotel
Glen Clunie, Scotland
Tel: 08167 34209

B

BOURNEMOUTH
HOTEL MON AMI
ST MICHAELS ROAD, WESTCLIFF
Phone: (0202) 292801 or 290647
'Happy Christmas assured'

Friendly Hotel. 2 minutes walk to the beach. 100 bedrooms, ballroom and live entertainment, cabaret. Residential licence, en-suite rooms available, car park facilities, lift, baby/radio listening in rooms. Games room, colour TV and video in rooms.

Discount available for children (£178 per person inclusive VAT, 4 nights 24th December-28th December).
All inclusive

Ask for our Christmas and New Year Programme.

C

Celebrate Hogmanay
in the heart of Scotland with a menu of traditional fare and entertainment – Superb value
3 days from £95.99 F.B.
Half price for children – dogs welcome
Write for New Year details or BOOK NOW
RAC ★★★ AA
THE INVERCAULD ARMS HOTEL
Braemar, AB3 5YR. Tel (04868) 20015

D

STAY ON LUNDY ISLAND

Off the coast of North Devon, for Christmas, New Year or winter breaks. No cars, but wonderful walks, bird-watching, archaeology, silence, sea & space. The natives are friendly. Handsome, small & comfortable Millcombe Hotel & self catering cottages, remarkable pub. Boat from Bideford or Clovelly, or helicopter (7 mins.) from Hartland Point. Ring:

LANDMARK TRUST

Write to Mrs B. Glover,
Shottesbrooke, Maidenhead,
Berks. 062-882-5920.

E

. A Grand Christmas for all the family

All the fun and none of the work – just imagine it. A Christmas full of traditional celebrations, superb food in plenty and wines at reasonable prices. Parties, dancing, discos and competitions and an unrivalled range of free sports facilities including large heated indoor pool, squash, badminton, flood-lit tennis, snooker, table tennis, pitch and putt. All rooms have en-suite facilities, colour TV with video channel and central heating.

Ask now for our Christmas brochure. Tel: 0271 870418

NARRACOTT
GRAND HOTEL, WOOLACOMBE, DEVON

F

WHY NOT SPEND NEW YEAR WITH US IN PICTURESQUE NORTH CORNWALL
From £14.50 per night DB & B

Small peaceful owner-managed hotel overlooking bay and cliffs of Port Quinn. Surrounded by Nat. Trust and Cornish coastal path. All rooms superb sea views and ch, log fire in bar, excellent wine list at modest prices. Good home cooked meals. Open all year. No children under 10. Also: one twin room left for our Christmas programme. Write:

THE TREVOSE HOUSE HOTEL
Port Quinn, Port Isaac,
N. Cornwall, or
Tel: 0206 883773

---

2 Here are details about four families who are looking for a place to spend Christmas. Using the information given, write 4 paragraphs explaining what you think would be the best choice for each family. You will probably need about 50 words for each paragraph.

a Carol and Mike **Ballard** have two children (Tom aged 12 and Susan aged 15) who are very energetic and sometimes quite difficult to keep amused during the holidays. Tom loves swimming and Susan is fond of dancing. Their parents are both keen on keeping fit. They would like a holiday they can all enjoy without spending too much money.

b Barbara and Bruce **Fellows** also have two children (Jason aged 12 and Danny aged 7). Although they live in a big city, the whole family loves the outdoor life. They hate large hotels and would like a quiet holiday near the sea at a reasonable price.

c Tim and Mary **Gilchrist** want to combine Christmas with a celebration of their 40th wedding anniversary. They would like to be able to relax and enjoy a really special occasion without too many noisy children around! They are also hoping for some traditional Christmas entertainment.

d Dick and Lesley **Brown**, their two-year-old son and Dick's mother, who can't climb stairs, are looking for a hotel where they can all have an enjoyable time.

	You could begin like this:	**Useful**
Paragraph 1	I think the Ballard family would enjoy a holiday . . .	**Language**

Write three more paragraphs in the same way

Paragraph 2 The best holiday for the Fellows family seems to be . . .

Paragraph 3 In my opinion, the best holiday for the Gilchrists would be . . .

Paragraph 4 As for the Browns, I recommend . . .

Note You should give reasons for your choices.

My reason for choosing this hotel is that . . .
I feel they would be happy there / the hotel would suit them as/because . . .
The main advantage of this hotel is . . .

► Vocabulary review

Choose the word or phrase which best completes each sentence.
All the correct answers come from texts in this unit.

1 Judging by the smell, this can seems to be filled .... petrol.

   a by   *b* from   *c* of   *d* with

2 I don't get much chance to read books .... when I'm on holiday.

   a only   *b* except   *c* just   *d* until

3 The main .... of a camping holiday is that it's extremely cheap.

   a reason   *b* profit   *c* advantage   *d* good

4 You must be ready to leave at a moment's .... in case there's an emergency.

   a notice   *b* call   *c* advice   *d* instruction

5 He's always complaining .... the noise the neighbours make.

   a for   *b* from   *c* of   *d* about

6 Don't forget to put .... with your address on them on all your suitcases.

   a notices   *b* tickets   *c* labels   *d* badges

7 Her reason .... was to save time.

   a to fly   *b* of flying   *c* about flying   *d* for flying

8 I'd be no good at First Aid because I can't .... the sight of blood.

   a have   *b* bear   *c* look   *d* resist

9 My wife and I are very keen .... Scottish dancing.

   a on   *b* of   *c* in   *d* about

10 He's a good friend and he never .... to send me a birthday card each year.

   a ignores   *b* stops   *c* fails   *d* misses

11 There's always a lot of office work to .... after the holiday.

   a take over from   *b* get away with   *c* catch up with   *d* set out on

12 After he had finished his medical course, he .... research into the causes of heart disease.

   a did   *b* made   *c* took   *d* followed

13 The bank robber was described by the police .... dark-haired and in his late twenties.

   a for   *b* as   *c* like   *d* with

14 I've found the dishwasher so useful that I don't think I could .... without it now.

   a go   *b* pass   *c* get   *d* do

15 I only bought the book because I was .... by its cover.

   a interested   *b* attracted   *c* invited   *d* pleased

UNIT 2A Other people's jobs

▶ Lead-in 1

The drawings below represent ten different jobs.
Work with a partner to decide what the ten jobs are.

Now discuss: Which job . . . needs the most training?   is the best paid?   is the most satisfying?
                       is the most useful?   is the least pleasant?   is the hardest?

▶ Lead-in 2

Have you ever wanted to try someone else's job?
The writer, Danny Danziger, recently spent a week working in each of four different jobs
to see what they were like. Below are short extracts from the four articles he wrote about
his experiences.

1 Read the four extracts and try to guess what job he is describing in each one. Discuss
your ideas with another student.

A   Alan never seemed to get bored by the same old questions. But he did confide to me, "no one should do
this job more than three years, because after a while you look at the people, and they're not people,
they're the broken tap in room 23 or the lost wallet in room 7 or the couple who want to fly home because they're
not having fun."

B   The third gallery was the Time Measurement exhibit. Water clocks, sun-dials, sand glasses, watches and
chronometers. I saw my life ticking by, second by micro-second.
   Working in a more popular gallery you might be approached more frequently, but the range of questions is
unvarying. People only want to know the same thing. "Where's the nearest toilet/lift/cup of tea?"

C   During the week I went to bed early so I would not appear too awful in the morning light, and each day
started with an agony of indecision as I wondered what to wear. I never lost my embarrassment at
meeting people whose prime interest was in my physical appearance.

D   The pace starts off leisurely enough. With my crisp white apron and valet's jacket I would feel cool and
confident. It's quiet enough at 12.15 to notice the famous faces who are lunching. By one o'clock, the
place is jumping. As fast as tables are vacated new faces are slipping in. No time to enjoy the thrill of a film star
lighting a big cigar . . . the sous-chef is screaming that the food for table 166 is getting cold.

From The Sunday Express Magazine

2 These are the four places where he was working. Can you match the place with the extract, and add the name of the job?

Place	Extract	Job
Photographic Studio		
Museum		
Restaurant		
Holiday Resort		

Again, check your answers with another student.

3 Now answer these questions:

a In which job(s) did Danny have to wear special clothes?
b In which job did he have to work the fastest?
c Which job made him feel most anxious?
d Which job(s) involved dealing with people's problems?
e Which job did the writer seem to find most boring?
f In which job did Danny find the customers especially interesting?
g Which job did he discuss with an experienced worker?

Discussion points

4 *a* Individually decide:
  ● which of the 4 jobs you would choose to do if you had to, and why.
  ● which you would **least** like to do, and why.
b With a partner discuss your answers to question *a*.
c Here are some advantages and disadvantages for job *A* – the travel representative.

Advantages	**Disadvantages**
opportunity to travel	losing touch with friends at home
practising foreign languages	dealing with difficult clients
meeting people	low pay

With your partner write down 3 advantages and 3 disadvantages for the other three jobs.

Disagreeing

5 Expressing a different point of view

Look at the table below:

Yes,		on the other hand . . .
I agree,		even so . . .
I know,	but	what about . . .?
(perhaps) You're right,		don't forget that . . .

For example, you could discuss the travel representative like this.

A As a travel representative, you'd have plenty of opportunity to travel.

B – Yes, but on the other hand you'd probably lose touch with all your friends at home.
  – I know, but what about all the difficult clients you'd have to deal with?
  – I agree, but don't forget that you'd have to deal with some very awkward people!
  – Perhaps you're right, but even so it's not a very well-paid job.

Change your partner and discuss the other three jobs. Take it in turns to talk about advantages and disadvantages.
Use your notes and try to include some of the expressions above.

6 Imagine you had the chance to work for one week only in **any** job of your choice. Which job would it be, and why?

Focus on grammar 1 · Adjectives and adverbs

USE

Exercise 1 Complete the story by putting one word from the list below in each space.

complete	helpfully	modern
closely	previous	quickly
terribly	confident	unfortunately
straight	carefully	loud
nervous	firmly	

I still remember the first lesson I ever gave. I had planned it very ....*carefully*.... (1) but as the time to start approached, I began to feel ....*terribly*.... (2) ....*nervous*.... (3). There were ....*loud*.... (4) voices coming from the classroom but when I opened the door, the noise died down ....*quickly*.... (5) and by the time I reached the front of the room, there was ....*complete*.... (6) silence. I introduced myself in what I hoped was a ....*confident*....(7) voice and then turned to write my name on the board. It was a ....*modern*.... (8) whiteboard and the ....*previous*.... (9) teacher's notes hadn't been cleaned off. A pupil pointed ....*helpfully*.... (10) to the board cleaner and explained that I had to press ....*firmly*.... (11) on a button on the top to release a spray of water. ....*unfortunately*.... (12) I didn't look at it ....*closely*.... (13) enough and when I pressed the button a jet of water went ....*straight*.... (14) into my eye!

Now, with a partner, read the story again, underline all the adjectives and put a circle round all the adverbs.

Adjectives give information about nouns and are used
a before nouns. *For example:* A confident voice.
b with certain verbs. *For example:* There was complete silence.

Some common verbs in this group are **be**, **seem**, **appear**, **look**, **feel**, **sound**, **taste**. *For example:*

The test seemed easy.
You look rather tired.
This coffee tastes horrible.

Adverbs give information about verbs and adjectives. *For example:*

I had planned it very carefully.
I began to feel terribly nervous. (also: awfully, extremely etc)

FORMATION

The following table shows how adverbs are formed from adjectives. Fill in the missing examples.

regular	patient	patiently	**no change**	straight	late
	wise	....		hard	
	sudden	....		fast	
change of spelling	happy	happily	**irregular**	good	well
	sensible	....			
	helpful	....			
	true	....			

Note Be careful with some adjectives that end in -ly. They cannot be used as adverbs. Use a similar adverb or adverb phrase. *For example:*

He gave me a friendly smile.
He smiled at me in a friendly way.

Now use **silly**, **ugly** and **lovely** in similar sentences of your own. Use a different verb in each sentence.

THE COMPARISON OF ADJECTIVES AND ADVERBS

helicopter   bicycle   car   rowing boat   skateboard

1 Look at the pictures above and complete these sentences. Check your answers with a partner. You may disagree!

A .... is cheaper than a ....

A .... is more convenient than a ....

A .... can be parked less easily than a ....

The least reliable method of transport is a ....

2

	Comparative	Superlative
Adjectives of one syllable: cheap	. . . er than	(the) . . . est
Adjectives of two or more syllables: convenient Adverbs: easily	more . . . than less . . . than	(the) most . . . (the) least . . .
Irregular Forms: good bad far (distance) (time)	better worse farther further	(the) best (the) worst (the) farthest (the) furthest

Now make sentences of your own about the pictures using these words:

safely   expensive   comfortable   quickly   economically   hard

For example, you could begin like this:

You can go . . .   It's .... to learn to use . . .
     get about . . .   repair . . .
     travel . . .   steer . . .

Exercise 2   Put the adjective or adverb in brackets into the form which best suits the meaning of the sentence.

a In your opinion, what is (stressful) aspect of being a doctor?
b Who is (useful) to society, a policeman or a social worker?
c I think women drive (carefully) than men.
d Please talk a bit (quietly). You're disturbing everyone.
e He feels much (fit) since he stopped smoking.
f There's nothing (annoying) than losing one's door key.
g Michael prefers to be alone. He is (sociable) person in the office.
h He did not do very well, but at least he tried (hard) than last time.
i That really is (bad) food I've ever eaten!
j I bought her (expensive) present I could afford.

STUDY BOX 1 The use of articles 1

NO ARTICLE		**DEFINITE ARTICLE**
a *meals:* We had breakfast at 8 o'clock. lunch, tea, supper, dinner	*but*	**The** breakfast on the train was awful.
b *times of day:* We left at sunrise. dawn, midday/noon, lunchtime, sunset, night, midnight.	*but*	in **the** morning/afternoon/evening
c *methods of travel: For example:* by air. by sea/boat/train/coach/bus/car/bicycle, etc.	*but*	We came by **the** early train/**the** 140 bus/**the** express coach.

▶ Text 1 · Waiter for a week

Study the following questions and then read the text through fairly quickly in order to answer them in your own words. Note which paragraph the information can be found in.

a What exactly did the writer's job involve?
b What seems to be the worst part of a waiter's job?
c What made his job more difficult?
d What did he dislike about the customers' behaviour?

I was to be a commis waiter* for my week at the restaurant. There are 50 waiters. Commis waiters and waiters work as a team. The waiter is the front man, taking orders, chatting to the customers; the commis, rather less glamorously, runs to the kitchen to bring up the orders and assist in serving them at the table. Although the commis will actually do more physical work, they share the tips equally. All in all this is fair, as it must be pointed out that the senior waiter is actually responsible for keeping a running account of the bills and if he makes a mistake, or undercharges, the fault is rectified through *his* wage packet. It's an important working relationship.

I reported for work at 11 am. That may sound like a relaxed time to start the day, but the hours, I was soon to learn, are hell. The last client at lunchtime may not leave until half past three, or later, and the evening shift starts at 6 pm. What can you do in 2½ hours, especially if you don't happen to live in central London? Once or twice I didn't get home until 4 am. The hours, it was generally agreed, are the worst thing about waitering.

The commis takes the orders from the table down to the kitchen. He places the order for hot food under the nose of the sous-chef who is shouting out orders to the cooks, while orders for cold dishes and salad go to a separate counter, and desserts are from yet another area. The kitchen is two flights of stairs away from the restaurant. The commis then comes up to see if any more orders have been taken while the previous one is being prepared. At the same time, dishes have to be cleared or put on the table, glasses refilled, ashtrays emptied, and somehow there always seems to be a new table with six or eight new orders to be filled – two flights away in the kitchen.

Hell, I rather imagine, is like the kitchen of that restaurant. Yelling chefs, endless banging of pots and crockery, steaming casseroles, hissing frying pans, men with red shining faces, trays with loads heavy enough to break your wrists. And running. Always running. Up and down, down and up. And since everyone is running, and always with loaded trays, you need the co-ordination of a gymnast to stay out of trouble.

I spent as much time as possible in the dining room itself. I noticed that wearing a uniform somehow transformed me into a role. It wasn't play-acting. Customers become sir or madam. Deference, a quality I usually lack, became the order of the day. I became very sensitive about the way I was treated. I hated being summoned by the click of the finger or the bend of the index finger. It was hurtful if conversation deliberately stopped as I served the meal, and yet unkind if it continued as if I didn't exist. I began to notice if people said please and thank you, and then whether they looked at me when they said it.

*an apprentice or trainee waiter

From The Sunday Express Magazine

1 There are a number of quite difficult words in the text but you should be able to work out what they mean from the context. Choose the most likely meaning for the following words or expressions:

1 *glamorously* (line 5) A glamorous job is

   a an active, energetic one.
   b an exciting, attractive one.
   c a difficult one.

2 *rectified* (line 12) ". . . the fault is rectified through *his* wage packet." means

    a the money is taken from his earnings.
    b he has to pay a fine for his mistake.
    c he must pay back the money to the customer.

3 *yelling* (line 36)

    a working.
    b singing.
    c shouting.

4 *co-ordination* (line 41)

    a skill.
    b courage.
    c strength.

5 *deference* (line 46)

    a being tidy.
    b showing respect to people.
    c fighting back.

6 *the order of the day* (line 47)

    a the most popular dish of the day.
    b the programme of work for the day.
    c the normal way of behaving.

7 *summoned* (line 48)

    a answered.
    b touched.
    c called.

2 Say whether the following statements are true or false, and why.

  a A commis waiter has to be careful to add up bills correctly.

  b The senior waiter earns more in tips than the commis waiter.

  c It was hard for the waiter to make use of his free time.

  d The commis waiter has to wait in the kitchen while the food is prepared.

  e The kitchen was extremely noisy.

  f There was a danger that waiters would crash into each other.

  g The writer normally finds it easy to be respectful to people.

  h He felt that some customers behaved rudely to him.

Discussion points

A

1 The writer didn't like customers to click their fingers to call for service. How do you normally call a waiter in your country? Do you know any different methods of attracting a waiter's attention in other countries?

2 Why did the writer feel hurt when conversations stopped as he served a meal? Do you stop speaking while a waiter is serving you, or do you carry on?

3 Do you like a waiter to be extremely polite to you or do you prefer more casual service?

B

1 When is it normal to give tips in your country? Which people do you always tip, and which do you tip if the service was especially good?

2 Do you approve of tipping, or do you think it should be stopped? Why?

3 Have you ever had a job where you received tips?

4 Have you ever refused to tip someone who expected a tip? If so, what happened?

▶ Focus on listening 1

Fill in the information you hear in the spaces below.

1 COURSES AND CAREER OPPORTUNITIES

a 'Start' course: Dates 7–11 May; Cost ....

b Young Engineer of the Year Competition: closing date: ....
prize: ....

2 LOCAL JOB OPPORTUNITIES

TAUNTON

Job Description *Trainee sales person*

Number of Vacancies *1*   Part Time ☐

Full Time ☑

Wages/Salary *£3,000 a year*

Age ....

Additional Information ....

WELLS

Job Description *Groom*

Number of Vacancies .... Part Time ☐

Full Time ☐

Wages/Salary ....

Age *Open*

Additional Information *Experience is necessary*

WARMLEY

Job Description ....

Number of Vacancies *20*   Part Time ☐

Full Time ☐

Wages/Salary ....

Age *Over 16*

Additional Information ....

EASTON

Job Description *Trainee baker*

Number of Vacancies *1*   Part Time ☐

Full Time ☑

Wages/Salary ....

Age *Open*

Additional Information ....

▶ Focus on grammar 2 · The simple past

Use   The simple past tense refers to actions or situations which began and ended in the past. There is no connection with present time. It has two main uses:

● It refers to a definite time or period of time in the past. *For example:*

I bought this car last July.
It snowed three times last week.

There are many ways of expressing a definite time in the past. Look at the following examples.

He went to America in 1984.
two years ago.
when he was a student.
during his last year at college.

Exercise 1 Complete the following sentences by choosing the correct word from the list below. There may be more than one possible answer.

at   in   when   for   before   on   ago   during   after   until

1 He got married .... 1985.

2 He was President .... the period 1964–1967.

3 How long .... did you last see him?

4 The fire started .... 6 o'clock.

5 I was ill .... three months.

6 They had to use candles .... there was a power cut.

7 He read a book .... he fell asleep.

8 She left Spain .... four years.

9 Fortunately they left the building .... the bomb exploded.

10 Didn't you see the match .... Saturday?

Note The time is not always mentioned but it is still clear that the action or situation is now ended. *For example:*

> I opened the door, looked out into the darkness and saw the same face again. Then I . . .

● The simple past tense refers to past habit. *For example:*

> I worked in London for three years.
> She lived abroad for most of her life.
> He smoked twenty cigarettes a day as a student.

Exercise 2 Complete these sentences:

1 When I was at school I ....

2 If he behaved badly when he was a child, his mother ....

3 A hundred years ago people ....

4 I hate sport now but when I was younger ....

5 At school which subjects .... ?

Form **1 Regular verbs** Infinitive + **-ed.** *For example:* work – work**ed**

There is a change in the spelling of the simple past form of **some** regular verbs. For example: fit – fitt**ed**

Complete the following table.

dance	danced	stop	stopped	prefer	preferred	try	tried
argue	....	tap	....	occur	....	apply	......
use	....	rot	....	travel	....	study	......

2 Irregular verbs. There are some rules, but as they are quite complicated the best approach is just to learn the irregular forms.

Fill in the gaps in the table below and compare your answers with a partner.

Infinitive	Past	Past Participle	Infinitive	Past	Past Participle
....	became	....	....	....	heard
bite	....	....	....	laid	....
....	....	broken	....	lost	....
....	caught	....	put	....	....
....	....	chosen	....	rode	....
cost	....	....	....	....	shot
....	drove	....	steal	....	....
fall	....	....	....	....	taught..........
....	....	felt	tear	....	....
fly	....	....	....	wrote	....

▶ Communication activity
Working can be a health hazard

Stress is the mental strain which we feel when we have to cope with difficult, unpleasant or dangerous situations.

Some jobs involve a lot of stress because of the nature of the work. A construction worker, for example, working on a new building high above the ground, is in constant danger. What special stresses would be suffered by:

a a traffic warden?　　*b* a prison officer?

Some jobs are stressful because of the circumstances. You may enjoy your job but if the new boss is bad-tempered and criticises everything you do, you will probably suffer from stress too, after a time.

Other jobs are much more relaxed. It's hard to imagine a gardener suffering from serious stress. What other low-stress jobs can you think of?

Stress can cause high blood pressure and lead to mental illness or heart disease. It also causes problems for employers like strikes and accidents.

Recently, a British university made a study of a number of different jobs to see how much stress workers suffered. Here is a list of 26 of the jobs they studied.

Work with a partner to:

1 Decide which job involves by far the **most**, and which by far the **least** stress.
2 Put the other 24 jobs in three groups according to whether they have High, Medium or Low stress.

actor	film producer	manager (commerce)	politician
architect	fireman	miner	postman
bus driver	professional footballer	museum worker	salesman, shop assistant
dentist	hairdresser	pop musician	secretary
doctor	journalist	nurse	soldier
engineer	librarian	pilot (civil)	teacher
farmer		police	

When you have finished, compare your answers with another pair and discuss your reasons.

Finally, turn to page 217 for a complete list of results.

STUDY BOX 2

Expressions with **Do** and **Make**. . . . if he **makes a mistake** . . . (*Text 1*)
It's a **duty** that has to be **done** (*Text 2*)

	Make			**Do**	
money	a complaint	a choice	good	one's best	
war	an inquiry	a mistake	harm	one's duty	
certain	an excuse	a charge	damage	one's bit	
sure	an offer	a discovery	business	a favour	
a journey	the bed	use of	work	a test	
a trip		fun of	homework	an experiment	
		room for	housework	the washing-up	

23

▶ **Text 2** Look at the notes about traffic wardens in six different parts of the world.

1 Find this information as quickly as possible.

 a Which of the traffic wardens is the oldest?
 b In which city are traffic wardens least well paid?
 c Which city has the highest parking fine?
 d Which city has the highest towing away fee? *Rotterd*
 e Which cities do not have parking meters? *SP + R*

Michiko Demizu, 25. **Wage:** £338·60 monthly. **Previous job:** police admin. Now patrolwoman, Parking Counter-measures. Chalk-on stick means she can mark road next to offending tyre without leaving car. **Meters** are few. **Towing** fines total £28·50 (Japanese hold world towing record - three minutes from calling truck to car removal.) "It's a duty that has to be done, no matter how hard you work, you don't get praised"

Elly van Driel, 23. **Wage:** £442 a month. **Previous job:** welfare worker. Despite the fact a car driver once tried to run her down, takes real pleasure in her work with old people. Top rate **meters** are 7p for 15 minutes, and **fines** £7·75 an infringement with **towing away** £45. It's unusual to call out **clamps** – they're for serious concerns, such as stolen cars but pavement and tyres get chalked in order to check if the car has been moved

Marina Di Generoso, 32. **Wage:** basic £154, with additions, £380. **Previous job:** secretary. Pleased that Italy's top fashion designers are redesigning the uniform. No **meters**, parking discs for windscreens instead (small boys earn money by altering time for drivers) but these almost forgotten about as too many double and triple-parked cars to concentrate on. Top parking **fine** is £36, **towing away** fine, £16. **Nickname:** Vigilessa

Valdeci Pola da Silva, 24. **Wage:** £180 monthly. **Previous job:** assembly line supervisor. Reckons it's the drivers with the expensive cars who get up to the most ticket-avoiding tricks. **Meters** once tried, but used wrongly or not at all, replaced with books of cards (2 hours each for 6p) which wardens and news stands sell – because of pickpockets, she deposits this money in bank several times a day. **Nickname:** Blue Zone girl

Ahn Ong-Chul, 39. **Previous job:** factory labourer. **Wage:** £211 monthly. Dislikes the long working hours involved (11 a day), especially in sub-zero temperatures in the winter, and views his job dispassionately. "How can I like it? It's for an uneducated man". Only 190 **meters** in Seoul, maximum charge is 75p for 120 minutes, the **fine** is double the meter charge. **Towing away** only takes place from no-go zones and totals £20

Sandra Goldgraben, age not given. **Wage:** £1,019 monthly. **Previous job:** nurse and aspiring actress. Unusually prefers to walk her beat – most colleagues ride three-wheelers. Has the distinction of ticketing six Rolls-Royces in minutes on one half block stretch and of moving on Cary Grant. **Meters** are 4½p for 20 minutes, **fine** £8 for a lapsed one and £27 for **towing away**, which is done by private contractors

Now read the notes more carefully and answer the following questions:

2 Which traffic warden seems to enjoy the job most?

 a Marina Di Generoso   *c* Michiko Demizu
 b Valdeci Pola da Silva   *d* Elly van Driel

3 In Sao Paulo traffic wardens have to call regularly at banks because

 a they collect more money than they   *c* there is a danger that they will be
    can carry.   robbed.
 b their superiors do not trust them with *d* they need to get supplies of small
    a lot of money.   change.

4 In which city do traffic wardens seem to have the worst working conditions?

 a Tokyo   *c* Rome
 b Seoul   *d* Sao Paulo

5 Which city seems to have the worst parking problems?

 a Rotterdam   *c* Rome
 b Sao Paulo   *d* Beverly Hills

6 Which city seems to be most efficient in dealing with parking problems?

 a Tokyo   *c* Seoul
 b Rotterdam   *d* Beverly Hills

7 Only one traffic warden mentions a really bad experience. This warden was

 a tricked by a dishonest driver. •   *c* badly beaten up by an angry driver.
 b insulted about the nature of the work. *d* almost knocked over by a car.

▶ Focus on grammar 3 · The past continuous

Form was ....ing/were ....ing

Use The past continuous tense describes actions and situations which are unfinished at a particular point in the past. We have no information about the exact starting and finishing time. *For example:*

When I woke up, the sun was shining through the window and someone was making breakfast.

In diagram form the sentence looks like this:

The main function of the past continuous is, therefore, to provide the background to specific events in the past, and it is most commonly used:

1 To refer to longer actions which are interrupted by shorter actions. *For example:*

The taxi arrived while I was having breakfast.

25

Notice the difference between:

a I was standing at the bus stop when the accident happened.
(I was already standing there at the moment when the accident happened.)

b When the accident happened I ran to phone for an ambulance.
(I ran to the phone the moment after the accident happened.)

2 To refer to two or more longer actions happening at the same time. *For example:*

While I was chatting on the phone, the dinner was burning.

3 To describe a scene or the background to a story. (The main events in the story are in the simple past.) *For example:*

The wind was increasing in strength and the sea was beginning to get rough. A few seagulls were circling overhead. Then the boat started to take in water.

4 To show that an action started before and continued after a particular time in the past. *For example:*

This time last month we were getting excited about our holiday and now it's all over.

5 To emphasise how long the action continued. The length of time is more important than the action itself.

Compare these two sentences:

He was talking to a policeman for two hours. I began to get worried.
He talked to a policeman at the door and then went into the building.

Note For a list of verbs that cannot be used in the continuous form, look back at Focus on grammar 2 (Unit 1A) page 11.

Exercise 1 Complete the following sentences using a verb in either the simple past or the past continuous tense. Add any other necessary words.

A suitable verb is suggested for the first five.

1 While I was working hard my lucky sister .... (enjoy)

2 I couldn't answer the phone when it rang because I .... (have a bath)

3 When Jane's husband left her she .... (sell)

4 I didn't hear a thing because I was watching television when the burglar .... (break in)

5 The bus was late as usual so when I got to work everyone else .... (already/work)

6 Before cars were invented people ....

7 Just as I was parking my car another driver ....

8 When I finally passed my driving test I ....

9 Look at the rain! It's hard to believe that at this time last week we ....

10 While David was waiting outside one cinema his girlfriend ....

Exercise 2 In the following passage put the verb in brackets into the most suitable tense (simple past or past continuous).

One of the most embarrassing incidents in my early career as a doctor (1) .... (happen) when I (2) .... (work) in the Accident Department of a large city hospital. I (3) .... (usually, cycle) to work when the weather was fine as I (4) .... (try) to lose weight. That particular morning it (5) .... (just, begin) to rain as I (6) .... (leave) the house but I (7) .... (think) I could reach the hospital before the rain (8) .... (get) too heavy. I (9) .... (cycle) down the hill, (10) .... (turn) into the main road and (11) .... (head) for the city centre when the bus in front of me (12) .... (begin) to slow down. As I (13) .... (move) out to overtake it, there was a loud bang and everything (14) .... (go) black. When I (15) .... (come) round, I (16) .... (lie) on the pavement and a crowd of people (17) .... (stand) around me. Then I (18) .... (hear) an ambulance in the distance and my heart (19) .... (sink). Five minutes later I (20) .... (arrive) at the hospital and was carried into the Accident Department on a stretcher.

▶ Focus on listening 2 · A life at sea

For questions 1–6, tick (√) whether you think the statements are true or false.

	True	False
1 John didn't want to join the Merchant Navy at first.		✓
2 He suddenly decided to leave his first ship just before it sailed.		✓
3 His training course taught him how to serve at table.		✓
4 The life at the training school was hard.	✓	
5 As a bellboy, he had to ring the ship's bells.		✓
6 He often regretted joining the Merchant Navy.		✓

(handwritten notes: 1 — "he did decide"; 3 "lay at"; 5 "16-18")

For questions 7–10 put a tick next to the correct answer.

7 The total time John spent in the Merchant Navy was

a 2 years.
b 4 years.
c 6 years.
d 10 years.

(handwritten: 12, 6 + 4)

8 The worst thing about being a merchant seaman was

a the low pay.
b the accommodation.
c the other seamen.
d the time away from home.

9 On one occasion the ship was delayed outside Hong Kong because

a it had lost important equipment in a storm.
b there were too many ships already in the harbour.
c it was impossible to enter the harbour.
d conditions in the harbour were too dangerous.

10 He finally left the Merchant Navy because

a he wanted to go and live in Australia.
b he was tired of the life at sea.
c he was persuaded by friends to leave.
d he was offered the chance of a new career.

STUDY BOX 3

Phrasal verb **Put.**   Was there anything you found really hard to **put up with**?

(Listening 2)

put aside – save (especially money/time). We've **put** some money **aside** for a holiday.
put away – store/tidy. Please **put** your toys **away** now, children.
put off – postpone. They've **put** the wedding **off** for a month.
                discourage/distract. When I heard how difficult the exam was, it **put** me **off** entering for it.
put on – get dressed. Why don't you **put** a thicker jumper **on**?
                increase (especially in weight). He eats like a horse but never **puts on** weight.
put out – extinguish. Firemen managed to **put** the fire **out** after two hours.
put through – connect. Could you put me **through** to the Manager, please?
put up – provide accommodation. My sister will **put** me **up** while I'm in London.
put up with – tolerate. I will not **put up with** your rudeness!

▶ Focus on writing · Informal letters

Writing Bank: page 220

1 Each country has its own conventions in letter writing. These concern the way that the sender's address is written, for example, and where different parts of the letter are placed on the page.

With a partner, decide where the following parts of a letter should be:

Dear...

Yours etc.,

Your Address

The Date

Check your result with your teacher.

2 Now copy these details on to the letter below so that you have a correct model.

Yours,

Flat 2,
9 Wood Road,
Barrington,
Somerset TE3 4LL,
England.

Dear Gill,

10th Sept. 19—

It's been ages since I've seen you and quite a lot has happened!
First of all, I've got a new job with an advertising company. It's much harder work but more interesting and better paid than my old job.
I've also moved to a new flat as you'll see from my address. It's quite a lot bigger and I've now got a spare bedroom for guests!
Why don't you come and stay for a weekend so we can catch up on each other's news? It would be lovely to see you.
Looking forward to hearing from you.

3 Read the following notes and make sure that your model letter is perfectly correct!

Notes

1 Never write your name before your address.
2 Put a comma after each line of your address and a full-stop at the end.
3 It's better to write the date in the form 2(nd) Feb(ruary) 19— rather than 2/2/19—.
4 Never begin a letter with 'Dear Friend'. Always use a name.
5 Write the first line of the letter (Dear . . .) next to the margin.
6 Each paragraph of a handwritten letter should be indented, that is it should begin about a centimetre after the margin.
7 Most letters have a brief sentence on a separate line before the end. 'I look forward to hearing from' you or just 'Best wishes' are common.
8 The end of the letter 'Yours sincerely' etc is written near the middle of the page.
9 'Yours sincerely' is a suitable ending for informal letters to people you don't know too well. 'Yours' is suitable for closer friends and 'Love' for very close friends and family!
10 Notice that 'Yours' is always written with a capital 'Y' and 'sincerely' with a small 's'. This ending is followed by a comma.

Now write the numbers above on the model letter next to the parts they refer to.

4 Writing task

Imagine that you have received the letter on page 28 from an English friend.
Write a reply either accepting the invitation or turning it down (with reasons).

Notes

1 Follow the layout of the letter on page 28.

2 Remember to: ● thank your friend for the letter and invitation.
● say you can or can't come (and why).
● comment on your friend's news.
● give some news about yourself.
● **either** suggest a date and time for your visit, and say you're looking forward to it.
or say how sorry you are that you can't come, and make an alternative suggestion.

▶ Vocabulary review

Choose the word or phrase which best completes each sentence.

1 I only left my car on double yellow lines for 5 minutes and now I've got a £10 .... to pay.

a fee   *b* fare   *c* bill   *d* fine

2 My speech isn't ready yet but I'll have time to prepare it .... the journey, I hope.

a for   *b* through   *c* in   *d* during

3 He enjoyed playing computer games at first, but after .... he got bored with them.

a little time   *b* no time   *c* a while   *d* while

4 The advantage of this remote control television is that you can change the channel .... leaving your chair.

a rather than   *b* without   *c* instead of   *d* by

5 You drove right at me! Were you trying to .... me down, or what?

a get   *b* hit   *c* run   *d* push

6 I'm afraid I didn't hear the doorbell when you rang. I .... in the garden at the time.

a worked   *b* have worked   *c* was working   *d* have been working

7 If you want to .... the date on that cheque, you'll have to sign your name as well, or the bank won't accept it.

a alter   *b* exchange   *c* remove   *d* revise

8 .... how hard I work, I never seem to get any praise.

a No matter   *b* Regardless   *c* Not counting   *d* Even

9 Each student must be .... for his or her own belongings.

a interested   *b* responsible   *c* careful   *d* aware

10 I have two assistants in my department and we work together as a ....

a crew   *b* team   *c* band   *d* gang

11 He soon realised that his girlfriend's only interest was .... his money.

a for   *b* about   *c* with   *d* in

12 I wouldn't mind if he didn't .... me like a servant.

a treat   *b* behave   *c* pretend   *d* speak

13 I was so worried about the news that I couldn't concentrate .... my work.

a to   *b* in   *c* on   *d* about

14 The watch I bought is fine but the strap won't go round my ....

a waist   *b* wrist   *c* ankle   *d* elbow

15 .... we do the same work, she earns more than I do.

a Despite   *b* However   *c* In spite   *d* Although

UNIT3A Enthusiasms

▶ **Lead-in**   Below are pictures of twenty different items connected with five different sports or hobbies. Write the name of each activity in the place provided below together with the four items connected with it.

Activity	sewing	painting	cooking	gardening	tennis
Item 1	sew machine	palette	whisk	boots	racket
2	scissors	picture	knife	watering can	ball
3	needle	brush	scales	plant	shoes/trainers
4	cotton	easel	saucepan	spade	net

▶ **Text 1**

1 In this section, four well-known people describe an activity which they are enthusiastic about.

The four activities are: windsurfing* running breeding budgerigars* tennis

Below are the four people concerned, with clues about their hobby. Try to guess who has which hobby.

Sally Oppenheim
Member of Parliament

She has become more aggressive in her hobby since she entered politics.

 tennis

Rosalind Plowright
International opera singer

Her hobby allows her to be completely alone with nature.

windsurfing

Bill Sirs
Trade unionist

His doctor disapproves of his hobby.

running

Geoff Capes
Shot put* champion

He describes his hobby as the absolute opposite of what he does in his sport in terms of aggressiveness.

 breeding budgerigars

windsurfing or board-sailing: the fastest growing water sport in the world. Windsurfers stand on a flat board and hold on to a bar on the sail to direct their course.
budgerigars are small birds, usually blue or green and originally from Australia. They are often kept as pets and breeders keep them in numbers in order to produce young ones, and sometimes to enter them in shows.
shot put: a competition to throw a heavy metal ball the furthest distance.

2 Now read through the four articles as quickly as possible to find out the correct answer.

Rosalind Plowright

A

I think windsurfing is better than swimming. More exhilarating. You can really get away from it all. I love being alone with nature, and when you're out there on the water you can come around a headland and suddenly find that you're completely alone. Just me and the sea and the wind in my hair. Once, when I was working in San Diego, I suddenly felt I'd had enough of opera – studying the role and the claustrophobia of the rehearsal rooms – and found going out windsurfing a tremendous escape.

I think most of my singer colleagues are rather amused by the idea of me windsurfing. However, these days, at least 50 per cent of singers keep physically fit in some way – playing golf, or working out in gyms. A few years ago they tended to be a lot fatter, but now they are conscious of the need to keep fit.

Geoff Capes

B

I find the hobby gives me relaxation and peace of mind – it's the absolute opposite of what I do in my own sport in terms of aggressiveness. You can't be noisy and loud with budgerigars; but I'm as competitive when I'm showing my birds as when I'm competing with my iron. I say to the judge "Tell me why that bird has won and not mine." That is the way to learn.

You should put in at least one and a half hours work on your budgerigars a day if you want to be successful, especially in preparation for shows. You have to wash them in diluted washing up liquid and then rinse them. You blow-dry them with a hairdryer – not right up close, just a gentle blast of air. Or put them in front of the fire to dry naturally. But you get them more fluffy if you blow-dry. Those birds are better looked after than some human beings.

46 secs.

2 mins.

Bill Sirs

C

Apart from keeping you fit, the great thing about running is that it releases the tensions of work. You can't worry when you're running, and you can see all your problems from afar, making it easier to find solutions. During the 13 week steel strike in 1980 I ran a lot, thinking things out.

Recently, a senior hospital consultant looking at my knee shook his head and said, "I don't really approve of all this running, you know. How long have you been doing it?" I told him 32 years, to which he replied, "In that case, I give up." With a bit of luck, I'll still be running in the next 15 years – unless, of course, I drop dead.

Sally Oppenheim

D

Social tennis is what I like best. Playing doubles with about eight regular friends for fun. It's generally a noisy, boisterous kind of game, with constant shouts of frustration.

We have long, loud arguments about line decisions, followed up by long arguments about the score. We're all pretty aggressive, and I think I make it worse, actually. I have noticed that since I entered politics my game has got a lot more aggressive, and I am very argumentative about the score.

The wonderful thing about tennis is that when you are playing it, you can't think of anything else. Your mind is totally absorbed in the game. And when you do that really good shot the elation is incredible. On the other hand, however, there is probably no frustration greater than the muffed shot at the net.

From The Sunday Times Magazine

3 Find a phrase or sentence in each passage which explains why each writer finds their hobby so important.

Is there anything they all have in common? *Relaxing – escape from work*

4 Answer these questions by circling the correct letter(s). There may be more than one correct answer. The letters refer to the writers of the four passages.

a Who mentions the health aspect of their hobby?   A B C D

b Who doesn't always want their hobby to take their mind off their work?   A B C D

c Who describes their hobby in the most detail?   A B C D

d Who mentions other people's reactions to their hobby?   A B C D

e Who mentions an annoying moment experienced while enjoying their hobby? A B C D

f Who mentions the pleasure and excitement their hobby can give them?   A B C D

g Who seems to want to become more expert in their hobby?   A B C D

h Who mentions the difficulties of their job?   A B C D

i Whose hobby involves an element of competition?   A B C D

When you have finished, compare your answers with another student's and discuss any differences.

Vocabulary 5 The four writers use several words describing emotions. Find words in the passages which mean the same as:

a very exciting (adjective) ....exhilarating............

b feeling of being enclosed in a small space (noun) ....claustrophobia............

c feelings of worry or anxiety (noun) ....tensions............

d feeling ready for a quarrel or fight (noun) ....aggressiveness............

e feeling of annoyed disappointment when you are prevented from doing something (noun) ....frustration............

f feeling of joy or pride (noun) ....elation............

Discussion points 6 Work with one or two other students to discuss the following:

a Which of the four activities:
  ● would be the most expensive to do regularly?
  ● requires the most patience?
  ● would be the easiest to take up?
  ● requires the most skill?
  ● needs the most physical strength?
  ● is the most dangerous?

b Which would appeal to you most and which least?

▶ Focus on grammar 1 · The present perfect simple

Look at these examples from Text I:

> Tell me why that bird has won and not mine.
> I have noticed that since I entered politics my game has got a lot more aggressive.

The present perfect tense is used whenever there is a strong link between the past and the present. It gives information about the present as well as the past. Though the action happened before now, we are often more concerned with the present result or effect. *For example:*

I've mended the cooker.	= You can use it now.
She's been to Japan.	= She has some experience of the country.
We've already eaten.	= We are not hungry.

Suggest the present result or effect in these examples:

> My car has broken down.
> I've spent all my money.
> The bus drivers have gone on strike.
> She's passed all her exams.
> There has been an earthquake.

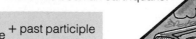

Form

| has have | + past participle |

Use There are two main uses of the present perfect:

I a to refer to an action which began in the past and has continued until now. *For example:*

> He has worked hard all his life.

b to refer to a number of individual actions which have happened up to the present (and may happen again). *For example:*

> She has changed her job three times in the last five years.

| so far |
| recently |
| lately |
| up to now |

Notice that the present perfect is often used with time expressions that refer to a period up to the present. The most common ones are shown in the box on the left. Underline the other examples used in *a* and *b* at the bottom of page 33.

In addition the present perfect is often used with 'for' and 'since'. *For example:*

I've lived in London for ten years (and still do)   (for + a period of time)
I've lived in London since 1976 (and still do)   (since + a point of time)

In a diagram the two sentences can be represented like this:

```
                        for 10 years
                    ┌──────────────────┐
                    I have lived in London
────────────────────●──────────────────●──────────────────▶
                   1976 ◀──since 1976──▶ now
```

Exercise 1   Add **for** or **since** to the following sentences.

a He has been unemployed . . . *since* he left school.

b I've known her *for* six years.

c The phone has been out of order *for* a long time.

d I haven't had a cold . . . *since* last November.

e Where have you been . . . *since* 12 o'clock?

2 to refer to an action which was completed in the past but where the time is not given. When the exact time is given, use the simple past.

Compare: I've found a new job!
I found a new job last week.

Look at these two pictures of David Sage and notice the changes that have taken place in recent years. Complete the sentences below with a suitable verb

Exercise 2

Since 1979 . . .

a he *'s lost* . . . a lot of hair.

b he *'s grown* a moustache.

c his eyesight *has got* . . . worse.

d he *'s put on* . . . weight.

e he *'s changed* . his style of dress.

| just |
| already |
| before |

Notice that the present perfect is used with these words when they refer to an indefinite time in the past. *For example.*

We've already done that exercise.
I think I've been to this restaurant before
She has just had a baby.

● Again, the **present** result is important.

Exercise 3

| ever |
| never |
| yet |
| still |

These words are also often used with the present perfect but in questions and negative sentences. In the following examples put the word in brackets in the correct place.

a Have you been to the opera? (ever)
b Have they arrived? (yet)
c She has learned to drive. (never)

d I haven't finished that book. (still)
e Your father hasn't phoned. (yet)

Exercise 4   Match the two parts of these sentences so that every sentence is grammatically correct and makes sense.

homework?

pres. perf / simple
simple past

pres. perf i	**1** I've had a headache	*a* for several years.
past simp. h	**2** The cost of living increased by 10%	*b* yet.
pres. perf j	**3** The television has gone wrong	*c* this morning?
past simp g	**4** Cars replaced horse-drawn vehicles	*d* last night.
pres. perf b	**5** I haven't passed my driving test	*e* in the last few weeks.
past simple d	**6** I didn't sleep very well	*f* at least an hour ago.
past simple f	**7** You're too late! The film began	*g* nearly a hundred years ago.
pres. perf a	**8** He's been a vegetarian	*h* last year.
past simple c	**9** Did you have breakfast	*i* since lunchtime.
pres. perf. e	**10** He has become more sociable	*j* several times in the last month.

Focus on listening 1

5mins.

You are going to hear information about three different leisure activities: Judo, Budgerigar breeding and Windsurfing.

Before you start listening, study the table below and read through the notes carefully so that you know what specific information to listen for.

As you listen, fill in the missing details.

1

Activity	First Introduced	Made an Olympic Event		Costs	
Judo	1882	1964	Judo suit to buy / Judo suit to hire	£ 15 / £5 a month	
Windsurfing	1969	1984	Beginners board / A racing board	£300 / £ 1000	
Budgerigar Breeding	1840	✗	Price range for birds	£ 7 £ 500	

2 *a* The ....headquarters.... of the International Judo Federation is in Paris.

    b The season for windsurfing in Britain is ....March - Sept....

    c At other times you need to wear a ....dry suit....

    d The telephone number of the Budgerigar Information Bureau is ....01 - 137 3444....

    e The most highly prized colour would be ....Pink....

Focus on writing 1 · Speeches

Writing Bank: page 231

For this type of writing you must imagine that you are going to speak to one or more people for five minutes or so, without interruption. It could be an informal situation, like giving advice to a small child, or it could be a more formal occasion like making a speech of welcome for an important visitor to your school or college.

Whatever kind of speech you're going to give, it's important to think carefully about the following points before you start:

a Who are you?   What kind of speech are you expected to give? What is your relationship with your audience?

b Who are you talking to?   Is it a large group or only one or two individuals? How old are they? How well do you know them?

c Where are you?   Is it a formal or an informal occasion? Is it important to speak loudly and clearly or would it be better to be more chatty?

d What are you talking about?   Is it a serious or a light-hearted subject? Can you include any humour? Are you explaining, persuading, describing, encouraging, or what?

Exercise 1 Look at the following possible speech topics and decide what the answers to the four questions *a–d* above are for each one.

    1 You have been asked to give a talk to a group of 10–12 year-old school children about your favourite hobby. Write what you would say.

    2 Some English friends are planning to tour your country and have asked for your advice on where to go and what to see. Write what you would say to them.

3 Two new students have joined your English class and you have been asked to show them round the school and explain what they need to know. Write what you would say as you walk around.

4 The school your children go to is considering giving up the teaching of English. Write the speech you would give at the Parent-Teacher's meeting which has been called to discuss this change.

Language Remember that spoken English, even for a formal speech on an important occasion, will be different from written English. Informal speeches will be even more different in style, of course.

Look at the two examples below and compare the two ways of giving the same information:

> **Written**
> Eggs are date-stamped by the packing stations with the relevant week number, the week of January 1st being Week 1, so their freshness can be checked when buying. Fresh eggs can be stored for 3 weeks in a cool larder or refrigerator. Whole eggs in the shell cannot be frozen.

> **Spoken**
> If you look at an egg box, you'll notice a date stamp which has been put on at the packing station. This shows the week number and it's easy to understand because the week of January 1st is Week 1, and so on throughout the year, you see. That's how to make sure that the eggs you buy are really fresh. By the way, you can store fresh eggs for up to 3 weeks in a cool larder or refrigerator, but you can't freeze whole eggs at all.

Exercise 2 Now say whether the following statements are true or false:

Spoken English uses –

a more contractions like 'I'll', 'it's' etc.
b more examples of the passive voice.
c more 'filler' phrases like 'you see'.
d more words to say the same thing usually.
e more slang.
f more phrasal verbs like put back (for replace) etc.
g more long words.

Exercise 3 Read the written instructions for poaching an egg and then write what you would say to someone if you were actually showing them how to do it.

> An egg for poaching should be broken carefully into a cup or saucer. Heat 2.5 cm of water in a shallow pan (a frying pan is suitable). Do not add salt or vinegar or the white will be tough. Bring the water to a gentle boil and slide in the egg gently. Cook for about 3 minutes or remove the pan from the heat, cover and leave for 3½–4 minutes.

Exercise 4 Imagine that you have been asked to give a short talk about your favourite sport or hobby to a group of ten English schoolchildren who are on an exchange visit to your country. The children are all aged from 14 to 16 and it will be a fairly informal occasion. Write what you would say.

(120–180 words)

Notes 1 You should try to cover all the main points of your subject, so first of all, make notes. Some of the following headings may be useful:

Cost   Equipment   Training   Time   Qualifications
Skills needed   Advantages/Disadvantages

36

2 Remember that you'll be talking (not reading aloud!). You should include typical features of spoken English like contractions and 'filler phrases' to make your talk sound natural. Make it clear, too, that you're speaking to someone by referring to your audience from time to time. *For example:*

> I don't know if any of you have ever been climbing?

3 As well as the practical side, you should also describe the enjoyment you get from your sport or hobby and try to share your enthusiasm for it with your audience.

4 Your approach will depend on the kind of hobby you have. If it's fairly unusual, you will need to spend more time explaining it. If it's a well-known one, then concentrate on describing your personal experiences (remember, a little humour helps!)

5 The talk should leave your audience with a clear idea of what your sport or hobby involves and how to take it up themselves if they should want to. Your talk should also have been entertaining!

STUDY BOX 1

1 Adjective/noun + preposition: opposite

the opposite **(of)** – a person or thing which is completely different from another
    'It's **the** absolute **opposite of** what I do in my own sport.' (*Text 1*)

opposite **(to)**   – completely different from
    My opinion is completely **opposite to** yours. The **opposite** sex.
    – facing
    The bank is **opposite (to)** the post office. The man sitting **opposite**.

2 Verb + preposition   'I don't really **approve of** all this running.' (*Text 1*)

(dis)approve **of**	listen **to**	**remind** somebody **of/about** something
describe **as**	pay **for**	**warn** somebody **of/about** something
complain **about**	rely **on**	
concentrate **on**	depend **on**	

Focus on grammar 2
The present perfect continuous

Look at this example from Listening 1:
    Windsurfing is very simple to describe, but, as I've been discovering, not so easy to do!

Form
    $\dfrac{\text{has}}{\text{have}}$ + been + $\dfrac{\text{present}}{\text{participle}}$

Use   The continuous form of the present perfect tense is used

1 to suggest that a situation is temporary rather than permanent.

    Compare: I've worked in this office for eight years.
                I couldn't find a full-time job so I've been working part-time.

2 to show that an action is not finished.

    Compare: I've been waiting to see him since 10 o'clock. (I'm still waiting)
                I've waited long enough! (I won't wait any longer.)

3 to emphasise that an action has only just finished, particularly when explaining results that can still be seen. *For example:*

> Why are you covered in oil? – I've been mending the car.
> Why is the floor so wet? – The washing machine has been leaking again.

Exercise 1   Now answer these questions in the same way:

    a Why are Jane's eyes red?
    b Why are you out of breath?
    c Why does Guy's back ache so much?
    d Why do you feel so tired?

[handwritten: treat with caution]

Note   ● Some verbs cannot be used in the continuous form. Look back at page 11 for a list of the most common examples.
     ● The present perfect continuous cannot be used when a quantity is mentioned.

    Compare: I've been writing letters this evening.
               I've written five letters this evening.

Exercise 2   Complete the following sentences with the correct form of the verb in brackets. Use the simple past, present perfect or present perfect continuous. Where more than one tense is possible, decide which is more appropriate.

[handwritten margin: temp/unfinished]
1 I .....*have been sharing*..... (share) a flat with two friends since I ....*came*....... (come) back to England but I'd like a place of my own.

2 After John ....*left*....... (leave) the army, he ....*applied*.... (apply) for a job in a bank and *has worked / been working* ... (work) there ever since.

3 I ....*saw*........ (see) the film a few weeks ago but I .....*have never read*..... (never, read) the book. *[handwritten: experience]*

[handwritten margin: temp/ unfinished]
4 You look frozen! How long *have you been*... (you, stand) out here in the cold?

[handwritten margin: pres. perf. simple]
5 Car workers .....*have been*..... (be) on strike since September when the company .....*rejected*....... (reject) their claim for a 20% pay rise. *[handwritten: standing]*

6 *Have you heard* (you, hear) the news? Simon Jones and Sally Drew *have announced* (announce) their engagement. They *have been* ....(go out) together for ages but nobody ....*thought*........ *[handwritten: normally simple form]* (think) they would ever get married. *[handwritten: going]*

7 What *have you been doing* (you, do) lately? This is the first time I *have seen* ...... (see) you since we ....*met*......... (meet) at the Smiths' party last May.

[handwritten margin: simple]
8 There ....*have been*.... (be) heavy snowfalls in the West Country in the last twenty-four hours and the police *have warned* (warn) drivers to take great care. Two serious accidents ...*have*............ (already, occur) on the M5 motorway and the forecast is for more snow on the way.

9 I still *haven't heard*. (not, hear) from Geraldine even though I ....*wrote*....... (write) to her three times last month.

10 Food prices *have risen*... (rise) steadily since Britain ......*joined*.... (join) the Common Market in 1973.

STUDY BOX 2

Adjectives with numbers.   '... the **13-week** steel strike ...' (*Text 1*)
                            '... **21-year-old** Cathy ...' (*Text 2*)

When a plural expression with a number is used as an adjective, (as before a noun), it becomes singular.
a 5-mile walk (a walk of 5 miles)   a six-foot man
a 10-pound cheque   a 4-storey house
a 5-litre can
Now change the following in the same way:
a letter with 8 pages   a break of 20 minutes
a mountain which is 3,000 metres high   a baby of 3 months
a ticket which cost $20
Note: A hyphen is usually used, as in the examples.

▶ Text 2 · A new way to jump

1 Read the following text through fairly quickly to answer these questions:
  a How much did it cost to make a parachute jump? *£385*
  b How long did the training last? *Sat a.m → Sun pm.*
  c Did the jumps go well? *Yes*
  d How did David and Cathy feel about the experience? *Fantastic*

Until a few weeks ago neither David nor his wife Cathy had ever been in an aeroplane. Then one recent Saturday morning they left their house in Dorchester and drove to an aerodrome near Maidstone in Kent. The next afternoon
5 they got into an aeroplane and flew up to around 10,000 feet and jumped out.

At 7.15 a.m. they climbed into their old red Marina and set off. The car is **on its last legs** and they had saved more than £700 towards a new one. They could have stayed at
10 home and bought a replacement car, but the chance of a once-in-a-lifetime experience was too inviting, although it was going to cost Cathy £385 to have it.

Cathy was so nervous during the drive that her hands shook too much for her to hold the map to **navigate**. They
15 arrived at 11.15 and within a short while, the instructors at the centre had not only **allayed their fears** but had persuaded Dave that he should have a go as well.

Once they had made up their minds, training began **in earnest.** First they were shown a video of a novice making
20 his first jump. Then the instructor showed them photographs of every stage of the jump, from sitting with legs dangling out of the plane 10,000 feet up, to landing five minutes later.

They were then introduced to their gear. This proved
25 surprisingly neat and easy to handle – "just like a big haversack, with all vital controls on the front". They were shown how to pull the toggle which operates the main parachute. In case it does not work – which seldom happens – there is a reserve parachute.
30 They were then taught the right **posture** to adopt for jumping and landing, and after lunch started working from a **mock-up** of the side of an aeroplane in the barn. They practised exits by sliding off the side to the ground below. Then they were suspended from a beam in harnesses and

35 made to practise steering a parachute. The various preparatory drills are repeated over and over again until they become **second nature**.

Next day at about lunchtime, David put on his gear and climbed into the aeroplane, sandwiched between his two
40 instructors. At 12,500 feet David and his two instructors jumped – and everything went like a dream. He was so relaxed he was able to wave and smile. After 50 seconds of free fall David opened his parachute. A few minutes later he landed close to where his wife was waiting; in fact, he
45 landed so well that he remained upright and did not fall over.

Cathy jumped a little later, firmly hitched on either side to her two instructors. They detached themselves only when her parachute had opened safely. The instructors
50 then continued their free fall, releasing their parachutes later so that they could land before their pupil.

"It's extraordinary", says Cathy. "There's no sensation of speed because there's nothing to relate to. You're not flying past anything. You can't hear anything. Everything is
55 done by hand signals. And as soon as I put up my parachute, I shut my eyes and screamed: it's just like putting on the brakes, only worse. You feel as though you're going upwards".

Cathy turned this way and that and found herself saying
60 "This is fantastic", before making a perfect landing. "I wouldn't have missed it for the world", says 21-year-old Cathy.

She has been told that she is the first woman in Britain to have done what she did, and Dave is only the second man.
65 "We saved up for a car", he says, "and **blew it all** jumping out of an aeroplane".

But the couple from Dorchester have no regrets.

From The Sunday Telegraph Magazine

2 Say whether the following statements are true or false and why.

F *a* Cathy and Dave had saved up to pay for their parachute jump.
F *b* Cathy wasn't at all worried before the training began.
T *c* There was less equipment to carry than they expected.
T *d* They each had two parachutes.
F *e* They made their first jump together.
T *f* Cathy's instructors descended more quickly than she did.
T *g* They both fell for some distance before their parachutes opened.
F *h* Cathy's landing was less successful than her husband's.
F *i* Cathy had always disliked flying before.

3 Eight words or phrases which you may not know are in bold in the text.

- Study them carefully and say what you think they could mean in the context.

- Below are eight explanations for them but they are **not in the same order**.

  Match the explanation to the correct word or phrase.

  a full-size model   *mock-up*
  b reassured them   *allayed their fears*
  c nearly worn out   *on its last legs*
  d position of the body   *posture*
  e spent a sum of money in one go   *blew it all*
  f give directions   *navigate*
  g a firmly fixed habit   *second nature*
  h seriously   *in earnest*

4 Choose the answer which you think fits best.

1 During their training, Cathy and Dave

a were given a short demonstration flight
b were shown how the controls of the plane worked
c were taught how to get out of the plane correctly
d were tested to see how fit they were

2 Dave's jump 'went like a dream' (line 41). This means that

a it was over extremely quickly
b it went exactly as planned
c it fulfilled a long ambition
d it didn't seem to have been real

3 The main role of Cathy's instructors during her jump was to

a operate her parachute correctly for her
b hold on to her until it was safe to let go
c tell her what to do at every stage
d help her to make a safe landing

4 Cathy screamed when her parachute opened because

a she wasn't expecting it to happen
b it made such a loud noise
c she was afraid it wasn't going to work
d it slowed her down so suddenly

Discussion points

- Could you have done what Cathy and Dave did? Why/why not?
- What do you think it is that people enjoy about parachute jumping and free falling?
- What kind of person do you have to be to enjoy a sport like parachute jumping, in your opinion?
- Do you think Cathy and Dave made the right decision when they spent their savings on parachute jumping rather than on a car? Why/why not?

▶ Communication activity · 20 questions

Work as a class or in groups.

Instructions 1 Think of three sports or hobbies and write them down. (Don't choose activities which are too obvious – for example football – or ones that you know nothing about!)

2 Choose one student as 'Subject' to start. He or she picks one activity from their list. The rest of the class (or group) must ask the Subject questions about the activity in order to guess what it is.

> Rules: *a* You can ask each Subject a maximum of 20 questions.
> *b* The questions should be ones with Yes/No answers. *For example:* Do you need special equipment? not What special equipment do you need?
> *c* All the questions should be in correct English! The Subject needn't answer questions which are incorrect.

Note If you want to make this activity into a competition, allow the Subject to score 1 mark for every question asked. The highest score wins at the end of the activity.

Preparation Here are some of the range of questions you could ask.

a Is it expensive   to do/play?
    dangerous
    difficult

Do you do it on your own.

b Can you do this indoors?

....
....

c Do you need special equipment?

Do men + women play it together

....

d Would other people enjoy watching it?

....

e Could you do it in this town?

Does it need a lot of space

....

f Do you need to be very strong?
Do you have to practise very often?

Do you have to run fast

....
....

Imagine that the Subject's activity is football. What other questions would help lead you to the answer?

▶ Focus on listening 2

You are going to hear a runner describe the route he took round the city of Bristol. Before you listen, study the map below and the four questions which follow.

1 As you listen, mark the route which the runner took and then choose the correct answer for questions 2–5.

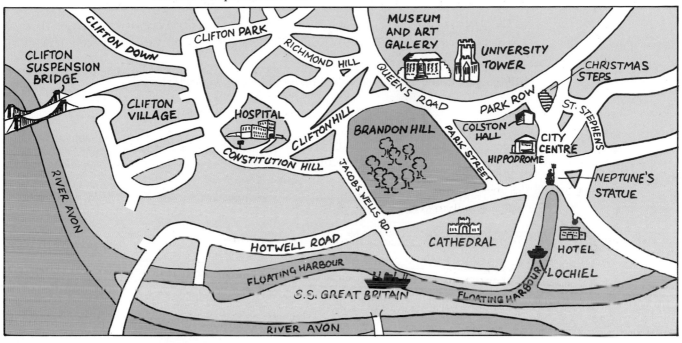

2 Ned didn't cross the Suspension Bridge because

- *a* he didn't want to waste time.
- *b* he couldn't pay the fee.
- *c* he thought it was too expensive.

3 The Hippodrome in the city Centre was probably

- *a* a shop.
- *b* a theatre.
- *c* a race course.

4 The distance he ran was

- *a* the same as he had intended.
- *b* less than he had intended.
- *c* more than he had intended.

5 The only disadvantage of the Bristol run is

- *a* the difficulty of following the map.
- *b* the distance involved.
- *c* the number of hills.

STUDY BOX 3

The order of adjectives. *For example:* '. . . their old red Marina . . .' (*Text 2*)

Age Size Temperature Texture etc.	Shape	Colour	Origin	Material	+ noun

A new white Chinese paper lampshade
A huge circular blue plastic swimming pool

Put the following adjectives in the correct order.

cat black, fat, Persian
package paper, brown, thick
jumper old, woollen, blue
jug green, tiny, glass
dining table wooden, round, large

▶ Focus on grammar 3 · Modal verbs 1: ability

Can, Could and Be able

Use   **1** Present. **can** is more commonly used than **be able** to express ability. *For example:*

> I can drive but I can't ride a bike.
> How many mistakes can you find?

2 Past. In affirmative sentences there is an important difference in meaning between **could** and **was/were able to**. **Could** refers to general ability whereas **was/were able to** is used in cases of specific ability.

Consider the following situation.

Eric and Adam were both keen cyclists. At the weekend they often cycled from Bournemouth to Southampton, a distance of more than 20 miles. When they set off together last Sunday, the journey took Eric two hours. Adam's bike had a puncture just after he began the journey so he had to go back home.

> Both Eric and Adam could cycle 20 miles. (They were both fit enough to do it)
> Last Sunday only Eric was able to cycle that far.

Note   **managed to** can replace **was able to**

In negative sentences **could** is normally used in both general and specific cases of ability. *For example:*

> The sea was so polluted that we couldn't swim.
> I couldn't walk until I was two and a half.

3 Perfect and future tenses. These are formed with **be able to** because **can** has no infinitive or past participle. *For example:*

> I'll be able to visit you more next summer.
> He hasn't been able to solve the problem yet.

Similarly, **be able to** is the only possible infinitive. *For example:*

> I'd like to be able to offer you a job but there are no vacancies at the moment.

4 Could have done. **Could** + perfect infinitive is used to show that someone had the ability to do something but didn't do it. *For example:*

> She could have been a model but she became a nurse instead.
> He was so rude I could have hit him.

Exercise 1   Complete the following sentences using **can**, **could**, **could have** or a suitable form of **be able to**.

a I .... play the piano much better when I was a child than I .... now.

b The doctors say he .... (never) walk again.

c Fortunately he .... swim quite well so he .... save the little girl from drowning.

d He had a ticket so he .... come to the match but he was too busy.

e .... (you) stand on your head?

f I .... (not) write since I broke my arm.

g Although she was not very tall, she .... reach the book she wanted by standing on a chair.

h He was so confused that he .... (not) remember who he was.

i I don't think that I .... mend it but I'll try.

j He .... get out of the smoke-filled room by crawling on his hands and knees.

Focus on writing 2 · Directed writing

Writing Bank: page 234

Below is a page from a catalogue of new books and notes on four people's special interests. Using the information given, continue each of the paragraphs started on the next page. Give your reasons for your choice of each book in about 50 words.

NATURE WATCHERS
Rachel Lawson
over 100 colour photographs
£15.00

Written to accompany an exciting new 13-part ITV television series, *Nature Watch*, this book describes the people who spend their lives working with the birds, animals and plants in various parts of the world. Their infectious enthusiasm is irresistibly evident, and is brought to life with their own outstanding colour photographs. Hints on nature watching for the amateur are found throughout.

DO IT YOURSELF!
Editor Bob Dillard
150 colour photographs and 490 colour illustrations
£9.95

Just the book for the job! With over 600 colour photographs and illustrations it covers the most popular DIY tasks around the home – painting, wallcoverings, stripping and finishing furniture and woodwork, tiling, putting up shelves, framing pictures, plumbing, and wiring. Full of handy tips and clear instructions.

COMPUTING DAY BY DAY
£4.95

Week to a page. A handy reference book for the home and micro computer user. This pocket diary provides a wide range of information for the enthusiast.

LEARN TO PAINT WILDLIFE
Martin Ferguson
colour throughout
Paperback £6.95

Another title in the popular and practical *Learn to Paint* series, this beautifully illustrated book shows you how to paint animals, birds, fish and butterflies in the studio and in the field.

HOUSEPLANTS THROUGH THE YEAR
Cynthia Wildman
12 double-page colour paintings
170 line drawings
£12.95

A fresh and eminently useful approach to indoor gardening. A month-by-month guide to jobs to do, plants to look for, planning ahead and enjoying seasonal variations – to give year-round colour and foliage in the home. Illustrated by original paintings for each month and an identification glossary of 150 houseplants. Includes herbs, bulbs and annuals.

SUCCESS IN WRITING AND STUDY
Conrad Ellis & Richard Hopkins
Paperback £6.50

A guide to success in written work, study and examinations for students in all subjects at colleges, universities and polytechnics. Topics covered include: grammar, punctuation, and spelling; sentence and paragraph structure; research and library work; graphs, tables, charts, and diagrams; essays, reports, and exams; letters, CVs, and application forms; listening and note-taking; talking and reading skills.

Jim Laughton (40)
He bought a home computer earlier this year and he's become very enthusiastic about it, spending hours each evening 'playing' with it, as his wife says. Unfortunately, he's getting a bit forgetful about things he's promised to do!

Freda Laughton (38)
She prefers action to reading or watching TV. She's planning to redecorate the lounge and she isn't expecting any help from Jim! She loves flowers, though, as the family lives in a first floor flat, there's no garden for her to grow anything in.

Susan Laughton (17)
She's taking 'A' Levels in English, History and Art next year and if she passes, she's hoping to become a teacher.

Tony Laughton (12)
He's very interested in animals and at the moment he wants to be a vet when he grows up.

a Jim would probably be very pleased to receive ....

b I think Freda would enjoy either ....

c I'd suggest giving Susan ....

d The present I'd recommend for Tony would be ....

Vocabulary review

Choose the word or phrase which best completes each sentence.

1 I heard that the .... at the end of the match was 2–0.
   a account   *b* total   *c* score   *d* number

2 Most people .... to pay their bills by cheque nowadays.
   a tend   *b* used   *c* require   *d* practise

3 My company is very .... of the importance of advertising.
   a interested   *b* anxious   *c* keen   *d* conscious

4 When I first started learning to play golf it was just .... fun.
   a for   *b* as   *c* in   *d* by

5 All this running up and down stairs will keep me ...., if nothing else!
   a able   *b* fit   *c* sound   *d* fine

6 I just can't make up my .... which course to take at college.
   a idea   *b* mind   *c* opinion   *d* decision

7 He doesn't take much exercise, ... from walking the dog.
   a alone   *b* besides   *c* except   *d* apart

8 My new job is the complete opposite .... the one I had before.
   a for   *b* from   *c* of   *d* to

9 Will he be good enough to .... in the Junior Championships?
   a attempt   *b* enter   *c* compete   *d* go

10 I don't .... of smoking at all.
   a agree   *b* approve   *c* allow   *d* accept

11 Of course, it may rain and in that .... we'll organize indoor events.
   a case   *b* weather   *c* condition   *d* occasion

12 You're bound to feel a bit .... before you take your driving test.
   a disappointed   *b* shy   *c* frightening   *d* nervous

13 I'll let you know my answer .... I've spoken to my wife.
   a as   *b* once   *c* until   *d* while

14 The children really loved .... down the snow-covered hillside.
   a sliding   *b* slipping   *c* skating   *d* spilling

15 They tried to .... me to see their point of view.
   a insist   *b* suggest   *c* explain   *d* persuade

▶ Lead-in

The Morris family, who live at number 37, are away on holiday. Number 35 belongs to the Bowen family. Their Scottish cousins, who are on a touring holiday, are staying with them overnight. They've all gone to the seaside for the day in the Bowens' car. The families have left a number of invitations to burglars. Work with a partner to see how many you can find. There are 10 in all.

STUDY BOX 1

Rob vs. Steal

1 You steal things (**from** people, organisations or places).
   Thieves stole the radio from my car.   My watch has been stolen.

2 You rob people or institutions (**of** things)
   He tried to rob a bank once.   Two men robbed her of her money.

   Note also
   The army robbed them of their youth.
   You have robbed me of my success.

▶ Text 1

1 Read the following article fairly quickly.

Seven banks a day are robbed in LA

John Barnes on a city's remarkable record

OCTOBER 4, 1979, Is a day of fond memory for FBI agents in Los Angeles. It's the last day that the city did not have a bank robbery.

5 Last year there were 1,844 bank robberies in the city and its suburbs, an average of about seven every business day, and a quarter of all the bank robberies committed in the United States. 10 The total haul was around four million dollars.

There are several reasons why Los Angeles heads the bankrobbery league – way ahead of San Francisco, second with 15 546, and New York third with 443. The place has an awful lot of banks – 3,300 and many stay open until 5 or 6 in the evening and at weekends. They are also very informal. "You need a warm, invit- 20 ing place to do business," says Stephen Ward of the British-owned Crocker Bank. Bank robbers are particularly appreciative.

The robberies are usually quite gen- 25 teel, with none of the machine-gun violence of the old movies. Usually, the robber passes a stick-up note to a teller, pockets the cash while the surveillance cameras click away, then makes a get- 30 away via the nearest freeway. Tellers have orders to hand over the money immediately. "The banks believe, quite rightly, that you can replace money but you can't replace lives," says one FBI 35 man.

Most of the robbers are drug-addicts. But they also include "pregnant women, one-legged men, husband-and-wife and father-and-son teams," according to 40 Joseph Chefalo, who heads the FBI's bank-robbery squad.

The FBI is particularly keen to find the "Yankee Bandit", who may have earned a place in the Guinness Book of Records 45 with 65 bank hold ups. Before making his getaway, he always doffs his Yankee baseball cap, with a smile in the direction of the cameras. For a while, the FBI thought he had retired with his haul of 50 155,000 dollars. He was not seen over the Christmas holidays. But when the first working day of the new year started off with 14 robberies, there he was, smiling for the cameras, Yankee cap in one hand, the cash in the other.

From The Sunday Times

2 Now cover the article and see if you can answer these questions:

a How does Los Angeles compare with other American cities as regards bank robberies?
b What was special about October 4th 1979?
c Are there any reasons why L.A. has so many bank robberies?

3 Find words or phrases in the article which mean the same as:

Paragraphs 1–3
a affectionate ....
b amount stolen ....
c is at the top of ....
d a list or class..............................
e grateful...................................

Paragraphs 4 and 5
f polite.......................................
g cashier in a bank ....
h takes (dishonestly) ....
i close watch ....
j escapes................................
k wide, high speed road....................
l is leader of ....
m group of people working as a team .....

Paragraph 6
n robber ....
o takes off...................................

4 Say whether the following statements are true or false, and why:

a Seven banks are robbed every day in Los Angeles.
b Bank robbers frequently injure bank staff or customers.
c Banks tell their staff not to try and resist robbers.
d The F.B.I. disapproves of the banks' advice to staff.
e The F.B.I. has no idea what the "Yankee Bandit" looks like.
f There were no bank robberies in Los Angeles before 1979.
g Bank robbers don't usually need to speak to bank staff.
h Los Angeles banks have a more relaxed atmosphere than banks in other U.S. cities.

5 Now answer these questions in your own words:

a What makes the "Yankee Bandit" exceptional?
b Why do most Los Angeles bank robbers rob banks?
c How do most robbers escape?

6 Finally, discuss the following points:

    a Why is the F.B.I. 'particularly keen' to find the *Yankee Bandit?*

    b What would be written on a stick-up note?

    c What would you do if you were i) a bank teller ii) a customer during a bank raid?

▶ Focus on grammar 1 · Modal verbs 2: obligation

Read the following passage and underline any phrases that express an obligation.

Accommodation is always arranged with an English family. A single room costs between £40 and £45 a week and you have to pay a month's rent in advance. You should allow £10 a week for bus fares and other extras. Breakfast is provided and you don't usually have to pay extra for heating. You must complete and return the enclosed form as soon as possible but you needn't send any money until we find you a suitable family.

Must

● **must** and **have to**

In the present **must** is used when the obligation comes from the speaker. **Have to** is more common when the obligation comes from someone else, often a law or a rule. *For example:*

    You have to pay a month's rent in advance. (This is a general rule)
    You must complete and return the enclosed form. (This is the agency's rule)
    In Britain, motorcyclists have to wear a crash helmet. (This is the law)

In the future and the past **have to** is the only way of expressing obligation. *For example:*

    There was a bus strike last week so I had to walk to work.
    If they move to the country, they'll have to buy a car.

Exercise 1

Complete the following sentences by choosing the most suitable form of **have to** or **must**.

    a My cough is terrible. I .... stop smoking.

    b The bus .... turn back because there was so much snow.

    c I .... take these tablets every day since I was a child.

    d Everyone who works .... pay income tax.

    e You .... work harder if you want a better job.

    f In the army you .... obey orders.

● **mustn't** and **needn't/don't have to**

mustn't expresses a negative obligation (= the action is forbidden).
needn't and **don't have to** indicate that there is no obligation. Notice the difference between **needn't** and **don't have to**: *For example:*

    You mustn't drink alcohol while taking these tablets.
    You don't have to have a licence to own a cat. (No legal requirement)
    You needn't wash up. I'll do it later. (No obligation)

Exercise 2

Complete these sentences by putting **mustn't**, **needn't** or **doesn't/don't have to** in the spaces.

    a You .... ask me when you want to use the telephone.

    b This plant .... stand in direct sunlight or it will die.

    c Students .... attend cookery classes if they don't want to.

    d The doctor says I .... get overtired but I .... stay in bed.

    e You .... park your car on double yellow lines.

Should/Ought to

Should and **ought to** are interchangeable and are used when the obligation is not so strong. Often they express advice or duty. *For example:*

    You should write to your family more often.
    I ought to stay in and work tonight.

Need

● In the present tense **need to** expresses a weaker obligation than **have to** and **must**. It is used mainly in questions and negative sentences. *For example:*

    Need I really do it all again?
    You needn't finish your lunch if you are not hungry.
    In hot weather you need to water the grass every day.

● **Needn't have (done)** and **didn't need to**

In the past **needn't have (done)** is used to show that an action was performed even though it wasn't necessary. *For example:*

> We needn't have booked seats for the show because the theatre was half empty. Next time we won't bother.

Now suggest why the following actions were a waste of time:

You needn't have cooked all that food.
He needn't have taken his umbrella.
I needn't have bought two bottles of suntan lotion.

Didn't need to also refers to an action that wasn't necessary but, in this case, it wasn't performed. *For example:*

> I didn't need to pay by cheque because I had plenty of cash.

Note   **Didn't have to** is preferred when the obligation is imposed by someone else. *For example:*

> I didn't have to go to work yesterday so I stayed in bed till lunchtime.

Exercise 3   Comment on each of these situations using the appropriate form of the word in brackets and **needn't have**, **didn't need to** or **didn't have to**.

a Patrick and Annie decided to go to France for a holiday. He went to evening classes to learn the language but she already spoke French well.

  She .... (go) to evening classes.

b George was invited to a formal party but had nothing suitable to wear and no money to buy new clothes. Fortunately a friend lent him a suit.

  He .... (buy) new clothes.

c It took Alan four hours to do his homework. The next day his teacher said his essay was rather long. She had asked for 200 – not 2000 – words.

  He .... (write) so much.

d Sidney was ill. The doctor gave him some medicine to try but suggested that an operation was probably the only solution. The medicine worked and Sidney got better very quickly.

  He .... (have) the operation.

e Judy looked through her bag several times but couldn't find her door key so finally she kicked the door down. Later she noticed the key lying on the path.

  She .... (damage) the door.

Exercise 4   Using a suitable expression of obligation write what you would say in the following situations.

a There's a no-smoking sign in the room. Your friend takes his cigarettes out of his pocket.
b A friend is planning a holiday in the U.S.A. and he thinks he can get a visa when he arrives there.
c You invited some friends to dinner and spent all day preparing a wonderful meal. They telephone you at 8 p.m. to say they cannot come.
d You are looking after two children while their parents are out. It's 11 p.m. and the children are still watching television.
e Your parents have decided to go out for a meal. You recommend an excellent restaurant that never gets too crowded. They wonder whether they should reserve a table.

▶ Focus on writing 1 · Speech

Writing Bank: page 231

> You are a Crime Prevention Officer and you have been asked to give a talk on local radio explaining how people can help to prevent their homes being burgled.

Use ideas from the Lead-in to this unit and write the speech you would make (120 – 180 words). Before you begin, refer back to the introduction to this kind of writing on page 35.

First paragraph   Introduce yourself and your subject. Explain why it's important (rising rate of crime, etc.).
Middle paragraphs   Describe basic security measures (locks, alarms, safes, etc.) and explain how people can avoid actually inviting burglars to their homes (See Lead-in).
Last paragraph   Tell people that they can get free advice from their local police station and remind them once again of the need for security measures.

▶ Focus on listening 1 · Crime report

You are going to hear part of a local radio programme which deals with crime in the area.

1   As you listen for the **first** time, tick (√) any of the objects below which have been stolen.

2   As you listen for the **second** time, put a cross (X) by any objects which have been found by the police.

Put a tick or cross in the small box in the bottom right hand corner of each picture (You may need a tick and a cross for some objects).

▶ Text 2   Read the following advertisement and then answer the questions which follow.

You're already well equipped to prevent crime.

Everyone comes with their own built-in burglar alarm. It's called the sense of sight and sound.

Unfortunately, many of us go around with the alarm switched off.

We don't see the stranger loitering outside the house next door.

We overlook the kids trying the car doors.

We don't notice the sounds from the flat upstairs. (Weren't they supposed to be on holiday?)

The police can only do so much to prevent crime.

There never can be enough of them to guard every home in every town. So they need your help in combating the burglars, the vandals, the car thieves.

Not, of course, by setting out to 'have a go' every time you see something suspicious. It'll always be the job of the police to arrest criminals.

But by acting as a line of communication between them and your community.

For instance, you probably know far more about your immediate neighbourhood than the police ever could.

A stranger in someone's garden would probably be far more obvious to you than it would to even the local bobby.

Providing, of course, you were on the look-out.

And that's the whole idea behind the Neighbourhood Watch schemes now springing up around the country.

To create a spirit of watchfulness within a community, anything suspicious being reported to the police.

It's early days yet, but results so far are very encouraging. The crime figures are already dropping in many of the areas running a scheme.

And all due to people like you.

Don't let them get away with it.

From The Central Office of Information

1 The purpose of thc advertisement is to

   a warn people about the increasing risk of crime.

   b encourage people to join the police force.

   c advise people how to protect their homes from crime.

   d explain how people can assist the police.

2 The advertisement points out that many people

   a are not very keen to co-operate with the police.

   b are not as observant as they could be.

   c don't control their children properly.

   d don't tell their neighbours about their holidays.

3 One of the ways we could help prevent crime is to

   a keep the alarm system in our home turned on.

   b try to stop criminals from escaping.

   c watch out for people behaving suspiciously.

   d inform the police if we hear noises upstairs.

4 One disadvantage the police have is that they

   a don't know local people personally.

   b are too busy arresting criminals.

   c know communities less well than residents do.

   d can't see what's happening in people's gardens.

5 Results of the Neighbourhood Watch schemes suggest that

   a they are already successful wherever they are run.

   b they are likely to be a success.

   c they are not successful in certain areas.

   d they are not popular with the police.

Describing clothes

● **Present**
He's wearing a new pair of shoes.
I've got a thick sweater on.
We usually wear jeans at the weekend.

● **Past**
She was wearing a flowery hat.
He had a scarf on.
I always wore a uniform.

Choose words from the following list to label the pictures below.

dress	skirt	belt	cap	jacket	pullover
apron	overalls	shoe	slacks	shorts	vest
blouse	boot	collar	trousers	T shirt	
sleeve	socks	overcoat	shirt	raincoat	

Check your answers with another student. Make sure you know the meanings of **all** the words in the list!

> **STUDY BOX 2**
>
> Phrasal verb **Get** (1).   The thieves **got away** in a stolen green van. *(Listening 1)*
>
> **get across** – communicate.   Although I couldn't speak the language, I managed to **get** my meaning **across** when necessary.
> **get (a)round** – overcome or avoid a problem.   I'm sure we'll find a way of **getting round** the difficulties.
> **get (a)round** – become known.   The news of his arrest **got around** quickly.
> **get at** – reach.   The cupboard is too high for me to **get at** easily.
> **get at** – suggest.   What exactly are you **getting at**? Why don't you say what's on your mind?
> **get away** – leave/escape.   I didn't **get away** from the meeting till late. (See example above).
> **get away with** – escape with stolen goods.   The burglar only **got away with** a few pounds.
> **get away with** – escape from punishment.   He **got away with** his crime because of insufficient evidence.
> **get back** – regain possession.   The police think there's a good chance we'll **get** our car **back.**
> **get by** – manage, survive.   How will you **get by** on only a part time salary?
> **get down** – cause depression.   Don't let these problems **get** you **down.**

▶ Communication activity · Witness

Introduction   In this activity you must work with a partner.

Student A will study a picture for 30 seconds. Meanwhile Student B will time Student A by counting 'one thousand and one, one thousand and two,' and so on (silently, of course!) until one thousand and thirty is reached.

After that, Student B will find out how much Student A remembers of the picture.

Instructions   **Student A** Turn to page 56 and study the picture carefully.

Student B *a* Start counting!
b After 30 seconds, tell your partner to give you his/her book so that you can now see the same picture. Hold it so that your partner can't see it.
c Ask questions, using the past tense, about:
● what exactly the two people were doing at that moment.
● the two people's appearance – age, clothes, hair, expression.
● any other details of the surroundings.
d When you have finished, ask Student A to look at the picture and point out any mistakes.
e Make a note of any words you didn't know to ask the teacher.

Now change roles. The new Student A must look at the picture on page 57 and the new Student B must look at the instructions above.

● Who makes the best witness?
The two pictures on page 53 show how the scene in the first picture (page 56) was remembered by two different groups of people. The first were police officers and the second, members of the public. Both groups made mistakes but each group made a different kind of mistake.

Work with a partner again. Compare the two pictures with the real event on page 56 and discuss the mistakes each group made. *For example:*

The public said that the man had fair hair but in fact his hair was dark.

(You may find it useful to refer to the Language for Describing People in the Functions Bank on page 214 before you start.)

Police description

Public description

From The Sunday Times

When you've finished, decide what the main difference between the police officers' description of the scene and that of the public was.

Does the difference surprise you? Why/Why not?

▶ Focus on listening 2 · Bad start to a honeymoon

For most of the questions below, you have to fill in the missing information by writing short answers.

● For question 2, tick (√) the correct boxes.
● For questions 9 and 10, tick the correct answer *a, b, c* or *d*.

1 Where were Alan and Cheryl driving to when they stopped in Stratford-on-Avon? ....

2 Which of these things were stolen, according to Alan? Tick the correct boxes.

tickets	☐	credit card	☐
passports	☐	cash	☐
travellers' cheques	☐	cheque book	☐
flight bag	☐	driving licence	☐
suitcases	☐	marriage licence	☐

3 Who did Alan think had taken their things at first? ....

4 Where had Alan put the luggage in the car? ....

5 Why should Alan know what to do after a theft? ....

6 Were the police hopeful that they would get their belongings back? ....

7 What clothes did Alan have left? ....

8 What is Cheryl's job? ....

9 The travel agency helped them by

    a giving them their money back.   *c* arranging a different holiday for them.
    b issuing new tickets for the original holiday.   *d* making an insurance claim for them.

10 How do Alan and Cheryl feel now?

    a cheerful   *c* depressed
    b nervous   *d* angry

STUDY BOX 3 Phrasal verb – **Break.**   Thieves **broke into** Bell's toyshop . . . *(Listening 1)*

break down – fail to work.   My car **broke down** on the way to work.
break down – collapse (in tears).   She **broke down** in tears when she heard the news.
break in – enter by force.   See example above.
break off – end suddenly.   He **broke off** in the middle of a sentence.
break out – escape.   Seven prisoners **broke out** of Leeds jail last night.
break through – force a way through.   The crowds managed to **break through** the barriers.
break up – separate. She's **broken up** with her boyfriend.
break up – smash into pieces.   Can you help me **break up** this box to make firewood.

▶ Text 3   Read the following news item:

Granny, 70, holds up a bank!

A GRANDMOTHER of 70 tried to hold up a bank by grabbing a hostage and pretending she had a gun.

But she was overpowered by the hostage — and the "pistol" in her pocket turned out to be a perfume spray.

Bespectacled widow Peggy Barlow tried her raid after watching a TV programme about robberies.

She suffered from arthritis and could not walk without a stick, so she got out her pensioner's pass and took a bus to the bank in Kensington, London.

Hostage

First she grabbed a customer, warning her: "Keep quiet and you won't get hurt."

Then she pushed the perfume spray forward in her pocket to look like a gun, bundled her hostage into the manager's office and demanded: "Keep your hands above the desk. Give me all the money in the bank."

When the manager, David Ball, said he couldn't give her ALL the money, she asked for £85,000 and eventually settled for the £50,000 he offered.

But after Mr Ball left the office, Mrs Barlow was overpowered by her hostage, psychiatrist's wife, Mrs Julien Watkins, 48.

As Mrs Barlow was led away by police she apologised to the bank staff — and asked detectives if she could telephone some friends to cancel a bridge party.

She became desperate when her debts reached £70,000 after her husband — a bank manager — died in 1975, the *Old Bailey heard yesterday.

Recorder, Sir James Miskin, sentenced her to nine months jail, suspended for a year, after she admitted demanding money with menaces and assaulting Mrs Watkins. He told her,

"If you behave from now on, you can forget this dreadful affair."

Mrs Barlow said later: "I can still hardly believe it was me. I'm normally very timid."

She added: "I read a lot of Agatha Christie but no-one has written about a criminal as daft and unlikely as me."

*Old Bailey — the central criminal court of England.

From the Daily Mirror

1 Look at the twelve sentences below.
   a Three of them are incorrect. Cross them out. Be prepared to say why they are wrong.
   b Show the order in which the other nine events happened by writing the numbers 1–9 in the spaces to the left. The first is done for you.

...... In court, she denied that she had attacked a customer.
...... She pretended that she had a gun.
...... She was arrested.
...... She bought a ticket on the bus to Kensington.
...... She agreed to accept £50,000.
...1.. Mrs Barlow got into debt.

...... She took a customer as a hostage.
...... A court found her guilty.
...... She asked for all the money in the bank.
...... She asked to make a telephone call.
...... She saw a programme about robberies on television.
...... She told the judge that she was sorry.

Check your answer with another student.

2 Now answer these questions about Text 3 in your own words.

   a What made Mrs Barlow decide to rob a bank?
   b How did she convince the bank staff that she was serious?
   c What happened to end the bank raid?
   d What was the result of the court case for Mrs Barlow?
   e What does she feel about the affair now, looking back?
   f In what way(s) was this bank robbery different from those described in Text 1?

> **STUDY BOX 4**
>
> Compound adjectives formed with participles
>
> *a* Describing people:
>
> | | | | |
> |---|---|---|---|
> | well-spoken* | kind-hearted | well-brought up | middle-aged |
> | well-dressed | left-handed | well-behaved* | short-sighted |
>
> * *Note* These participles are unusual because they are active in meaning.
>
> *b* Describing clothes and materials:
>
> | | | |
> |---|---|---|
> | hard-wearing | well-cut | tight/loose-fitting |
> | long-lasting | short/long-sleeved | single/double-breasted |

▶ Focus on grammar 2 · Participles

1 The **present participle** consists of the **verb + ing**. *For example:*

I've been listening   You're lying   We'll be waiting

The **past participle** consists of the **verb + (e)d** or an irregular form. *For example:*

I was arrested You're sure to be promoted They had already left

2 Participles can be used like adjectives, before a noun. Underline the participles in examples from texts in this unit:

a You need a warm, inviting place to do business.
b But when the first working day of the new year started off . . .
c Everyone comes with their own built-in burglar alarm.
d Bespectacled widow, Peggy Barlow, tried her raid . . .
e She was able to sort out the problems about the stolen cheque book.

Note
● Present participles usually have an *active* meaning. An **annoying** problem is a problem which annoys you.
● Past participles usually have a *passive* meaning. An **annoyed** neighbour is a neighbour who has been annoyed by something.

Exercise 1 Use verbs from the following list to make present or past participles to be used as adjectives in the sentences below:

wear	break	frighten	last	help
know	warn	tire	light	grind

a It's been an awfully .... day. I must sit down for a moment.

b I prefer proper .... coffee to the instant sort.

c This perfume is supposed to be very long-..................

d Your jacket is rather .... on the elbows. You'll need a new one soon.

e Haven't you heard of him? I thought he was quite well-.................. as an actor.

f Don't tell the children a .... story or they'll never get to sleep.

g Do you need a .... hand with the washing up?

h She says she's got a .... heart but I'm sure she'll soon find another boyfriend.

i The streets are very brightly-.................. at night.

j I stopped speaking at once when I saw the .... look he gave me!

3 Participles can also be used in **participle clauses** to replace a subject and verb,

● to give more information about a noun. *For example:*

That's the whole idea behind the Neighbourhood Watch schemes now springing up around the country. (Schemes which are springing up)

The two men arrested for shoplifting were in their twenties. (The two men who were arrested)

● to give more information about a verb. *For example:*

> We all rushed out, thinking there was a fire. (We rushed out *because* we thought there was a fire)

> Driving home today, I got caught in the rush hour traffic. (I got caught in the traffic *as/when* I was driving home)

Perfect participles are used to show that one action was complete before another started. *For example:*

> Having spent five years in Portugal, I know the country quite well. (*Because* I spent five years . . .)

> Having reached the station, they found their train had already left. (*When* they reached the station . . .)

> Negative participles are formed with not.   Not caring . . .   Not having seen . . .

Exercise 2   Complete the following sentences with suitable present or perfect participles.
Add any other necessary words.

a .... the street yesterday, I nearly got knocked down by a bus.

b .... for ten years in a bank, she decided it was time to look for a more exciting job.

c .... the hotel window, I saw an amazing sight – a man with a bear on a lead!

d .... a bus the other day, I met a most interesting man.

e .... what present to buy you, I've decided to give you some money instead.

f .... all his money on clothes, he had nothing left to buy food with.

g .... the ambulance, I thought there had been an accident.

h .... unsuccessfully to phone you on several occasions, I thought I'd better write you a letter

Exercise 3   Rewrite the following sentences, replacing the part in red with a suitable participle. *For example:*

> He saw that I looked ill and told me to lie down.
> Seeing that I looked ill, he told me to lie down.

a As we were unloading the car after the holiday, we realised that we had left our tent behind.
b She rushed to answer the phone because she knew that it might be her husband calling
c The sergeant took my name and address and then asked me to make a statement.
d She didn't find anyone at home so she pushed a note through the letter box.
e As I had eaten a three-course meal already, I had to refuse their invitation to dinner.
f He tore open the letter and found a cheque for £100 in it.
g The shop assistant thought I had stolen the bag and called the police.
h As I wasn't used to the climate, I found it quite difficult to work at first.

See **Communication activity, page 52**

▶ Focus on writing 2 · Description

Imagine that your car broke down miles from anywhere one evening and that you had to spend the night in it.

Meanwhile, friends who were expecting you back got worried and went to the police to report you missing. Your friends were asked to write a description of your physical appearance and of the clothes you were wearing when they saw you leave earlier in the day.

In the two paragraphs, write the description which your friends might give.

Notes   1 Study the Language for Describing People in the Functions Bank (page 214) before you begin.
2 Use the clothes you are wearing now as the basis for your description.

Plan   **First paragraph:**   Physical appearance; height, build, hair, complexion, eyes, any distinguishing features.
Second paragraph: Clothes; colour, material, pattern, style, etc.

See Communication activity, page 52

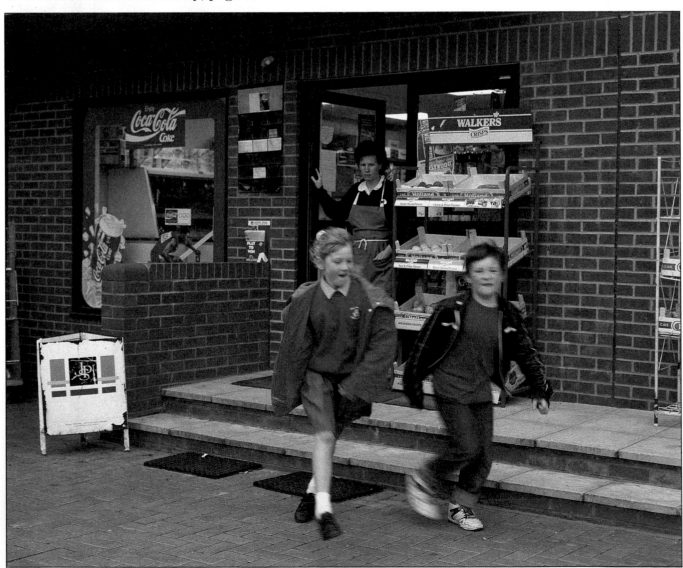

▶ Vocabulary review

Choose the word or phrase which best completes each sentence.

1   We started walking .... the direction of the town centre.

    a from   *b* to   *c* in   *d* by

2   My Company .... a lot of business in the USA.

    a takes   *b* does   *c* makes   *d* runs

3   I'm sure I made a(n) .... lot of mistakes in the test.

    a horrible   *b* awful   *c* bad   *d* serious

4   French .... the list of the most popular foreign languages taught in this country.

    a leads   *b* wins   *c* beats   *d* heads

5   When the police arrived, they forced the robber to .... his gun.

    a hand out   *b* hand in   *c* hand on   *d* hand over

6   We tied all the old newspapers into a .... for the dustmen to collect.

    a packet   *b* bunch   *c* heap   *d* bundle

7   The hijackers took seven .... before releasing the rest of the passengers.

    a prisoners   *b* hostages   *c* witnesses   *d* slaves

8   When she got back to the hotel, she found she had been robbed .... all her money.

    a from   *b* for   *c* with   *d* of

9   I found I couldn't afford a new car so I had to .... for a secondhand one.

    a settle   *b* decide   *c* choose   *d* agree

10 The judge gave him a 4 year prison .... for his crime.

    a time   *b* punishment   *c* sentence   *d* period

11 When I questioned him, he finally .... stealing my pen.

    a admitted   *b* accused   *c* accepted   *d* confessed

12 Although none of us wanted to go on the picnic, it .... to be quite enjoyable.

    a turned up   *b* turned out   *c* showed up   *d* showed off

13 Keep a(n) .... for the milkman. I don't want to miss him.

    a look-out   *b* outlook   *c* view   *d* sight

14 He's lost so much weight that if he doesn't wear a .... his trousers fall down!

    a strap   *b* band   *c* belt   *d* tie

15 I couldn't afford to buy any food but I managed to .... on some bread and cheese I had left.

    a get across   *b* get away   *c* get by   *d* get down

Waste not, want not

▶ **Lead-in** 1 What are the names of these containers?

Write the names against the letters *a-h* in the list. Then choose two items which you can usually buy in that container from the words below. The first has been begun for you.

a bottle   (perfume, ...)   *e* ....

b ....   *f* ....

c ....   *g* ....

d ....   *h* ....

matches	glue	chocolate	peaches	soup	envelopes
tea	honey	sugar	toothpaste	vinegar	
instant coffee	potatoes	cream	orange-juice	perfume	

2 **What is packaging for?**

Some packages have an important purpose. For example, the box that we buy matches in helps to keep the **contents** together. It also provides a way of using them, of course. Other packages are less important and may only be a way of attracting our attention.

Look at the examples of packages below and discuss with a partner what purpose they serve, if any. As you do this, fill in the table below.

a a box of chocolates
b a carton of long-life milk
c a plastic container of salt
d a box containing a bar of soap
e a packet of cake mixture

f a box containing a diet meal for slimmers
g a plastic bag containing oranges
h a packet containing 1 dose of medicine
i a bag containing a box containing a
   tube of expensive face cream

	What can a package do?	Is it important or unimportant?	
For example:	Keep the contents together.	✓	

▶ **Text 1** 1 Read the following text through fairly quickly and look for the answers to these questions:
a What does 'One-Trip' in the title refer to?
b What are the disadvantages of one-trip containers?
c Who benefits from one-trip products?

One-Trip Living

The product that most people throw out after using only once is packaging. This was not always true. The pottery or metal container used in Roman times and in most rural areas of the world today is a permanent and valuable household item. Unless a container is accidentally broken, it lasts a lifetime, despite the many journeys from home to market, farm or water-well and back. The growth of large cities and modern methods of food production changes all that. Because the food must be shipped from place to place while it is produced, and because of the increased variety of foods available and the convenience of pre-cooked meals, it is impossible for the customer to collect many foods in his own container.

It costs a great deal to provide a new container each time we buy milk, wine, beer and other drinks. Yet for a number of reasons the trend towards one-trip bottles for all these items is in full swing. The case of the vanishing returnable soft-drinks bottle shows how much these containers add to the rising tide of waste.

Until the late 1950s Americans had to borrow soft-drink bottles by paying a deposit each time they bought one. But several years later, soft-drink bottlers decided that it was more convenient for the customer to throw the bottle away instead. A returnable bottle lasting 30 or more trips was replaced with 30 one-trip cans or bottles. Sales of soft-drinks climbed and the container manufacturers smiled all the way to the bank. Glass companies gave soft-drink sellers a helping hand. The U.S. company,

Consumer Glass, made an arrangement with the bottler companies to reimburse them for much of the cost of one-trip bottles.

Other manufacturers have joined in promoting the throw-away spirit. The Aluminium Company of America announced that packages would soon replace pots and pans. Food packages were being designed with their own electric plugs. After you eat the food, just throw away the pan with the messy old grease. What about a camping holiday? You can make a bonfire on the last day with the disposable equipment that can now be purchased. In hospitals, there may well be a case on health grounds for disposable syringes. But is the use of one-trip sleeping bags and tents taking disposability too far?

The Soft Drink People

Last year, Schweppes dumped 250 million extra fragile non-returnable bottles all over Britain.
Please ask the children not to tread on too many. Broken glass hurts the company image.
Better still, help us make Schweppes take their bottles back.

Contact **Friends of the Earth.**

---

2 Find words or phrases in the text which mean the same as the following. (The paragraph numbers are given in brackets)

a in the countryside (adj) (1)

b intended to last for a long time or for ever (adj) (1)

c sent for some distance (1)

d tendency (1)

e the increasing amount (2)

f pay back (3)

g encouraging/helping to spread (4)

h large fire built in the open air (4)

i bought (4)

j intended to be used once and then thrown away (4)

3 Answer these questions.

a Why don't people in cities provide their own containers for food any more?
b Explain how Americans borrowed soft-drinks bottles before 1960.
c Was the change to non-returnable bottles popular with the public? How can you tell?
d What encouragement was there for the soft-drinks manufacturers to make the change?
e In what way are aluminium food packages supposed to be more convenient to use than pots and pans?
f What is the writer's attitude towards the fashion for one-trip products?

Discussion points

4 *a* What 'pottery or metal containers' (*line 3*) can you think of which would be valuable household items in country areas of the world?
b Make a list of one-trip products available now.
c Which items on your list do you use? What advantages do they have over traditional, more permanent items?
d What other everyday items could become one-trip products if manufacturers decided to produce them? What might the results be?

▶ Focus on grammar 1 · Conditional 1

ZERO CONDITIONAL

1 Look at these examples:

> If you press this button, an alarm goes off   You get 5p back if you return the bottle.

These are things which always happen, and **when** could be used instead of **if**.

Form

IF	Present form	Present form or Imperative

Note Present forms include the present simple, present continuous, present perfect simple and present perfect continuous. *For example:*

> Students only get a certificate if they have attended the course regularly.

2 This kind of conditional is used to describe general truths, including scientific processes. Complete the following:

a If you lower the temperature of water, it eventually ....

b Wood floats if you ....

c If water is heated, it ....

d If you strike a match, it ....

e Plants die if you ....

f You put on weight if you ....

3 This kind of conditional can also be used to give instructions. Match the **if-clauses** in Column A with the correct imperative from Column B, and revise your phrasal verbs!

A	B
1 If you make a mistake,	*a* tear it out.
2 If your car runs out of petrol,	*b* cut it down.
3 If you're not ready for your driving test,	*c* give it back.
4 If you see an interesting recipe in the magazine,	*d* cut it up.
5 If you receive the application form,	*e* rub it out.
6 If you've finished with his pen,	*f* put it off.
7 If you can't remember the 'phone number,	*g* tear it up.
8 If the meat's too big to go in the pan,	*h* fill it up.
9 If you get another threatening letter,	*i* fill it in.
10 If the tree's in danger of falling,	*j* look it up.

4 The **if-clause** may come first or second in a statement, as can be seen in the examples at the beginning of the section. When do you need to use a comma? Study some of the example sentences and say what the rule is.

CONDITIONAL 1

1 Look at these examples:

> If you plan to go on a walking holiday, you will need strong shoes.
> He will only get there in time if he leaves right now.

These are things which are possible and it's quite probable that they will happen.

Form

IF	Present form	Future form

Note Future forms include the future simple, future continuous, future perfect simple and future perfect continuous. *For example:*

> If he doesn't get the job, he will have done all this work for nothing.

2 Change the verbs in the following sentences into the correct forms.
a I (give) you a ring if I (need) any advice.
b He (only/can) come if the meeting (take) place on a Friday.
c If you (not/pass) the examination, you (take) it again?
d She (just/must) take a taxi if she (miss) the train.
e If you (go) to see him now, he (work).
f We (lose) our way if we (not/keep) to the main road.
g If the weather (be) sunny, we (bring) our umbrellas for nothing.
h If you (not/speak) clearly, he (not can) understand.

3 Write a conditional sentence for each of the following signs. *For example:*

If you buy 20 litres of petrol, you will receive a free wine glass.

SPECIAL OFFER
FREE WINE GLASS
with every 20 litres of petrol

A

LOST-BLACK CAT
(answers to the name of
'Tibbles')
REWARD £25

B

NO PARKING
by order
FINE £50

C

Enter our great
photography
competition
FIRST PRIZE
£1,000

D

NO ENTRY
without a visitor's pass

F

DANGER!
The contents of this bottle are
POISONOUS

E

SPECIAL SPRING DRY
CLEANING OFFER
2 GARMENTS
CLEANED FOR THE
PRICE OF ONE

OTHER CONDITIONAL LINK WORDS

4 **If** is not the only link word used in conditional sentences.

The box on the right shows other possible link words.

> **Unless** – if not
> **As long as**   if and only if/
> **Provided (that)**   on condition that
> **Suppose** – Imagine

Complete the following sentences:

a I won't interrupt you .... I have an important message to give you.

b .... you are stopped by the police, what will you do?

c He'll let you borrow his camera .... you take good care of it.

d The airship will make its first flight tomorrow provided ....

e Suppose ...... ,,,,............., will you have enough money to buy another?

f My parents don't mind what time I come home as long as .... ,,,,,.........

g I'll lend you the money you want provided that ....

▶ # Focus on listening 1
The sweet, short life of products

During the talk on the life-spans of modern products, answer questions 1 to 4.
For question 5 you will need to complete a table of information.

1 Which product is mentioned as lasting a much shorter time in the home than it does in a
factory? ....

2 What three changes can manufacturers make to persuade people to buy a new
model? ....
....

3 Which two industries have been most successful in persuading people to keep buying
new products? ....

4 Which item does the speaker say may soon be changed every year? ....

5 Complete the following table:

Products	The Useful Life of Products (in years)		
	Useful life of product (manufacturer's estimate)	Actual time in use in the USA	Actual time used in underdeveloped countries
a Washing machines and irons	......	5	25
b	11	2.2	......
c	25	2	......
d Construction equipment	......	8	100+
e	30	......	80+
f Photographic equipment	35	......	50

STUDY BOX 1

1 Phrasal verb **Wear.** Even the best products **wear out** in time. (*Listening 1*)

Wear off – pass away.   The pain **wore off** gradually.
Wear out – become useless.   My shoes are **worn out**.

2 Prepositional phrases

on foot	**in** sight	**under** control	**in** reach	**by** oneself
by car/boat/bus	**out of** sight	**out of** control	**out of** reach	**out of** doors

▶ Communication activity 1 · Pollution

Work in pairs for this activity:

Student A   Look at the instructions below and the picture on page 71.
Student B   Look at the instructions below and the picture on page 215.

Instructions   The picture on page 71 is the same as Student B's except that 8 small changes have been made.

1 Try to find 5 of the differences by describing your pictures to each other. Do not let your partner see your picture!
Take it in turns to describe a section of the picture in detail. Be prepared to ask each other questions in order to be sure that what you see is exactly the same. When you discover a difference, make a note of it.

2 When you have found at least 5 differences, look at the two pictures together with your partner, and spot the ones you have missed.

"I can remember when all this was unspoilt countryside."

▶ Text 2 · Recycling

Recycling means taking something that has already been used and treating it so that it can be used again. For example, old newspapers can be treated by removing the ink and mixing them with water under pressure so that they become pulp and can be made into paper again.

Read the following information about recycling and then answer the questions which follow.

From The Observer Magazine

Note Compost is a mixture (usually made of vegetable matter) which gardeners use to make the soil richer.

1 The information tells us that a huge quantity of rubbish in Britain is

a burnt.   *c* buried.
b recycled.   *d* piled up.

2 The most difficult material to recycle is

a paper.   *c* aluminium.
b glass.   *d* plastic.

3 People in Oregon return more drinks containers than they used to because

a they have been taught to be less   *c* there is a law which says they have to.
   wasteful.   *d* there is a financial advantage in doing
b they can't buy non-reusable bottles   so.
   any more.

4 Bottles collected from bottle banks are

a cleaned and used again.   *c* taken away and buried.
b made into new bottles.   *d* burnt to provide energy.

5 The problem with recycled paper is that sometimes

a it is dearer than new paper.   *c* there isn't enough to satisfy demand.
b it is less strong than new paper.   *d* there is too much imported from
                                   abroad.

6 The passage suggests that one thing the reader should do is to

a mix rubbish with oil and burn it as fuel.   *c* find out where waste materials can be
b grind up rubbish and bury it in the   taken.
   garden.   *d* send all metal cans to Alcoa in
                                    Birmingham.

You may not know the exact meanings of the following four words which appear in the text. Look at the context again, and then choose the most likely meanings. The letters in brackets refer to the section of the text.

7 *nourishes* (A)
   a supports   *b* creates   *c* provides

8 *fluctuates* (G)
   a rises   *b* falls   *c* moves up and down

9 *compressed* (H)
   a mixed together   *b* bent into a shape   *c* forced into less space

10 *ores* (J)
   a large factories which separate and melt metals   *b* rocks from which metal can be
   obtained   *c* mines where metals are found

STUDY BOX 2

Plural-form nouns   A package can protect the **contents**.

The nouns below have no singular form.
a Plural-form nouns which take the plural form of the verb:

clothes	jeans	shorts	earnings	pyjamas	trousers
contents	outskirts	surroundings	goods	scissors	

b Plural-form nouns which take the singular form of the verb:

crossroads	maths	news	physics

▶ Text 3   Read the following short text about the Friends of the Earth organisation and then answer the questions which follow.

Friends of the Earth Trust is an educational charity set up to help people of all ages become aware of the threats to our environment. Pollution is just one of these. The destruction of wildlife and wasting our natural resources are others.

In Britain, the countryside is disappearing or being destroyed – modern farming, mining and quarrying, motorways and power stations are all adding to this destruction. By the year 2000 about half the world's animal and plant species could be extinct.

Every year a forest the size of Wales is cut down to make paper for use in Britain. If more people used recycled paper fewer trees would be cut down, and there would be less waste to dispose. Another important benefit would be the new jobs created in the collection of waste paper.

In Britain it is almost impossible to get away from noise. Even in remote areas low-flying aircraft shatter the peace.

Friends of the Earth Trust Ltd.
377 City Road, London EC1V 1NA
Telephone 01-837 0731

New jobs would also be created if there was a large programme to save energy in buildings. It is cheaper to save energy than to produce electricity, but vast amounts of money are spent on nuclear power. From the mining of uranium to the disposal of radioactive waste there are a number of threats to the environment. In addition there are close connections between nuclear power and nuclear weapons. There are safer sources of energy.

Energy could also be saved if more short journeys were made by bicycle. This would reduce pollution and traffic congestion. Cycleways should be built to make cycling safer.

The threats to our environment are all related. For instance building cycleways instead of unnecessary new roads would save energy, reduce pollution and the destruction of our wildlife.

by P. Robey and C. Frere Smith. A registered charity, No. 2816811 Reg in London. Company No. 1533942

Say whether according to the advertisement the following statements are true or false and why.

a The aim of Friends of the Earth is to warn about pollution.
b The main danger to the British countryside is from roadbuilding.
c Many types of animals are likely to have disappeared by the end of the century.
d Large parts of Welsh forests are being destroyed to produce paper.
e Recycling paper would increase unemployment.
f More power is used in homes, shops and offices than necessary.
g People should travel by bicycle instead of by car.
h Special routes for cyclists are needed.

▶ Focus on grammar 2 · Conditional 2

Look at this example from Text 3:

If people used more recycled paper, fewer trees would be cut down.

The 'if' event here is **possible** but much **less probable** than in a conditional 1 sentence. The conditional 2 is also used for **unreal** events. *For example:*

If I had more time I'd help you.

Form

IF	past simple or continuous	would, could, might + infinitive

Note   The correct form for the verb **to be** in the if-clause is **were** (*For example:* If I **were** you, **I'd** complain), but **was** is also possible and is often heard in conversation.

Exercise 1   Put the verbs in brackets into the correct form to make conditional 2 sentences.

a Your uncle would really appreciate it if you (go) to see him.
b If she (make) more effort to help herself, I (have) more sympathy with her.
c Chris (not/take) a day off work unless he (be) really ill.
d If you (know) her as well as I do, you (not/rely) on her at all!
e We (must) reduce the price if we (want) to sell our house quickly.
f If electric cars (not/have) such large batteries, they (be) faster to drive.
g If you (call) the Fire Brigade, how long (it/take) them to arrive?
h I (not/carry) your wallet around in your pocket if I (be) you!

Exercise 2 The picture below shows Martin ready for an interview for a job as a bank clerk. Although he's bought a new suit for the occasion, he's not likely to make a very good impression!

Make sentences to explain what he could do to improve his chances at the interview. *For example:*

If he had his hair cut, he | would / might | make a better impression.

▶ Focus on writing · Discussion

Writing Bank: page 227

> Describe some of the ways in which pollution affects our lives and suggest what can be done about it.

Preparation

1 Work with one or two other students.

 a Look again at the picture on page 71 and make a list of the different examples of pollution that are shown.
 b Put the different examples into groups according to the kind of pollution they represent (*For example:* air pollution, noise pollution, etc).
 c Add any more examples you can think of to the groups on your list.
 d Compare your results with other students' and add any examples you hadn't thought of.

2 *a* Make notes on your list about the causes and **who is responsible** for the different kinds of pollution.

 b Explain to each other the causes, using expressions from the table below:

Cause/result links

Smoke from factory chimneys is | **due to** / **caused by** / **the result of** | modern industrial processes.

There is more rubbish these days | **as a result of** / **because of** | the amount of packaging used.

The reason for the increase in rubbish **is . . .**

---

3 Discuss with your partner(s):

 a what effects pollution has on our daily lives and which types of pollution are the most serious. Use expressions from the table below:

Addition links

Rubbish in the street is | **both** / **not only** | unpleasant to look at | **and** / **but also** | unhygienic.

Besides, / **What is more,** / **Furthermore,** | it can also be dangerous if it contains sharp metal or broken glass.

---

 b how pollution could be reduced. *For example:*
   A law could be introduced to make smoking illegal.
   If bottles were reusable, there would be less rubbish.
 c what difficulties there might be. Practise talking about these, using expressions from the table below:

Concession links

Although lead-free petrol would be dearer, it would be less harmful.

Lead-free petrol would be dearer **but** it would be less harmful.

Lead-free petrol would be dearer. | **However,** / **In spite of this,** / **Despite this,** | it would be less harmful.

Plan **First paragraph:** Introduce the subject. *For example:*
– with a personal experience.
– by commenting on the increase in pollution in recent years.
– by mentioning the increase in public concern about pollution.

Middle paragraphs: Describe the main types of pollution – their causes and effects. Suggest ways of reducing this pollution, explaining the difficulties there might be.

Final paragraph: Emphasise the importance of fighting pollution and sum up, perhaps, by saying whether this fight is likely to be successful or not.

▶ Communication activity 2 · Follow the country code

Look at the pictures below and then do the exercise which follows.

Enjoy the countryside and respect its life and work.

Make no unnecessary noise.

1 Match the instructions from the Country Code below to the pictures above. Do this by writing the correct number in the box after the instruction.

Keep your dogs under control. ☐

Help to keep all water clean. ☐

Take your litter home. ☐

Fasten all gates. ☐

Leave livestock, crops and machinery alone. ☐

Keep to public paths across farmland. ☐

Guard against all risk of fire. ☐

Take special care on country roads. ☐

Protect wildlife, plants and trees. ☐

Use gates and stiles to cross fences, hedges and walls. ☐

2 When you have finished, compare your answers with another student's and discuss any differences.

3 Now say what **would, could, might** happen if you didn't follow these rules.
For example: If you didn't keep your dog under control, it might frighten cattle.

Write 5 similar sentences.

▶ Focus on listening 2

You are going to hear a conversation in an information office.

As you listen, answer the questions below.

Part one

1 The first national parks in England were established in
   a 1920   *b* 1949   *c* 1951   *d* 1957

2 To answer questions *a-h* below, use the letters in red from five of the national parks on the right. The first one is done for you.

   a Which national park is suitable for rock climbing? *L.D.*

   b Which has the highest mountain in England and Wales? ....

   c Which is divided into two sections? ....

   d Which has most people living in it? ....

   e Which receives most visitors each year? ....

   f Which has interesting Roman remains? ....

   g In which national park could you visit several castles? ....*S*

   h Which is the most remote from towns and cities? ....*N*

National Parks in England and Wales

Part two In this part, you must match the signs to the name of the correct national park.

Seven signs will be described. Write the number of the national park under the sign. Write X by those which are not described.

1 Brecon Beacons
2 Dartmoor
3 Exmoor
4 Lake District
5 Northumberland
6 Peak District
7 Yorkshire Dales

A ....

B   ....

C ....

D ....

E ....

F ....

G   ....

H ....

I   ....

J   ....

▶ Focus on grammar 3 · Modal verbs 3: permission

1 TALKING ABOUT PERMISSION   CAN, MAY, COULD

Can and **may** are both used to talk about what is and isn't permitted in the present.

Only **can** is used in questions. **Could** is used to express past permission. *For example:*
   He said I could borrow his car for the day

Complete the following examples by referring to the Countryside Access Charter below.

a You may walk freely on .... but you may not ride a horse or bicycle on them.

b You can .... along a right of way but you can't ....
   ....

c Can you .... on commons? (Yes, you can sometimes)

d Originally commons were areas of wild, uncultivated land where country people ....
   take their animals to feed.

Now, with a partner, ask and answer four more questions about what you are allowed to do in the countryside.

Countryside
COMMISSION

YOUR RIGHTS OF WAY ARE
- Public footpaths – on foot only. *Sometimes waymarked in yellow*
- Bridleways – on foot, horseback and pedal cycle. *Sometimes waymarked in blue*
- Byways (usually old roads), most 'Roads Used as Public Paths' and, of course, public roads – all traffic. *Use maps, signs and waymarks. Ordnance Survey Pathfinder and Landranger maps show most public rights of way.*

ON RIGHTS OF WAY YOU CAN
- Take a pram, pushchair or wheelchair if practicable
- Take a dog (on a lead or under close control)
- Take a short route round an illegal obstruction or remove it sufficiently to get past.

YOU HAVE A RIGHT TO GO FOR RECREATION TO
- Public parks and open spaces – on foot
- Most commons near older towns and cities – on foot and sometimes on horseback
- Private land where the owner has a formal agreement with the local authority.

IN ADDITION you can use by local or established *custom or consent*, but ask for advice if you're unsure: Many areas of open country like moorland, fell and coastal areas, especially those of the
- National Trust, and some commons
- Some woods and forests, especially those owned by the Forestry Commission
- Country Parks and picnic sites
- Most beaches
- Canal towpaths
- Some private paths and tracks.
Consent sometimes extends to riding horses and pedal cycles.

2 ASKING FOR, AND GIVING PERMISSION

Informal	Can I	(possibly) ...
	May I	
↓	Could I	
	Might I	
Extremely formal	I wonder if I could	
	I wonder if I might	

Yes, (of course) you can/may.

No, (I'm afraid) you can't/may not

Can is the least formal. **May** and **could** are more formal and **might** is extremely formal.

The addition of **possibly** or the use of the form **I wonder if I ...** make the request more polite.

Only **can** and **may** are used in replies. Some replies may use neither. *For example:*

   Can I ask a question?   Yes, of course. Go ahead.
   Could I go early today?   No, I'm afraid not. There's a lot of work to do.

Practice   What would you say in the following situations? Choose suitable forms to ask for permission and give suitable replies – with **reasons** where appropriate! See Functions Bank page 210.

a You need to borrow your friend's ruler.   **(Answer: No, because...)**

b You want to speak to your boss. You open the door...   **(Yes)**

c Your car has broken down and you'd like to telephone the garage. You're outside a very grand house.   **(Yes)**

d You're trying to find your way to the station and you see a man looking at a map...   **(Yes)**

e There's a short cut from your camp site to the river across a field. You are just going to take it when you see the farmer!   **(No!...)**

f Your friend has a fantastic new sports car. You'd love to drive it.   **(No...)**

g Some colleagues of yours are having an important meeting. You need to interrupt in order to give one of them a message.   **(Yes)**

h You urgently need to borrow £100 (but only for 2 days). Ask a friend. **(No...)**

See **Communication activity 1, page 63**

STUDY BOX 3

Phrasal verb **Set.**   How were the national parks **set up**? *(Listening 2)*

set down – write down on paper.   Could you **set down** your reasons in writing?
set in – start and seem likely to continue.   The rain's **set in** for the day, I'm afraid.
set off/out – begin a journey.   Don't **set off** without me!
set off – start.   This has **set off** a chain reaction.
set off – cause an explosion.   Don't **set** the fireworks **off** too near the house.
set out – begin a course of action.   He **set out** to beat the world record.
set up – establish.   The society was **set up** in 1906.

▶ Vocabulary review

Choose the word or phrase which best completes each sentence.

1 If you can't keep your dog .... control, you shouldn't bring him to the park.

   a on   *b* under   *c* in   *d* with

2 Leave that machine ....! You might get hurt if you touch it.

   a apart   *b* along   *c* aside   *d* alone

3 As long as we .... to the footpath, we won't get lost.

   a keep   *b* stay   *c* follow   *d* remain

4 He's been trying to persuade his father .... him a bicycle.

   a buy   *b* buying   *c* to buy   *d* for buying

5 My old riding boots served me well for eleven years before they finally ....

   a wore off   *b* wore out   *c* broke down   *d* broke up

6 How much water does that tank ....?

   a include   *b* keep   *c* consist   *d* contain

7 I don't think I can help you .... you tell me all the facts.

   a provided   *b* if only   *c* unless   *d* if

8 The island has many natural ...., including oil and copper.

   a resources   *b* sources   *c* fuels   *d* materials

9 This information pack is designed to make children more .... of the things they can see in the countryside.

   a interested   *b* aware   *c* curious   *d* awake

10 I think you're .... your energy by sweeping up those leaves. The wind will only blow more down.

   a speeding   *b* spoiling   *c* losing   *d* wasting

11 Tomorrow will be mainly sunny. There may be a few showers but these are not expected to .... long.

   a take   *b* stay   *c* last   *d* survive

12 '............. you ride a horse along a public footpath?' 'No, it's forbidden.'

   a May   *b* Can   *c* Might   *d* Must

13 I don't know what I can have spent all my money ....!

   a on   *b* for   *c* at   *d* in

14 It's a great shame all those old oak trees are going to be ....

   a cut up   *b* cut off   *c* cut down   *d* cut out

15 The supermarket has .... the old milk bottles with new cardboard cartons.

   a changed   *b* removed   *c* withdrawn   *d* replaced

▶ Lead-in

1 Look quickly at the advertisement for the OMNIBOT to find if there are answers to the following questions:

    a Is the advertisement aimed at scientists?
    b Where can the OMNIBOT be used?
    c What provides its power?
    d How much does it cost?
    e Where can it be bought?

Check your answers with another student.

WHAT WAS ONCE SCIENCE FICTION IS NOW SCIENCE FACT

Once, robots programmed to obey their master's every whim were found only in science fiction novels and films.

Now the fantasy has become reality.

Because now there is OMNIBOT, the world's first home entertainment robot.

This technological marvel has its own 7 day linear programmable memory, onboard micro computer for movement control, voice and electronic sound transmission, digital display and multifunction alarm system, audio broadcast facility, and multifunction remote control.

OMNIBOT is complete with carrying tray, master control unit, home base, charger and re-chargeable battery.

So get OMNIBOT to help and entertain you and your guests. He will fetch and carry drinks, deliver messages, talk to your friends, play your favourite cassettes and even wake the kids up on Saturday morning — in fact be everything that you have ever wanted from your very own personal robot.

Get to know your friendly OMNIBOT at any of the outlets listed and see how he can be the best behaved house companion anyone could own. OMNIBOT, only from Tomy.

Omnibot   TOMY

The most advanced Home Entertainment Robot

■ AVAILABLE FROM   HARRODS ■ HAMLEYS ■ SELFRIDGES ■ FENWICK ■ FREEMANS MAIL ORDER ■ LIGHTNING ■ LITTLEWOODS MAIL ORDER ■ SELECTED TOYMASTER OUTLETS AND OTHER LEADING TOMY STOCKISTS ■

2 Now look at text again and study the picture. Which of the following can the OMNIBOT do, according to the advertisement?

a speak
b play with the children
c serve drinks to visitors
d tell you the time
e move in different directions
f write down messages

g broadcast music
h remember commands for one week
i help prepare food
j stop you from oversleeping
k answer the telephone
l do the washing up

Discussion   3 Read the questions through and decide on your own answers first. Then discuss them with a partner or with the rest of the class.

a The advertisement says that OMNIBOT can be everything you ever wanted from a personal robot. Can you think of any important tasks it can't do?
b What kind of person might buy a personal robot, in your opinion?
c If you were given a personal robot like this as a present, would you be pleased? What would you use it for?
d If you had one to give away as a present, who would you give it to? Why?

▶ Focus on grammar 1 · Talking about the future

Look at these examples below and underline the verb forms used to talk about the future:

a We're having a party next Saturday. Can you come?
b Be careful! I think that car is going to pull out in front of you.
c What time does our flight leave?

1 The **present continuous** (a) and the **'going to' future** (b) are both used to talk about future actions or events which have already been planned.

Very often either form can be used. The **'going to' future**, however, tends to suggest a more personal intention and can also express determination. *For example:*

I know you don't want me to come but I'm going to, all the same.

Note   The **'going to' future** is not usually used with the verb *to go*.

Exercise 1   Fill the spaces in the following sentences with a suitable verb in the **present continuous** or with **'going to'**.

a Which dress .... for the party tonight?

b I'm afraid I can't give you a lift tomorrow because I .... my car repaired.

c I feel nervous already and I .... my driving test till tomorrow!

d We .... dinner at 8 o'clock. Is that alright?

e .... anything special tonight, or would you like to call round and see us?

f Why .... to work tomorrow? Is it a holiday?

g A friend of mine .... the guitar in a concert tonight.

h When .... your homework? It's almost 9 o'clock already!

2 The **'going to' future** is also used to talk about things which we feel sure are going to happen, because of the evidence that we can see, hear, feel or sense. *For example:*

Look at the sky! I'm afraid it's going to rain at any minute.
If she continues working like this, I'm afraid she's going to be ill.

Exercise 2   Complete the following sentences, using the **'going to' future**.

a Listen to that thunder! It sounds as if there ....

b You'd better buy another suitcase. The handle on that one .... before long.

c That dog doesn't sound very friendly. I hope it ....

d Cars come round this bend much too fast. One of these days there ....

e Look at the petrol gauge. I think we .... petrol any minute.

f Have you got a paper handkerchief? I think I ....

g No goals and only five minutes of the match left. I'm afraid the result ....

h The government is refusing to give the teachers any more money.

  I hope there ....

3 The **present simple** is used to talk about future events or actions which are part of a fixed programme or timetable.

  What examples of such a programme can you think of? *For example:*

  The train gets in at 7.30 tomorrow evening.

Exercise 3 Work with a partner. Imagine that you are going on holiday together, and you have received the following details about the programme. Take it in turns to ask and answer questions. *For example:*

  A What time do we leave London?   **B** We leave at 8.30 in the morning.

a How .... Dover?

b Which French port .... ?

c What time .... Paris?

d What .... the first evening?

e What.. Monday?

f Where .... Tuesday?

g What ....the afternoon?

h When .... Epernay?

i What else .... there?

j What time .... London?

k Where .... during the trip?

l Are there any extras that .... ?

---

5 DAY LUXURY COACH TOUR OF FRANCE

Sunday: 8.30 a.m. departure from Victoria Coach Station for Dover.

Travel by midday ferry to Calais, and then by train to Paris (arrival late afternoon)

Evening free.

Monday: a.m. Sightseeing tour of Paris.

p.m. Boat trip up the River Seine.

Tuesday: a.m. Departure for Orleans, a large city on the River Loire.

p.m. Visit to cathedral and famous rose gardens.

Wednesday: a.m. early start for the drive to Epernay, in the heart of the champagne country.

Evening tour of the cellars.

Thursday: Return drive to Calais, stopping off at Rheims to look at the magnificent cathedral. Stop for lunch en route.

Arrival in London: 21.00 hours.

Accommodation throughout this tour is in comfortable 2 and 3 star hotels. Our luxury coach has reclining seats, WC, refrigerator and tea and coffee making facilities.

Price does not include: Lunches, entry fees to rose garden.

▶ Text 1

1 Describe the picture on page 76 in as much detail as possible.
2 Look at the headline below and discuss what the story might be about.

The robot wine waiter that lost its head

A robot that was supposed to serve wine in a restaurant ran amok instead, knocking over furniture and frightening customers, until eventually its head fell off into a customer's
5 lap, the Court of Sessions in Edinburgh was told yesterday.
  The court was told that during its eventful career at a restaurant in Leith, Edinburgh, the robot spilled a glass of wine on its first
10 test run and became uncontrollable after 30 minutes, knocking over furniture.

It was said to have been erratic and uncontrollable again during tests the next day, when it spilled more glasses of wine and ended 15 dropping its head into a customer's lap, while its lights and voice cassette also failed.

The engineer who demonstrated the robot at the restaurant and showed a disc jockey how to use it, told the court:

20 "It just needed practice, and in time you can perfect it. It is almost like a conjuring trick. You speak into the microphone."

But he said that if the batteries were undercharged "the results would be cata- 25 strophic, because the radio-controlled signal would be too weak and there would be jerky movements."

The robot stood in court wearing a black hat and bow tie. It looked in a sorry state, 30 incapable of speech or movement. After the case was settled, it was taken from the court on a trolley, its internal wiring detached from its body.

From The Times

1 Say whether the following statements are true or false, and why.

a The robot waiter worked properly at the beginning.
b The restaurant staff couldn't stop the robot when it was working.
c The restaurant staff weren't shown how to use the robot.
d The engineer suggested it wasn't difficult to operate.
e He couldn't think of any reason why it had behaved so badly.
f The robot was powered by electricity.
g It is no longer in working order.
h The court did not make a decision about the case that day.

2 Find the word or phrase in the text which means the same as:

a behaved violently ....

b likely to do unexpected things ....

c stopped working ....

d learn to do something absolutely correctly ....

e an action done by a magician ....

f terrible/disastrous ....

g sudden/not smooth ....

h poor condition ....

i small table on wheels ....

j not connected to ....

Discussion points
● Would you like to be served in a restaurant by a robot waiter? Why/Why not?
● What other examples of automatic machines replacing people can you think of? Have they improved service or not?
● Have you ever had the experience of a machine going terribly wrong? What happened?

76

▶ Focus on listening 1 · Word processor mishaps

1 Fill in the missing words in the short text below. Then answer the questions which follow.

Word Processing

A word processor is a computer designed to make .... quick and easy to produce a perfect text. It .... a little time to learn to use a word processor but here are the main steps: first you .... the **keyboard** to type in the words, and these appear .... a screen (or '**monitor**'). .... you can **edit** your text, to get rid .... mistakes and make changes. With an ordinary typewriter this .... probably mean a lot of re-typing, ... with a word processor you can do it electronically, before printing. .... example, a word or phrase can .... removed, and the word processor will automatically close up the space left. Finally, when you are satisfied .... your work, you print out the finished text using a separate **printer**. You can also store your text on a **disk** .... future use.

a What is the advantage of using a word processor rather than a typewriter?

b How is the equipment for word processing different from a typewriter?

2 You are going to hear four people describing things that went wrong while they were using word processors. Answers questions *a–e* below.

		A	B	C	D
a	**Profession**	Cookery Writer			
b	**Make of Machine**	✕	Astra		✕
c	**What was lost**			2 Chapters	Script for a documentary

d The cause.   Tick (√) the correct box.

	A	B	C	D
A fault of the machine				
The speaker's mistake				
Someone else's mistake				
Another reason (say what it was)				

e Which speaker stopped using a word processor as a result of this experience? Write the correct letter . . .

▶ Focus on writing 1 · Instructions

The picture opposite shows you how to unpack part of a home computer and assemble the equipment correctly.

The equipment consists of a **monitor** (the part with the screen), a **systems box** (the computer and disk drives) and a **keyboard** (which has keys like a typewriter). When the equipment is assembled, the monitor can be moved to the left or right, it can turn, and it can tilt forwards (picture 8) so that the user can choose a suitable position.

Write a paragraph of instructions to replace the pictures. (Remember that the equipment is expensive, so care is needed!)

Begin: Congratulations! You are the owner of a new Tangerine. Your computer has been carefully packed to protect it during delivery. Please follow the instructions below for unpacking and assembling your computer. . . .

Useful language

| 1 **First** |
| 2 **Next, After that,** |
| ↑ **When** ⎫ |
| ↓ **Once** ⎬ you have (done that) |
| 5 **Before** ⎫ (doing) |
| ⎬ you (do) |
| 6 **Finally** |

remove	plug in
take off	connect
switch on	place
switch off	adjust

▶ Focus on grammar 2
Sudden decisions, offers, suggestions, threats

Look at this example:

> Have we run out of coffee? I'll go out and buy some.

The **future simple** is used here to express a sudden decision (taken at the moment of speaking), and is often an offer to do something.

Remember how the '**going to**' **future** is used and note the difference between the following sentences:

 a There's no need to walk. John's going to give us a lift.
 b There's no need to walk. I'll give you a lift.

 a This is a plan I have already made, and probably arranged.
 b This is a decision I have just made.

The **future simple** is also used to express:

 a Offers   Shall I post that letter for you?/I'll pay, if you like, etc.
 b Suggestions   Shall we go to Scotland this summer?
 c Promises   (I promise) I'll never do it again.
 d Threats   Don't tell that joke again or I'll scream!

Exercise   Complete the following sentences with a suitable verb in the future simple. In each case say whether it is a sudden decision, an offer, a suggestion, a promise or a threat.

a It's very hot in here, isn't it? ....?

b Doesn't anybody know what this word means? I know, I ....

c For the last time, turn that record player down! If you don't, ...!

d The dog's looking very thirsty. ....?

e Oh, I've spilt coffee on your jacket! Don't worry I ....

f I think there's someone knocking at the door. ....?

g The children have made a terrible mess in your living room. Never mind I ....

h I'm sure I can see smoke coming from the window of the house opposite. ....
...........................?

i £5 for a 5 minute taxi ride! If you don't tell me the correct fare, I ....!

j Are you going to drive back tonight, or .... hotel for you?

▶ **Text 2**   Telephones that you can use in your car are a relatively recent development, and they're not cheap!

Discuss the following points:
a Which people would find a car phone most valuable? Why?
b What sort of people would like to have a car phone whether it was useful to them or not?
c Can you think of any disadvantages to having a car phone?

Now read the advertisement for car phones below and then answer the questions which follow.

The £100* Car Telephone
Another first from THE Carphone COMPANY

Now, only the initial payment* of £100 brings you any one of our feature packed Cellular Car Telephones — and that's not all — the Carphone offer includes CONNECTION to the British Telecom system, the INSTALLATION, MAINTENANCE and INSURANCE plus the monthly Cellnet SUBSCRIPTION. How about that for the best deal in town!

Carphone 2000

A highly sophisticated yet economical cellular car telephone. Stylish and utterly reliable, it operates just like a modern office phone. Advanced features include automatic redial of engaged number, illuminated keypad for convenient night use, 10 digit number display of number being called. 16 number memory store.
Recommended Retail Price £1350 plus VAT
£75 per month plus VAT .... 5 year agreement
£89.50 per month plus VAT .... 3 year agreement

Carphone 4000

An advanced cellular car telephone with 'call alert' and numerous convenient and time-saving features. Up to 29 of your most regularly dialled numbers can be stored in the memory. Last number recall if engaged. Volume controls for ringing, call tone, and conversation. Call timer, stopwatch, charge time stored. Options will include handsfree use of the phone, dual handset, quick transfer to second vehicle.
Recommended Retail Price £1750 plus VAT

Carphone 6000

This superb cellular telephone has a 30 number memory store for fast abbreviated dialling plus an electronic notepad memory to allow you to key in a new number even during a conversation. On-hook dialling is possible, no need to lift handset until your call is answered. Illuminated keypad for night use. You can converse with both hands on the driving wheel! Conference call facility permits 3-way conversations.
Recommended Retail Price £1995 plus VAT

Carphone Portable

All the features of the most advanced cellular car telephones — and yes, the handset is cordless! This means you can carry the handset with you when you leave your vehicle and dial or receive calls. Digital display of number dialled. 30 number memory for abbreviated dialling. Electronic lock prevents unauthorised use of the phone.
Recommended Retail Price £2995 plus VAT

The Carphone Company makes it simple.

We'll tell you everything you want to know about modern direct-dial car phones. How they operate and how to select the right equipment. And all about the new 'Cellnet' system, nothing can approach it for clear reception and reliability — and the area it covers is spreading rapidly. Installation will be quick and simple too, usually within 24 hours. After all you're dealing with experts backed by a nationwide service network.

1 Once you have paid your £100, you will still need to pay extra for

    a the phone to be fitted in your car.
    b the phone to be serviced when necessary.
    c the cost of insurance protection.
    d the cost of the calls you make.

2 Which model allows you to adjust the level of sound?

    a Carphone 2000.
    b Carphone 4000.
    c Carphone 6000.
    d Carphone Portable.

3 Which model would you buy if you were worried about other people using your phone without your knowledge?

    a Carphone 2000.
    b Carphone 4000.
    c Carphone 6000.
    d Carphone Portable.

4 Which model gives you information about the cost of your call?

    a Carphone 2000.
    b Carphone 4000.
    c Carphone 6000.
    d Carphone Portable.

5 A feature only the Carphone 6000 mentions is the possibility of

    a calling engaged numbers again automatically.
    b storing the numbers you often call in a memory.
    c reading the number keys easily in the dark.
    d speaking to two people at the same time.

6 Which phone has a feature which should help prevent accidents?

    a Carphone 2000.
    b Carphone 4000.
    c Carphone 6000.
    d Carphone Portable.

▶ Communication activity 1 · Role play

Work in pairs. Student A should look at the notes below. Student B should turn to page 86.

Role A   You are a salesman/saleswoman for a small office equipment company. Your sales this month have been very good and you are sure that your boss will be pleased with you. You want him/her to agree to install a car phone in your company car. You think it would be useful and that it would also help the company's (and your!) image.

Your boss tends to be very cautious about new ideas but you've arranged to see him/her and you're hoping to produce a convincing argument.

Remember to introduce the subject gently – don't mention the car phone too soon! **Let your boss start the conversation**.

STUDY BOX 1

Phrasal verb **Let**.   When your computer **lets** you **down**, it can be just as bad as a broken love affair. *(Listening 2)*

let down – lower.   He escaped by **letting down** a rope ladder from the window.
          – disappoint.   See above.
let in – allow to enter.   They won't **let** you **in** without a ticket.
let off – allow to explode.   Don't **let** any fireworks **off** too near the house.
          – excuse from punishment.   The judge **let** him **off** with a warning.
let out – release.   Be careful not to **let** the cat **out** when you leave.

▶ Focus on listening 2 · The year 2000

You are going to hear the views of two groups of people on what life will be like in the future.

1 As you listen **the first time**, put a tick (√) in the boxes below to show the subjects that each group mentions.

As you listen **the second time**, look at questions 2–5 and choose the correct answer: *a, b, c* or *d*.

	First group	Second group
space travel		
robots		
computers		
nuclear weapons		
overpopulation		

	First group	Second group
test tube babies		
unemployment		
future places for people to live		
future forms of energy		
future forms of communication		

2 The people interviewed were probably

a children at primary school.
b pupils at secondary school.

c students at university.
d workers of mixed ages.

3 The first speaker thinks that by the year 2000

a robots may have disappeared.
b computers may be in control of the world.

c civilisation may have been destroyed.
d people will be living on the moon.

4 The first speaker in the second group is fairly hopeful about the future because s/he thinks

a computers will prevent nuclear weapons from being fired.
b nuclear weapons could never be fired by accident.

c nobody would want to start a nuclear war.
d nuclear weapons will disappear from the world.

5 The Presenter of the programme is surprised at the end because the two groups

a had such strange ideas.
b knew so much about technology.

c had such different opinions.
d mentioned such similar subjects.

▶ Focus on grammar 3 · Talking about the future 2

1 Look at these examples from Focus on listening 2 and underline the verb forms used to talk about the future.

In the year 2000, I think I'll probably be in a spaceship . . .
I may be in charge of a robot court.
There just won't be enough jobs to go around.
Perhaps we'll be able to convert brain waves into radio waves.

We use the **future simple** to express:

a future fact:	She will be nine years old tomorrow.
b prediction:	That man will be a millionaire one of these days.
c opinion about the future: (especially after verbs like think, expect, suppose, and doubt if, and also after 'probably' and 'perhaps')	I expect we'll be tired after the journey. I suppose you'll have to change trains. I doubt if he'll have time to speak to you.

Form	will
	won't

will / won't + infinitive (without 'to')

Note The future of **can** is **will be able to** and the future of **must** is **will have to**.

If we are less sure about an event in the future, we can use **may**, **might** or **could**. *For example:*
It could rain. If it does we'll hold the party indoors.

Exercise 1 *a* Work with a partner to talk about the future. Take it in turns to ask each other's opinion about the developments below. Give answers too! *For example:*

A: Do you think there will be giant televisions in every home by the year 2020?
B: Yes, I think there will/could/may/might (be) and I hope so because . . ./but I hope not because . . .
or No, I don't think there will (be)/could be because . . .

- Video telephones (where you see as well as hear each other).
- Robots that think.
- Personal flying machines.
- Day trips to the moon.
- People living on other planets.
- One world language.

b Now make predictions of your own about the subjects below. *For example:*

Education: (As far as education is concerned,) I think computers will replace teachers in the future. There probably won't be any schools by 2020.

- Transport
- Entertainment
- The Third World
- Nuclear power
- Working hours
- The weather
- Population

2 Look at these further examples from Focus on listening 2:

The population will have gone up so much that everyone will be living in big plastic domes . . .

We use the **future continuous** to express:

a an action which will be going on at a future time. *For example:*

At this time tomorrow, our plane will just be taking off

b an action in the future when the process is a continuous one. *For example:*

The buffet will be closing in about five minutes.
We'll be moving to London in a few months.

Note The **future continuous** is also used to ask a polite question about a person's plans. *For example:*
When will you be checking out, sir?
Will you be going to the party tonight?

Form	will be
	won't be

will be / won't be + verb + '-ing'

Exercise 2 Work with a partner to try and arrange a meeting. Imagine that you each have one of the diaries shown. *For example:*

A: When shall I call round? How about Monday morning? What if I drop in on . . .

B: No, don't call round then because I'll be . . . No, Monday morning's no good because . . .

Useful language

Call in	Come around	Drop by
Call round	Pop in	Drop in

A

	Morning	Afternoon	Evening
SUN			Homework
MON			Opera on radio
TUES		Preparation for dinner party	Dinner party
WEDS	Spring clean kitchen	Plumber (to install washing machine)	

B

	Morning	Afternoon	Evening
SUN	Guitar lesson	Wallpaper sitting room	
MON	Repair roof	Lunch with mother	
TUES	Accountant		
WEDS			'Dallas' on T.V.

3 The **future perfect** is used to express:

a an action or event which will be complete by a future point of time. *For example:*

The population will have gone up so much that everyone will be living in big plastic domes . . .

The course will have finished by July 22nd.

b the length of time that an action or an event will have lasted, at a future point of time (also future perfect continuous). *For example:*

I'll have lived here for 6 years by next autumn. (or 'been living')
He'll have been working here for a year by the 1st September.

Form

will have	Past participle	(done)
+		
won't have	been + verb + -ing	(been doing)

Exercise 3 **Work in pairs.** Using the information given, take it in turns to ask questions and give answers. *For example:*

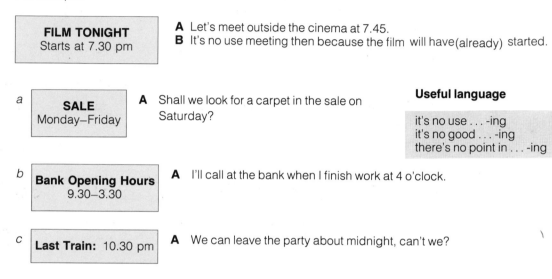

FILM TONIGHT
Starts at 7.30 pm

A Let's meet outside the cinema at 7.45.
B It's no use meeting then because the film will have (already) started.

a **SALE** Monday–Friday

A Shall we look for a carpet in the sale on Saturday?

Useful language

it's no use . . . -ing
it's no good . . . -ing
there's no point in . . . -ing

b **Bank Opening Hours** 9.30–3.30

A I'll call at the bank when I finish work at 4 o'clock.

c **Last Train:** 10.30 pm

A We can leave the party about midnight, can't we?

d **ARRIVALS** from London: 12.30 pm

A I'll be at the station to meet you at midday. (Careful!)

e **Cambridge First Certificate** Papers 1–3: 17th June

A I'll phone you on the 15th of June to see how you got on in your exam.

Exercise 4 Change the verbs in brackets into the correct form of the present continuous, 'going to' future, future simple, future continuous or future perfect. Make any other changes necessary.

Review

a Give me a ring on Thursday. I (hear) the results by then.

b This wind is so strong that it (probably/cause) some damage before long.

c I can't believe it! This time next week I (swim) in the Indian Ocean.

d Don't try to move that table all by yourself. Wait and I (give) you a hand.

e On 1st March we (be) married for a whole year!

f What do you think (happen) to their dog if they go abroad?

g Don't phone them now. It's only 7 o'clock in New York and they (just/get) up.

h I'm sorry to hear that you've lost your job. What (you/do) now?

i The builders (finish) work on the house by the weekend?

j I doubt if you (get) home before midnight.

▶ Communication activity 2 · Describe and draw

Work in pairs for this activity. You will each describe a picture of a house (one contemporary, one futuristic) so that your partner can draw it.

Before you start, look at the Functions Bank on page 212 (Describing Location and Describing Shape). Study the language briefly and then mark the place in your book for future reference.

Instructions
1 Turn your chairs so that you are facing each other. (You must not be able to see each other's drawings!)
2 Remember to describe your picture clearly, and in a way which is easy for your partner to follow.
  Begin with the size (how many floors, etc), shape and other general details.
3 The person who is drawing should ask questions to check if anything is unclear.
  For example: How big is the window (in relation to the door)?
                   Is the door in the middle? etc.

Student A should now turn to page 86 and look at the house. Start describing it as soon as you are ready.
Student B should take a clean sheet of paper and be ready to draw what **A** describes.

When you have finished, compare the two drawings and note any differences. Discuss how the description could have been improved.

After that, **Student B** should turn to page 216 and begin describing the house on that page.

▶ Focus on writing 2 · Description/discussion

> Write a description of what life will be like in the year 2020. (120–180 words)

Plan   **Introduction**

First paragraph   Here you can make general comments about likely developments, based on what is happening now. *For example:* advances in technology, population growth, etc.

Middle paragraphs   Choose 3–5 topics that you would find interesting to discuss in detail, and deal with them in separate paragraphs. *For example:*
   transport (public, private)
   communications (telephone, TV, satellite, computers, etc)
   employment (working hours, skills needed, retirement age, etc)
   domestic life (family size, house design, entertainment, equipment, etc).
   .... (Add your own ideas)

Final paragraph conclusion   Finish off with a general comment on the developments you've described. You might express your own feelings about them (excitement, anxiety, etc) or you could mention dangers you foresee, or you could explain why you feel your predictions may not be correct at all!

STUDY BOX 2   Phrasal verb   **Cut.**

The cleaning lady took out the plug. This **cut off** the electricity. (*Listening* 2)

cut across – take a short cut.   We'll **cut across** the park to save time.
cut down – bring down by cutting.   Several trees had to be **cut down**.
cut down (on) – reduce.   You ought to **cut down (on)** your smoking.
cut in – push in suddenly.   That red car **cut in** so suddenly in front of me that there was nearly an
                                 accident.
cut off – stop flow.   See above.
cut up – divide into small pieces.   They **cut** the old sheet **up** to make cleaning rags.

▶ Vocabulary review

Choose the word or phrase which best completes each sentence.

1 Oh dear, I've left my glasses in the garden. Could you go and .... them for me?

   a take   *b* carry   *c* search   *d* fetch

2 There's no .... to book tickets in advance. There are always plenty of seats.

   a problem   *b* matter   *c* need   *d* demand

3 We've told the children they can come to the party with us if they are well-.............

   a behaved   *b* behaving   *c* deserved   *d* deserving

4 I've tried hard to .... to know the neighbours but they don't seem very friendly.

   a get   *b* arrive   *c* manage   *d* succeed

5 Don't forget that .... to our new office by the time you get back from holiday.

   a I move   *b* I'll move   *c* I'll have moved   *d* I'll be moving

6 She decided to .... all her Christmas cards by hand to save money.

   a post   *b* deliver   *c* collect   *d* provide

7 If you don't pay your bill they'll .... your electricity.

   a cut down   *b* cut off   *c* cut in   *d* cut out

8 You can do whatever you like, as .... as I'm concerned.

   a much   *b* long   *c* far   *d* well

9 There's no point in continuing with the game if you won't .... the rules.

   a play   *b* keep   *c* listen   *d* obey

10 I think something's gone wrong .... the television. I can't get a picture at all.

   a to   *b* with   *c* about   *d* on

11 He got up so quickly that he almost .... his chair over.

   a hit   *b* carried   *c* knocked   *d* dropped

12 I've been ringing you all day but the line is always ....

   a occupied   *b* full   *c* used   *d* engaged

13 He was .... to attend a meeting yesterday but he was too busy to go.

   a arranged   *b* supposed   *c* intended   *d* obliged

14 If the music is too loud, you can adjust the volume .... by your bedside.

   a control   *b* switch   *c* button   *d* catch

15 They were offering ten free cassettes with the tape recorder, which seemed a very good ....

   a price   *b* exchange   *c* value   *d* deal

Communication activity 1
Role B

You are the director of a small office equipment company. Unfortunately things are not going too well at the moment – sales are down and you owe the bank quite a lot of money. You are even thinking of sacking some of your staff and selling their company cars in order to raise money.

One of your salesman/saleswomen, A, has asked to speak to you but you don't know what it's about. A's sales have been very poor until this month (when he/she managed to sell equipment to three members of his/her family). He/she also managed to damage a company car 2 months ago while parking. **You begin the conversation.**

See Communication activity 2, page 84

Going the hard way

▶ Lead-in ¹ᴬ

a Describe what you can see in each of pictures **A, B** and **C**.

b Describe the appearance of the people in each picture.

c In picture **A**, what do you think is the reason for the flag?

d What does the man seem to be doing? What might he be saying?

e In picture **C** the men have cycle panniers on each side of the front wheels of their bicycles. What might they contain?

f In picture **D** what kind of boat do you think this is?

2 Opposite are headlines from articles about the journeys which were made by the people in the pictures. There are also lists of the stores they took with them. Work with a partner to match the headlines and lists to the pictures and fill in the first three lines of the table which follows.

	Picture **A**	Picture **B**	Picture **C**	Picture **D**
1 Method of travel	skis	motorbike	cycle	boat
2 Destination	North p	Africa	Australia	China
3 Stores list	c	a	d	b
4 Extract	f			e

Headlines

My Lone
Walk to
the North
Pole

**Hard Track
to Africa**

*Slow Boats
to China*

**Australia!
– by pedal
power**

Stores lists

a clothes
    camping equipment
    5 gallon jerrycan of petrol
    1 week's food and water
    tools

c tent
    boots
    gloves
    balaclava
    goggles
    sleeping bag
    radio
    satellite relay kit
    compass
    200 kilos food
    camping stove
    pencils and notebooks
    rifle

b notebooks and ballpoint pens
    several novels
    2 Pentax cameras
    Polaroid camera
    metal suitcase with combination lock
    money belt
    zip-fastened bag
    medicines (septrin, mexaform and
    aspirin)
    thick-soled shoes

d tent
    sleeping bags
    clothes
    first aid kit
    tools
    cycle spares
    food
    £1000 in travellers' cheques

3 Which item/s from each list helped you to decide on your answers?

4 Look at the lists again and discuss:

a the meanings of any unknown words. For example, *balaclava* and *goggles* which can both be worn.
b why the various items were necessary. For example, why is there a Polaroid camera as well as two ordinary cameras on List *b*.
c how the lists differ from each other and why.
d whether there are any items which seem to be missing from the lists.

STUDY BOX 1   The use of articles 2

DEFINITE ARTICLE

oceans, seas, waterways and rivers	*mountain ranges*	*plural countries*	*roads*
the Pacific Ocean, **the** Sulu Sea	**the** Himalayas	**the** United States	**the** London Road
the Suez canal, **the** Channel	**the** Alps	**the** Soviet Union	
the Mississippi			

NO ARTICLE

cities	*mountains*	*countries*	*streets, squares, circuses*
New York, Hong Kong	Mount Everest, Ben Nevis	France, Argentina	Oxford Street, Leicester Square, Piccadilly Circus

5 Now look at these short extracts from descriptions of the four journeys. Match the extracts to the journeys and fill in the last line of the table on page 88.

a From Dubai, they travelled to Pakistan and India. There, while cycling through a small village on the road from Hyderabad to Khairpur, they met a young man who invited them back to his village 10 miles off the main road.

It was to be a memorable experience.

When they arrived at Talpur, Rick and David found themselves surrounded by the entire population of the village — more than 300 people.

b We cruised gently through France, Switzerland, Italy, Yugoslavia and Greece, getting the 'feel' of the bikes. With clothes, camping equipment, spares and enough tools to do practically a complete rebuild, we were loaded up fairly heavily, but we found that with good weight

distribution the bikes still handled excellently. Did they have enough in reserve, we wondered, to cope with the additional load of five gallons of petrol and a week's food and water, and with the extra strains of off-road riding?

c Where should I start? I went back to the lists again, but the decision was soon made. Not Rotterdam or Southampton; the Channel and the west Mediterranean were well-known and well travelled. I would start in Europe, but as close to Asia as possible: Athens. Friends had

told me of a steamer that shuttled passengers from Piraeus to the Greek island of Patmos, near Izmir in Turkey. From there I could find my way slowly to the Suez Canal, a first and formidable major hurdle.

d Now I was cold, tired and confused, the visibility on the frozen seawater was less than 10 yards in freezing fog. I could not contact my small back-up team in Resolute by radio, atmospheric conditions near the magnetic North Pole preventing that.

My compass was swinging steadily back and forth from

north to south. It was cold, about minus 15C, but the wind in the fog lowered this to nearer minus 45C.

But why was I there?

Because no one man had walked the place alone before. It was my Mount Everest and I was almost there, a miserable windswept icy hell somewhere where no one had ever stood alone.

6 Now work with a partner to answer these questions:

a In extract *a,* why did the two cyclists receive such a welcome from the villagers?
b What does the writer mean by *getting the 'feel' of the bikes* in extract *b*?
c What *spares* could the two motorcyclists have been carrying in extract *b*?
d How did they manage to handle their bikes with such heavy loads on them?
e Explain in your own words why the writer in extract *c* began his journey in Athens.
f What kind of boat did he plan to take first?
g Does he think it will be difficult or easy to pass through the Suez Canal? Which words give you the answer?
h In extract *d*, what problems was the writer facing?
i What reason does he give for making his journey? Is his reason understandable?
j If you had to choose, which of these journeys would you go on?

▶ **Text 1** **1** Here is another extract from the story of the two cyclists' journey to Australia. Read it through once, fairly quickly.

FREEZING

From Morocco, the two cycled on into Algeria — and it was there that their adventure almost turned to disaster.

For neither cyclist was prepared for the freezing temperatures in the hills of North Africa.

5 The nights became colder and colder until one night, they found it impossible to sleep.

"We lay there wearing every article of clothing we had with us and wrapped up in our sleeping bags, but it was no good. We just couldn't get warm.

10 "Since our tent had no groundsheet, we were lying on the frozen ground and it just seemed to get colder and colder."

By the early hours of the next morning, with their hands and feet completely numb, they could take it no longer.

"All I could feel was a terrible burning sensation in my
15 fingers," said Rick.

They decided to warm up by cycling on. But it only lasted for a few minutes. A mile down the road Rick, who was in front, came to a halt ... and keeled over to lie motionless in the snow.

Horrified, David jumped off his bike and ran to the rescue.
20 Desperately he worked to bring his companion round. For a while there was no response.

Eventually Rick opened his eyes ... but he was clearly in

danger. His face was blue and he was shivering violently. And they were miles from any town or village at 6 a.m.

Then something happened which they will never forget. 25

David was aware of something approaching. And before he had a chance to say anything, a huge figure was next to them. It was a man on a horse.

"He was wearing a brown cloak and a hood," said David. "He was Algerian and couldn't speak a word of English, but he took 30 control of the situation immediately."

The Algerian heaved Rick up on to his horse and began to ride off down the road.

David said: "It was rather frightening. I had absolutely no idea where he was taking him and the man made no effort to 35 explain."

With David wheeling the two bikes behind, the horseman rode for over a mile before stopping at a large camp in the mountains.

"I am convinced that Rick could have died if it had not been for that man," said David. "It took Rick three hours to thaw out 40 properly in front of the fire and all the time the Algerian fed us with milky coffee and biscuits.

"By about 10 a.m. we were back on the road after thanking the man profusely for everything he had done."

From 'How a stunning blonde stopped the marathon men' by Mark Elsdon Dew in The Sunday Express

2 Now say whether the following statements are true or false **without** looking back at the text.

a The two cyclists had no shelter from the cold during the night in North Africa.
b One night they became too cold to sleep.
c They had put on all the clothes they were carrying.
d Cycling made them feel warmer again.
e Rick fell asleep as he was cycling and collapsed in the snow.
f David didn't know what to do to help him.
g When Rick opened his eyes, David knew he was going to be alright.
h A stranger appeared out of the dark very quickly.
i David hadn't heard the stranger coming up to them.
j David is sure the stranger saved Rick's life.

3 Now read the text again more carefully to check your answers. Underline the word or phrase which gives you the correct answer.

▶ Focus on listening 1 · Overland to Australia

Listen to the interview on tape and answer these questions. For questions 2 to 6 below you must tick one or more of the boxes.

1 The part of Francesca's journey which will take the longest time is by

a car. ☐   *b* coach. ☐   *c* plane. ☐   *d* bus. ☐

2 Which countries will she pass through more than once?

Italy	☐	Turkey	☐	Jordan	☐
Greece	☐	Syria	☐	Iran	☐

3 Which countries did she have to obtain a visa for?

Turkey	☐	Iran	☐	Nepal	☐
Syria	☐	Pakistan	☐	Burma	☐
Jordan	☐	India	☐	Australia	☐

4 Where will she sleep?

a in a tent. ☐   *b* in the bus. ☐   *c* in the bus and in hotels. ☐
d in the bus and in a tent. ☐

5 The information Francesca received told her about

visas.	☐	clothes.	☐	injections.	☐
work permits.		luggage.		insurance.	

6 The price includes

hotel accommodation only.	☐	food.	☐	spending money.	☐
all accommodation.		transport.		the cost of visas.	

7 The whole journey takes

a 10 weeks. ☐   *b* 12 weeks. ☐   *c* 4 months. ☐   *d* 6 months. ☐

8 One reason Francesca gives for wanting to make the journey now is that

a she can't find work in Britain. ☐   *c* she'll be too old for the company's age limit soon. ☐

b she hasn't got anywhere to live in Britain. ☐   *d* she hasn't any responsibilities to prevent her from going. ☐

▶ Text 2

Here is another extract from the story of the motorcycle journey to Africa which Trisha Greenhalgh and her companion, Mat, made.

Read the text through once and find the answers to these questions:

a What difficulty did the two meet?
b How did they each react to it?
c What happened in the end?

TRISHA GREENHALGH tested her delight in danger on a motor-bike ride from England to the Sudan

One morning, when we had been riding in the blazing sun and stifling humidity for five hours, we came to a narrow, rickety bridge where the railway crossed a 5 stagnant pond. For 30 feet there was nothing but the widely-spaced wooden sleepers under our wheels, and nothing to stop us falling into the steaming bog below if we overbalanced. Right under the bridge 10 lay the body of a dead cow. I watched Mat as he approached the bridge and rode straight over, bump-bump-bump, without even slowing down. I stopped.

'What's up?' he yelled, from the other 15 side.
'I'm not riding over that thing. If I slip, I'll be in there with that cow!'
'There's nothing to it. I just did it, didn't I?'
20 'You're stronger, and taller. My feet don't touch the ground. You do it for me!'
Mat said strength didn't come into it and rode off, leaving me staring down into the sickly brown soup. He would be waiting 25 for me around the next corner, but I knew he would give me at least an hour before

coming to help. The sun burned my face; sweat ran off my forehead into my eyes and stuck my shirt to my body; big black tse tse 30 flies stung me through my clothes and mosquitoes flew into my mouth when I breathed. To remain stationary in this place was suicide; anyway, to sit around waiting for Mat to help was more than my feminist 35 pride could take. I rode back along the track a few hundred yards to get a good run-up, and over I went: bump-bump-bump. Mat was right: all the obstacles were in the mind.

From 'Hard Track to Africa' by Trisha Greenhalgh in The Observer

Now study the following 5 questions and then read the text again to find the answers.

1 The bridge looked dangerous to Trisha because

a there was a 30 foot drop to the water below.
b it had no barriers at the sides.
c there were pieces of wood all over the road.
d there was a railway line below.

2 Trisha stopped because

a she was exhausted.
b she suddenly saw the dead cow below.
c she wanted to let Mat go first.
d she was afraid of losing her balance.

3 Mat argued that

a the bridge was not at all difficult to cross.
b she had no other choice but to cross the bridge.
c the cow was harmless because it was dead.
d there was no difference between them in strength.

4 Mat rode away leaving Trisha because

a he didn't know what he could do to help.
b he felt she should overcome her fear by herself.
c he didn't believe she was really afraid.
d he couldn't wait any longer for her.

5 Trisha finally decided to ride across the bridge because

a she realised that it was easier than it looked.
b she was tired of waiting for Mat to come and help her.
c she knew she couldn't stay where she was any longer.
d she was afraid that Mat would go and leave her behind.

Vocabulary matching   Find the words in the passage which match the following definitions:

a burning brightly   ....

b making it difficult to breathe   ....

c not strongly built, likely to break   ....

d not flowing or moving, often bad-smelling   ....

e heavy pieces of wood supporting a railway track   ....

f an area of soft, wet ground   ....

g shouted loudly   ....

h causing a sick feeling   ....

i standing still, not moving   ....

j things which stand in the way of progress   ....

▶ Focus on grammar 1 · The gerund

The gerund, or **ing** form is a verbal noun. Gerunds can:

a stand on their own as nouns:Camping 's fine for a couple of weeks. (*Listening 1*)

b follow certain verbs: I enjoy camping very much.

c follow prepositions: I like the idea of camping

1 GERUNDS AFTER PREPOSITIONS

Exercise 1   There have been several examples of gerunds following prepositions in the texts so far. Choose the correct preposition from the list below to complete the sentences.

     of   after   before   without   by

a They decided to warm up .... cycling on.

b The horseman rode for over a mile .... stopping at a large camp in the mountains.

c By about 10 am we were back on the road .... thanking the man for everything he had done.

d David was aware .... something approaching.

e Mat rode straight over .... even slowing down.

⬤ In fact the gerund may be used after **all** prepositions. Here is another example:

It's just a case of changing the money as you get into the new country. (*Listening 1*)

Exercise 2   Complete the following sentences by adding the correct prepositions and the gerund form of a suitable verb. (There is a list of the missing prepositions below, if you need help.)

a I left home as soon as I was capable .... enough money to live on.

b I would never use your telephone .... your permission first.

c He explained that the machine was used .... bread into thin slices.

d I'm afraid I'm awfully bad .... names . What's yours again?

e She insisted .... her share of the bill.

f He gave up his job because he was fed up .... such long hours.

g My parents did nothing to prevent me .... a pop music group.

h I had some difficulty .... a taxi at the station.

     at   for   from   in   of   on   with   without

⬤ The gerund also follows **to** when it is used as a preposition. The phrases below are the most common examples of this use and are well worth remembering!

     look forward to   object to   prefer . . . to . . .   be used to

Exercise 3   Finish the sentences below with a suitable gerund form:

a There's a small entrance fee and so far no one has objected to ....

b Although he's a champion jockey, he actually prefers breeding dogs to ....

c Now I've got a really good camera, I'm looking forward to ....

d Don't worry about leaving me in charge of the children, I'm quite used to ....

2 GERUNDS AFTER VERBS

● The gerund is also used after certain verbs. *For example:*

Couldn't you delay sending the letter for a day or two?

The other common verbs which are followed by a gerund are listed below:

admit	dislike	involve	practise
appreciate	enjoy	keep	put off
avoid	finish	mention	resist
consider	give up	mind	risk
delay	can't help	miss	suggest
deny	imagine	postpone	can't stand

Exercise 1   Match the two halves of the sentences below so that they make sense:

a He had been considering
b The smell of the soup put me off
c In court she strongly denied
d He looked so funny that I couldn't help
e If you don't take a map, you risk
f Before our holiday we practised
g As everyone was away we postponed
h It's so hot, would you mind

1 meeting again till September.
2 getting completely lost.
3 starting his own company.
4 being anywhere near the scene of the crime.
5 wanting to taste it.
6 opening the window.
7 laughing out loud.
8 saying a few phrases in Greek.

Exercise 2   Complete the following sentences with suitable gerunds:

a If you seriously want to save money, you'd better give up ....

b I don't mind most housework but I can't stand ....

c The puppies looked so sweet that I couldn't resist ....

d If you want to learn to ride a horse, you won't be able to avoid ....

e Must you keep ....? It's really annoying!

f I'd hate to be a miner. Can you imagine ....?

g Can I have the newspaper if you've finished ....?

h The man the police caught finally admitted ....

i When he said he'd forgotten the phone number, I suggested ....

j My job as Tourist Officer for Birmingham involves ....

3 GERUNDS AFTER OTHER EXPRESSIONS

● Gerunds are also always used after the expressions in the following examples:

It's no use crying.   It's no good complaining to me!   The exam isn't worth worrying about.

4 GERUNDS AFTER POSSESSIVES

● Gerunds can be used after possessive adjectives and **'s**, as in the following examples:

I appreciated his meeting me at the station.   She mentioned Mike's telephoning last night.

It is also correct in informal spoken and written English to use the alternative forms:

I appreciated him meeting me at the station.   She mentioned Mike telephoning last night.

Note   Some verbs like **begin** and **continue** can be used with either gerund or infinitive with no change of meaning. Others like **stop** and **remember** can be used with either but there is an important change of meaning. This second group will be dealt with in Unit 5B.

▶ Communication activity · Quiz

John Ridgeway took his wife, Marie, on a 30,000 mile round-the-world yacht race. There were 12 other members of the crew, each chosen carefully by John, after a week-long selection process.

Do you have the qualities needed to undertake such a long and difficult journey?
a Do the special quiz on page 94 (set by John) and find out.

Read through for vocab

How do you rate as a round-the-world rover?

1 How old are you?

   a 18–25.
   b 25–35.
   c over 35 or under 18.

2 Are you

   a married and a parent?
   b single with a regular girlfriend or boyfriend?
   c single and unattached?

3 Do you prefer to spend your lunch hours

   a alone?
   b with one other person?
   c with a crowd in the canteen?

4 You are just arriving at a bus stop as a bus is leaving. Do you

   a run for the bus?
   b wait for the next one?
   c walk?

5 You discover that a borrowed book on your shelves belongs to a friend who has left the district. Do you

   a post it to him immediately?
   b write to him and ask if he wants it returned?
   c keep it as a souvenir?

6 You wake at 10 a.m., and were due at work at 9 a.m. Do you

   a risk getting into trouble by telephoning to say why you'll be late

   b go in, and blame everything on public transport?
   c go the next day and say you were too ill to phone?

7 The zip in your skirt/trousers breaks before an important interview. Do you:

   a tell the interviewer what happened?
   b buy a new pair of trousers?
   c buy a packet of safety pins?

8 Which of the following habits do you have?

   a smoking.
   b playing a musical instrument.
   c reading books.

9 There has been an argument in your office. Do you

   a keep well out of it?
   b sympathise with both sides separately?
   c suggest to each side that the other might just be in the right?

10 Are you doing your present job (or would you choose a job)

   a because it pays well?
   b because there was nothing better around?
   c because it fits your career plan?

11 You are staying in a youth hostel with friends. Returning to your dormitory after a hard day, you find you have an 'apple-pie' bed (as a joke, someone has made your bed in such a way that you can't get into it!). Do you

   a switch on the lights and demand to know who made it?
   b wait until morning to find out?
   c wait until next morning and make 'apple-pie' beds all round?

12 The company with which you have worked for 10 years is in serious financial difficulty. Do you

   a ask your union to fight for the highest possible redundancy pay?
   b leave immediately?
   c offer to give up your next pay rise to help keep down the company's costs?

13 What is the longest period of full-time training you have undergone since leaving school?

14 How many days have you had off work or study because of illness during the past year?

b Now compare your answers with those of another student. Discuss your reasons for choosing them.

c One answer in each question will earn the highest mark. This will be the answer which shows the qualities or attitudes needed by someone who is going on a long and difficult journey, as a member of a team. Work through the questions again, with your partner, and choose the answers which you think will earn the top mark. Be prepared to say **why** you have chosen them!

d When you have chosen your answers together, check the answers on page 217. Would **you** make a round-the-world traveller? How many correct answers did you and your partner choose? Did you choose them for the right reasons?

▶ # Text 3

Here is another extract from Gavin Young's description of his journey to China by sea. He is travelling across the Sulu Sea between Borneo and the Philippine Islands in a simple motor boat called a kumpit. He has been warned about the danger of pirates called Moros who attack boats in this area and sometimes kill the crew and passengers and now a group of wild-looking Moros has just boarded the kumpit.

Read through the text once and then answer the questions below.

It wasn't long before three of the younger Moros snooping about clambered onto the roof. They stopped dead when they saw me sitting on the rail; the last thing they'd expected to see was a white man. Then they slowly came forwards,
5 edging up to me without speaking – so surprised, I suppose, that they didn't know what to say. I waited until they were very near, and then I said, "Hello. How are you?" I put out my hand and the nearest Moro took it cautiously as if making an experiment and said, "You who? American?"
10 "No, English. You from Tawitawi?"
"From Jolo. You from England? Where you go?" He spoke with great hesitation; obviously his English was limited. There were bulges of what I took to be guns in their hip pockets, and two of them had long, big-handled knives
15 in their belts.
"I go Zamboanga."
"Zamboanga? You . . . ah . . . selling?"
"No, not selling, not merchant. Writer, writing book." I mimed someone scribbling.
20 "Ah, book?"
Another Moro asked, "Magazine also?"
"Sometimes."
At last the first Moro grinned. "Very famous, yah?"
"No. Not famous. Very poor man."
25 He sat on the rail so close to me that our shoulders touched, and they all laughed at me as if I were an exotic and possibly dangerous species of animal in a zoo.
"Very poor, yah?" he laughed. "So go in kumpit, no go aeroplane."
30 "That's right. A poor writer travelling in a kumpit. And you are – Moros?"
"Yah, Moro." He watched for my reaction.
I continued to smile. "Moro people very brave."

He asked, "England people say that? In England people
35 know about Moros?"
"In England not many people know. But in Singapore they know about Moros. Moros are famous."
The man next to me had spotted two Malaysian fifty-dollar notes in the breast pocket of my shirt; I had forgotten
40 they were there. Now he tapped the pocket with his finger and asked, "Malaysia dollar? Show me?"
I took out the two notes, each worth ten pounds sterling, and he took one and examined it, "You give me?" he asked politely.
45 'Yes, I give you that. This one" – I flourished the second fifty-dollar bill – "I keep this one. I need it for Zamboanga. Otherwise no money."
"Oh, yes," he nodded understandingly, one traveller to another. "You travel with little money. Maybe someone
50 steal."
"Yes. Carry very little money. Maybe pirates come on the kumpit. Any pirates here in Sulu Sea?"
The other two said something that sounded like "Mundo?"
55 Turning to me, he translated, "My friends say, yah, pirates here. Mundo means pirates in our language, Tausuq language. But Moro not pirate. Moro fighting Marcos. You scared?"
"Scared?" I said. "Why scared? You and me are friends."
60 "Ha! you good man." With a wide grin he threw an arm around my neck, jerked me down to his shoulder level and kissed me loudly on the cheek. "Good man. Friend," he informed the others with his arm around my shoulder. "Friend," he confirmed to me. "My name Musa. Your
65 name?"

From 'Slow Boats to China' by Gavin Young

1 Work in pairs to answer the following questions in your own words.

  a How do you think the writer felt when he saw the Moros boarding the boat?
  b How did he behave when he met them? Why?
  c What weapons did he know that they had? What weapons did he suspect that they had?
  d How did the writer make the Moros understand him even though their English was poor?
  e Why did the Moros believe him when he said he was a poor man?
  f How did they expect him to react when they said they were Moros?
  g Why did the writer say what he did about Moros?
  h How much money did the Moros take from him? How did he persuade them not to take any more?
  i Do you think he was really in danger?
  j How did he manage to make friends with the Moros?

2 Find the word or phrase in the text which means the same as:

  a searching around ....
  b climbed with effort ....
  c halted suddenly and completely ....
  d moving sideways, little by little ....

95

e carefully ....

f swellings ....

g guessed to be ....

h made the movements of writing quickly ....

i smiled widely ....

j strange and unusual ....

3 The Moros didn't speak good English and the writer sometimes also used a kind of broken English to make it easier for them to understand him. Look at the conversation in the text again and correct the English! *For example:*

From Jolo. You from England? Where you go?

Correct version: We're from Jolo. Do you come from England? Where are you going?

STUDY BOX 2

Verbs of perception   '. . . they **saw** me sitt**ing** on the rail' (*Text 3*)
see   watch   hear   notice   feel   observe

These verbs are followed by an object + **-ing** when they refer to part of an action.

I **heard** him sing**ing**. (I didn't hear the whole song)
We **watched** the man mend**ing** the road. (We didn't wait until the job was done)
I **felt** something crawl**ing** up my arm. (I didn't wait for it to reach the top!)

They are followed by an object + **infinitive** (without 'to') when they refer to a complete action.

Did you **see** that woman **steal** a watch? (take it and put it in her bag)
I **noticed** an old lady **cross** the road. (from one side to the other)

▶ Focus on grammar 2 · The past perfect

1 Look at these extracts from the texts in this unit. Underline all the examples of the past perfect tense in them.

a They stopped dead when they saw me sitting on a rail. The last thing they'd expected to see was a white man. (*Text 3*)

b The man next to me had spotted two Malaysian fifty dollar notes in the breast pocket of my shirt. I had forgotten they were there. Now he tapped the pocket with his finger . . . (*Text 3*)

c By about 10 am we were back on the road after thanking the man profusely for all he had done. (*Text 1*)

d One morning when we had been riding in the blazing sun and stifling humidity for five hours, we came to a narrow rickety bridge . . . (*Text 2*)

Form   **2** Now complete the tables below to show how the tense is formed:

Past perfect simple		Past perfect continuous
Had Hadn't +		Had Hadn't +

Meaning   **3** In each of the extracts above there are at least **two** actions in the past. The past perfect is used to show which one happened first.

Here is another example. The numbers show which action happened first and which happened later:

When the police arrived, the thieves had left the building.

a Did the police make any arrests? Why not?

b How would the meaning change if we used the past simple for both actions?

c Would the numbers change if we used the past simple for both actions?

Write the numbers 1 or 2 above the main verbs in the four extracts above to show which action(s) happened first, before the other action(s).

Note *a* The past perfect simple is used when one action has finished before another one starts and there is usually a time gap between the two actions. If one happens very quickly after another, or is the immediate result of the other, the past simple is used for both. *For example:*

When I heard his car arrive, I rushed out to meet him.

b If the order of events is clear anyway, it's not necessary to use the past perfect. *For example:*

I went to the doctor's surgery and then called at the chemist's.

c The past perfect continuous is used when the first action continued for some time or was unfinished. *For example:*

I knew by the look on their faces that they had been talking about me.

Exercise 1 Complete the following story by putting the verbs in brackets into the correct tense, past simple, past perfect simple or past perfect continuous:

I (just/finish)¹ writing a letter when the door bell (ring)². I (go)³ immediately to answer it because a neighbour of mine (tell)⁴ me she was going to call round. When I (open)⁵ the door, I (see)⁶ that there was no one there although I was sure I (hear)⁷ the bell. After I (look)⁸ up and down the street for a few minutes, I (shut)⁹ the door again and (begin)¹⁰ to wonder if I (dream)¹¹. I (decide)¹² finally that I (mistake)¹³ a car horn for the sound of the door bell. Just as I was turning round, I (notice)¹⁴ something white on the door mat. I (examine)¹⁵ it more closely and (realise)¹⁶ that someone (push)¹⁷ a note under the door. As I (never/see)¹⁸ the handwriting before, I (begin)¹⁹ to feel slightly alarmed.

Exercise 2 The past perfect tense is often used in **reported speech** where both the past simple and present perfect in the original words, are changed to the past perfect.

Change the following into reported speech:

a I hope you have read the instructions carefully.

The examiner said he hoped that we ....

b I'm not sure I've found the answer to your question though I've spent a week thinking about it.

She explained that she wasn't sure that she ....

c I can't shake hands with you because my hands are oily. I've been working on the car, you see.

He said he couldn't shake hands with me because his hands were oily and explained that ....

▶ Focus on listening 2

You are going to hear part of an interview with David Hempleman Adams, who walked alone to the North Pole.

For questions 1–10 tick (√) whether you think the statements are true or false. **True False**

1 David spent two years planning the first expedition.
2 On that expedition he succeeded in reaching the geographical North Pole.
3 Many people thought he wouldn't survive the cold.
4 He enjoyed making the expedition.
5 He missed the sense of danger after he returned to England.
6 He had air support[1] on both his expeditions.
7 He hadn't expected to be attacked by a polar bear.
8 The bear ate the Mars bar[2] before attacking him.
9 He immediately tried to kill the animal.
10 He regretted having had to kill it.

---

[1] regular supplies of food dropped by plane
[2] a type of chocolate bar

▶ Focus on writing · Formal letter

Writing Bank: page 222

Layout Working in pairs, put the following information in the correct places on the letter below.

a **Your Address:**
22 Green Lane, Bath, Avon

b **The Name and Address of the Person you are writing to:**
The Project Director, Amazon Expedition, 8 Bell St., London WC3 5YA.

c **The Date:** *d* **The Beginning:** *e* **The Ending:**
Dear Sir, Yours faithfully,

I was very interested in your advertisement in today's edition of The Evening Post and I should like to apply to be a member of the Amazon Expedition team.

I am twenty-three years old and have an honours degree in Botany from Bath University. Since leaving university I have been working in a research laboratory but my contract comes to an end in six weeks. I would particularly like to join the expedition for the opportunity it would give me to study the plant life of the area.

I enjoy several outdoor activities including rowing and rock climbing and I consider myself to be both fit and healthy enough to undertake such an expedition.

If you would like me to attend an interview, I would be able to come at any time convenient to you, as my employers have agreed to give me time off for the purpose.

I look forward to hearing from you.

Do you think this applicant is suitable? What questions would you ask him?

Style   This letter was sent in response to the same advertisement but it didn't create a very good impression! Read it through to see why not.

> Dear Sir,
>
> I noticed an ad. in the paper today which said you were looking for people to join your expedition team. It sounded as if it might be fun so I'm writing to say I'd like to come along.
>
> About myself: I left school at 16 because I couldn't stand the teachers and I wanted to earn a bit of money. After that I got a few part-time jobs as a waiter etc. but I didn't stick any of them for long. Recently I've been doing a bit of hitch-hiking round Europe so I've had some experience of travelling the hard way which should come in handy on the expedition you're planning.
>
> By the way, I'm a great guitarist so I can keep you all amused round the campfire at night.
>
> Let me know when I can call in for a chat about dates and other details etc.
>
> Yours
>
> David Morecambe

Work with a partner to underline all the features of style which are unsuitable in this kind of letter. When you have finished, check your result with that of another pair.

Note

A formal letter does not need to be written in very formal language these days. You should aim to express yourself clearly and concisely and to avoid slang, idiomatic expressions and abbreviations.

What else in the letter makes you think that David Morecambe would not be a very suitable member of the team?

Practice   *a* The first letter was from a botanist. What other members would be needed for the Amazon Expedition team? Discuss your ideas. *For example:*

A photographer would be needed because . . .

b Choose one of the members you have suggested, and write a letter of application from a suitably qualified person.

Remember to mention: ● why you are writing.
● your main qualifications and experience.
● your reason for wanting to join the expedition.
● any other relevant points (skills, interests, etc).

Follow the layout of the model letter on page 98.

STUDY BOX 3

Phrasal verb **Bring.**   '. . . he worked to **bring** his companion **round**.' (*Text 1*)

bring about – cause to happen.   Disagreements between the two countries finally **brought about** a war.
bring in – introduce.   The government is **bringing in** a new law.
bring off – to succeed in something difficult.   I didn't think he'd win the race but he **brought** it **off** magnificently.
bring out – make clear.   The way he read the poem really **brought out** its meaning.
bring round – help back to consciousness.   See example above.
bring up – raise a child.   I was **brought up** in the country.

Describing objects

1 Look at the following expressions and then use them to describe the objects below.

● **Materials**			● **Patterns**		
It's	made of	wool (It's woollen)	It's		spotted
		leather	They're		checked
		cotton			striped
They're		wood (It's wooden)			plain
		silk			
		plastic	● **Shapes**		rectangular
		etc.			circular
			It's		square
					oval
					triangular

See Functions Bank page 212 for these and other shapes.

2 Fill in the adjectives which have the opposite meaning to the following:

long	....	wide	....	expensive	....
hard	....	full	....	enormous	....
heavy	....	sharp	....	curved	....
thick	....	tight	....	dark (of colours)	....
smooth	....	hollow	....	bright (of colours)	....

Writing task

3 On a recent journey to Scotland for an adventure training course, one of your suitcases was lost by the airline. The picture below shows the case and some of its contents (but you should be able to remember a few more). Write a formal letter to the airline company (Customer Relations Officer, Beeline Travel Ltd., 26 Kingsway, Edinburgh, Scotland.) giving details of the case and the main items it contained so that the company can check to see if it has been found.

Plan

First paragraph: Explain why you are writing and give details of the flight (airports of departure and destination, date, time, flight number)

Middle paragraphs: Describe the suitcase and its contents giving the necessary details to help the company to recognise your belongings (size, colour, material etc.) Use from 1 to 3 paragraphs as necessary.

Last paragraph: Explain what you would like the airline to do (return your case or pay compensation).

▶ Exam practice A · Vocabulary

Choose the word or phrase which best completes each sentence.

1 The first job was to .... the car with the equipment they would need.

   a supply   *b* charge   *c* load   *d* stock

2 It's a good idea to carry a .... pair of shoes in case the ones you're wearing get wet.

   a repeat   *b* final   *c* double   *d* spare

3 Unfortunately the train .... by the time I reached the platform.

   a left   *b* has left   *c* had left   *d* had been leaving

4 The whole team .... a great effort to raise money for the expedition.

   a did   *b* made   *c* put   *d* took

5 Be sure to .... yourself up well if you're going for a walk by the sea.

   a wrap   *b* pack   *c* wind   *d* clothe

6 I've written to the company to complain but so far there's been no ....

   a repeat   *b* receipt   *c* return   *d* response

7 Someone fainted during the lecture and when we couldn't manage to .... him round, we called an ambulance.

   a take   *b* get   *c* bring   *d* pull

8 If you don't pay the fee now, you risk .... your place on the course.

   a of losing   *b* losing   *c* to lose   *d* lose

9 After the assassination of the president, the army .... control of the country.

   a gave   *b* made   *c* led   *d* took

10 Be careful you don't .... on the ice near the door.

   a swing   *b* slide   *c* sink   *d* slip

11 'What's .... ?' she called when she saw our anxious faces.

   a up   *b* on   *c* about   *d* out

12 Working in the midday heat made him .... so much that his shirt stuck to his body.

   a drain   *b* sweat   *c* strain   *d* transpire

13 Riding a horse isn't as difficult as it looks. In fact, there's nothing .... it!

   a to   *b* for   *c* in   *d* by

14 Our wet clothes .... as they dried in front of the fire.

   a smoked   *b* streamed   *c* thawed   *d* steamed

15 Please let me know your decision by Friday .... I'll have to offer the job to another applicant.

   a unless   *b* else   *c* otherwise   *d* in case

16 I'm really looking forward .... my new job.

    a start   *b* to start   *c* starting   *d* to starting

17 My knowledge of Spanish is rather ...., I'm afraid.

    a short   *b* limited   *c* scarce   *d* narrow

18 They were doing a simple .... with two gases when the explosion happened.

    a attempt   *b* trial   *c* experiment   *d* experience

19 When he stood up, he only came up to my shoulder ....

    a level   *b* length   *c* measure   *d* extent

20 She moved very slowly .... exhausted by her day's work.

    a although   *b* as   *c* like   *d* as if

21 He .... very gently on the window so as not to wake the whole house.

    a tapped   *b* pounded   *c* patted   *d* stamped

22 He's very .... of watching late night horror films.

    a keen   *b* interested   *c* fond   *d* mad

23 'The Times', ... is owned by News International, has recently sacked a lot of staff.

    a who   *b* which   *c* that   *d* whose

24 The company introduced a small electric car but it never .... with the public, and they stopped production after a few months.

    a caught on   *b* caught up   *c* took up   *d* took over

25 If you wear that red hat, I'll be able to .... you in the crowd.

    a pick   *b* spot   *c* discover   *d* realise

▶ Odd man out

In each of the following groups of words, there is one which does not fit. Work in pairs to choose the 'odd man out' in each group and say why it doesn't belong there.

Note There may be more than one correct answer!

1 steamers   liner   ferry   tram   yacht

2 cart   tractor   wagon   sledge   pram   (several possibilities!)

3 lorry   truck   car   van   petrol-tanker

4 taxi   tram   bus   coach   train

5 guard's van   carriage   sleeping car   track   runway

6 pilot   captain   conductor   engine-driver   cyclist

7 anchor   deck   cabin   platform   porthole

8 terminus   station   double-decker   bus-stop   driver

9 horse   ox   camel   dog   goat

10 Rotterdam   Southampton   Cairo   Bombay   Marseilles

HONEYSETT.

" Because it was you that forgot the flag, that's why."

UNIT2B Family life

▶Lead-in

1 Look at the pictures of two different family groups below. Describe each one.

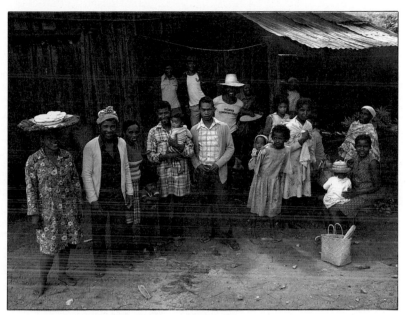

2 What are the advantages and disadvantages of growing up with several brothers and sisters in the family?

What are the advantages and disadvantages of growing up as an only child?

Questionnaire

There are 12 statements below. Read each one carefully and decide if you agree or disagree with it. Then write A (if you agree) or D (if you disagree) in the box on the right.

1 For women, financial support is one of the most important reasons for getting married. ☐

2 Women should work outside the home and make a financial contribution to the family budget. ☐

3 A husband should share his earnings fairly with his wife. ☐

4 A husband should help very little in the home, if the wife stays at home. ☐

5 If the wife works full-time, housework should be shared equally between both partners. ☐

6 Women should spend more time than men with children ☐

7 Mothers shouldn't go out to work while their children are small. ☐

8 A husband should have the last word on big decisions. ☐

9 A woman's career is just as important as a man's. ☐

10 Both husbands and wives should be free to have interests and friends of their own. ☐

11 Older children should help with the housework. ☐

12 Parents should always respect the wishes of their children. ☐

When you've finished, compare your answers with other students' and discuss the reasons for your opinions.

► Text 1

1 Read the following text through once, fairly quickly, to see what's unusual about this family's lifestyle.

A REALLY EQUAL PARTNER

John Holland/33/Part-time librarian/two children: Andrew 10, Thomas 8

John works two days a week in a London library – he job-shares with a woman colleague and spends the rest of the time at home. Pam, his
5 wife, is a full-time advisory home economics teacher with plenty of out-of-hours commitments. John looks after the children when Pam is at work, cooks the evening meal
10 twice a week and they share responsibilities during their holidays.

John comes from a large Belfast Catholic family and is one of eight children. "There was no question of
15 not **mucking in**," he remembers. "We all did, including my father. By the time I was 12, I could cook dinner for the family with help from my mother.
20 When his own children were very young, John worked full-time and Pam had part-time work, but when Pam was offered the opportunity of a responsible full-time job, they
25 didn't want to use childminders and so John decided it should be he who reduced his working hours to look after the children.

Although John does occasionally
30 resent getting so little financial reward for his work and misses the responsibility he lost, he feels he is well-suited to the arrangement he and Pam now have. "We know that
35 other couples are **better off** than us," he says, "and that we are unlikely to have a house with all **mod cons** or an expensive car, but that doesn't worry us. I suppose it
40 might do later. Right now being with the children is just more important to me than a successful business career and a fast lifestyle."

When it's Pam's turn to cook the
45 evening meal, John tackles other household **chores**, and once a week he does a big supermarket shop, usually on Friday nights. "That's Pam's time to be with the
50 children," he says.

Pam has learnt not to be too concerned about the standard of housework. Most of it simply doesn't get done at all, but of what is ac-
55 complished, John is responsible for about 60 to 70 per cent, because he has more time. He's **by no means** a great fan of laundry work.

But it is John who **throws a minor**
60 **fit** if anything happens to make the washing even more of a chore than it is already. "If Pam buys a red garment which will run in the wash, I make my disgust pretty clear," he
65 says "As for the ironing, I'll do anything to get out of it!"

Interestingly enough, despite his great involvement with Andrew and Thomas, John feels that Pam is still
70 the "mother" of the family and that the boys look to her more than to him for affection. Pam thinks this is *a* **throwback** to a long tradition: "Women are freer to express all
75 emotions: to **cuddle and 'mumsy'** their children. John is affectionate, but showing it doesn't come naturally to him – or to most men I suspect. He has to make an effort."
80 They seem to **have it all taped**, but reaching this level of smooth co-operation has been **an uphill struggle**. "Pam and I are very different people," says John, "with strong
85 views on all kinds of subjects, particularly politics and religion. To get this far we've had to talk it all through at every stage."

by Edwina Conner in Good Housekeeping

2 Say whether the following statements are true or false and why.

a John does all the cooking for the family.
b He had had no experience of helping in the house before.
c There are times when he feels a bit dissatisfied with his situation.
d He would rather have a full-time job than look after his children.
e John does most of the housework.
f He keeps the house very clean and tidy.
g The children are more fond of their mother than of him.
h John and Pam have the same opinions about most subjects.

3 Ten words or phrases which you may not know are in bold in the text. Study them carefully and say what you think they could mean in the context. Below are ten explanations for them but they are not in the same order. Match the explanation to the correct word or phrase.

a gets very angry ....
b have the situation well organised (slang) ....
c joining in to help (slang) ....
d not at all ....
e small duties which are uninteresting or difficult ....
f hold in one's arms and show affection to ....
g in a more comfortable position, financially ....
h a difficult task, needing continuous effort ....
i modern conveniences (abbreviation) ....
j a return to an older type ....

Read the text again and answer the following questions.

4 When his wife was offered a full-time job, John decided to look after the children because
    a he enjoyed being with them more than his wife did.
    b he didn't want a stranger to care for them.
    c his wife would earn more money than he could.
    d he only had a part-time job.

5 One regret that John sometimes has is that
    a he can't afford to buy a car.
    b he sees so little of his wife.
    c he has less responsibility at work than before.
    d he has given up an extremely successful career.

6 The job John seems to like least is
    a cooking.
    b shopping.
    c washing.
    d ironing.

7 Pam feels that women differ from men in that they
    a take more pleasure in housework.
    b show their feelings more openly.
    c find small children less tiring.
    d lose their tempers more often.

8 According to John, the arrangement he and Pam have for sharing duties in the home
    a has been difficult to achieve.
    b resulted from their political beliefs.
    c still leads to many disagreements.
    d developed naturally from the start.

STUDY BOX 1

Phrasal verb **Look.**   John . . . reduced his working hours to **look after** the children
    (Text 1)

look after – take care of.   See above.
look for – try to find.   I'm **looking for** my keys. Have you seen them?
look in – visit.   I'll **look in** and see you next week.
look into – investigate.   Police are **looking into** several burglaries in the area.
look out – take care (usually imperative).   **Look out!** There's a car coming.
look through – examine.   **Look through** the contract carefully before you sign it.
look up – search for information.   I had to **look** the spelling **up** in the dictionary.
look up to – respect.   He's always **looked up to** his elder brother.

▶ Focus on grammar 1 · The infinitive

THE INFINITIVE WITH 'TO' IS USED:

● to express purpose. *For example:*

He . . . reduced his working hours to look after the children. (*Text 1*)
To get this far, we've had to talk it all through at every stage. (*Text 1*)

Exercise 1 Complete the following sentences, using an infinitive with **to**.

a He's got to go on a diet ....
b We've decided to employ an architect ....:...
c They telephoned the police ....
d There's a plumber coming tomorrow ....

e I went to the doctor's....................................
f We had to call the Fire Brigade ....
g He joined the army..
h .... the team will have to play extremely well.

● after **adjectives**. *For example:*

We know . . . we are unlikely to have a house with all mod cons.
Women are freer to express their emotions.

● also with **too** + **adjective**, and **adjective** + **enough**. *For example:*

This tea is too hot (for me) to drink
Are you strong enough to lift that by yourself.

Exercise 2 To complete the following sentences, choose an adjective from List A and a verb from List B. Don't forget to use **to** with the infinitive.

List A					List B			
delighted	certain	simple	important		meet	check	know	use
hard	amazed	anxious	disappointed		believe	be	hear	see

a They told me in the shop that this camera was ...., but I can't get used to it at all!
b I was .... from his mother that he didn't get the job he wanted so much.
c I'm sure you're all very .... what your exam results are.
d You can wait for him if you like – he's .... home before 6 o'clock.
e It's .... it's June when you see all this rain!
f I've learned so much about you and I'm .... you at last.
g We were all .... your picture in the paper. How on earth did that come about?
h It's very .... that the electricity is switched off before you start.

Exercise 3 Complete the following sentences:

a This case is too heavy for me . . .
b There aren't enough eggs . . .
c Is the runway long enough for the plane . . .

d The weather is too bad for the ship . . .
e He's too short-sighted . . .
f Have you had enough practice . . .

● after **main verbs**. *For example:*

Pam has learnt not to be too concerned about the standard of housework. (*Text 1*)
They seem to have it all taped. (*Text 1*)

Other common verbs which take an infinitive with **to** are:

afford	ask	expect	help	manage	prepare	refuse
agree	begin	fail	hope	offer	pretend	
arrange	choose	happen	intend	prefer	promise	

● after the **object of a verb**. *For example:*

He taught me to play the piano.

Other common verbs which take an object followed by an infinitive with **to** are:

advise	encourage	force	intend	order	recommend	want
allow	expect	get	invite	persuade	remind	warn
ask	forbid	help	leave	prefer	tell	

Exercise 4 Complete the following sentences with suitable verbs from the two lists above. Fill in an object where necessary.

a We did everything we could to .... come with us, but he refused.

b Would you .... have tea or coffee?

c If you .... see him, please give him my regards.

d Could you .... set the alarm for 6 am? It would be terrible if I overslept.

e When I was a child, my parents .... play in the street, though I wanted to.

f Are you sure you can .... buy a new car? Wouldn't a second hand one be wiser?

g He .... take a course in typing and said it would be very useful for me.

h When I leave school, I .... get a job in a television studio.

i If you take on an assistant, it will .... get through your work more quickly.

j I .... climb the tree, but you ignored me. Now I don't know how we'll get you down!

● after some **auxiliary verbs**.   *For example:*

He has to make an effort.   You need to take more care.

Other verbs in this group are: be, ought, used

● as the **subject of a sentence**.   *For example:*

To try to escape would be foolish!

THE INFINITIVE WITHOUT 'TO' IS USED:

● after **modal verbs**.   *For example:*

You should come and see us more often.

Other verbs in this group are: will, shall, would, should, can, could, may, might, must

● after **make and let**.   *For example:*

You can't make me do anything!   Let the next patient come in now.

● after **would rather**, **had better** and **why not** ..?   *For example:*

I'd rather take a train (than fly).   You'd better stay in bed.   Why not come with us?

Exercise 5   The following passage describes the attitudes of two families, one French and one British, towards money. Put the verbs in brackets into the correct form: **Infinitive** with **to**, **infinitive** without **to**, or **gerund**.

'What's the point in (worry 1) too much about the future?' says Francine Beudet. Francine, her husband Hervé and daughter, Marine, live 100 miles south of Paris. 'We don't save much. We prefer (spend 2) our money now on (have 3) a good life.'

In England Gordon and Fiona Robinson take the same approach to money. Fiona decided (stay 4) at home (look after 5) their daughter, Chloë, who is nearly 3. 'I have considered (take 6) a part-time job, but as it's impossible for Gordon (be 7) home at a set time each evening, it's too difficult (arrange 8) at the moment.'

On the other side of the Channel, Francine has found an ideal solution to the problem of (combine 9) work with (run 10) a home and (bring up 11) children. She's a nurse and she works part-time at an old people's home. Although the hospital is close to Francine's home, she needs a car (get 12) there quickly.

Hervé is expected (buy 13) his own car but he does receive hotel and petrol expenses for his work, which involves (drive 14) an enormous distance each year. He organises his work so that when Francine is on night duty, he can (get 15) home every evening (take 16) care of Marine.

Gordon's car is provided by his employer and he is lucky enough (get 17) a new one every two years. He also spends each working day (travel 18) around his area, but instead of (stay 19) overnight in hotels, he manages (get 20) home.

From 'Vive la différence' Mail on Sunday magazine

▶ Communication activity

Work in pairs for this activity:

Student A — Look at the instructions below and the picture on page 218.
Student B — Look at the instructions below and the picture on page 219.

Instructions

The pictures are the same except for 10 small differences.

You must find the differences by describing your pictures to each other. Do not let your partner see your picture!

Take it in turns to describe a section of the picture in detail. Be prepared to ask each other questions in order to be sure that what you see is exactly the same. When you discover a difference, make a note of it.

▶ Focus on listening 1 · Children speaking

You are going to hear 3 children being interviewed. As you listen, fill in the missing information in the table below.

	Age	Brothers/ Sisters	Pocket Money	Spends Pocket Money on...	Help in the house	Punish- ment	Bed Time	
							Earliest	Latest
First Child		2 brothers		Sweets	— — — — and laying the table.	gets sent to bed or gets a smack.		11pm
Second Child	7			sweets	— — — — wiping up + putting things away.		8 or 9pm	
Third Child			£1 – £2		— — — — and bring the knives and forks.			11pm

Discussion points

1 Work with a partner. Tell each other:

a How much pocket money you got as a child, and what you used to spend it on.
b What you did to help in the house.
c What time you went to bed when you were 8 or 9 years old.
d How your parents punished you if you were ever naughty!

2 a What time should an 8-year-old child go to bed? What exceptions would you make?
b Should you smack naughty children? What other punishments can be used?

▶ Text 2 · Working mothers: what children say

In the two texts below, children give their opinions about having a working mother.

1 Look at the five questions below and then read the text about Debbie Hollobon to find the answers. (Don't worry about difficult words or phrases at this stage).

a Why was it a difficult time for Debbie when her mother started working full-time?
b How did she feel about her sister at that time? (Which words give you the answer?)
c What did she soon enjoy about the new arrangement?
d Does she feel that her mother neglected her in any way?
e What advantages does Debbie think there were in having a working mother?

Debbie Hollobon, aged 21, comes from Daventry, Northamptonshire. Her mother, head of the mail room in a staff agency, has worked full time since Debbie was aged 13 and her sister, Sarah was ten.

5 'I didn't like it a bit when she took a full time job and, as the elder sister, I had to look after Sarah. Everything seemed to come at once: we'd just moved to Daventry and I was in my second year at comprehensive school and meeting new people 10 and making new friends. I felt I had enough on my plate without having Sarah tagging along every time I went out. I went through a stage where I couldn't stand her; she seemed to get in the way of everything I wanted to do.

15 'I never told my mum how I felt. I knew she'd have been miserable sitting at home alone in a town where she didn't know anyone, so the job was very good for her. Once the initial shock wore off, I got to like it, being trusted with my own key and feeling grown up and independent.

'However much she had to do, coming home to 20 the cooking and cleaning after a day's work, she always had time for us when we wanted to talk. There was never a time when she shrugged us off because she was too tired or too busy.

'I probably helped around the house more than I 25 would have done with a stay-at-home mother, but she never told me to do any chores before she got home. I did what I felt like when I felt like it and I knew she wouldn't nag if it wasn't done.

'Since I got married, last June, I've appreciated 30 the extra independence that came from looking after myself for part of the day. I know what things cost because I'm used to shopping and I know how much work goes into running a house. A lot of the girls I grew up with, who never learned to fend for themselves, must have come down to earth 35 with a bump. When I have children I just hope I can do as well as my mother, but I don't know if I'll have enough patience and energy.'

From Living Magazine

2 Now work with a partner to ask and answer the five questions about Debbie. Try to use your own words.

3 Now read the five questions about Peter Swift and the text below.

   a What does he dislike about having a working mother?
   b What did his mother agree to before she started work?
   c Does he feel that his mother has neglected him at all?
   d What advantages does Peter think there have been in having a working mother?
   e Does he think the advantages make up for the disadvantages?

Peter Swift, aged 15, lives near Leeds. His mother has worked as a graphic designer for the last three years. 'I hate it; I've always hated it. Mum disappears at 7.30 am and doesn't get home until
5 about 7.30 pm, so we come home to an empty house. It doesn't worry my sister Elizabeth. She's a year older than me and has loads of homework, so she sits upstairs working and I'm left on my own.
10   'When she first had the chance of going back to work we all talked about it and she said that it was only a trial period and if we weren't happy with it she would give it up. But it wasn't a fair test because in the beginning it was all rather thrilling being on our own; like a big
15 adventure. I didn't realise what it would be like long term.
  'She started her new job two days before I started at comprehensive school and I had to go by myself, when all the other boys had their mothers with them. Of course, everybody was much more interested in what had happened at the new job
20 than what had happened at the new school.

'Elizabeth and I both have our own chores. I load the dishwasher and I sometimes wash the car or mow the grass. Elizabeth does the ironing – well, she says she does, but she never seems to get round to ironing my shirts. We get extra pocket 25 money because we help out, so I suppose it's fair, but all my friends do absolutely nothing around the house.
  'There is a good side to it. Mum has lots of interesting things to tell us and I like to hear her 30 talk about the people she meets. We probably get more freedom, too – I can make my models on the table without getting told off. We wouldn't have as much money for trips to France or hobbies like photography if she didn't work, but I'd swap all that if it meant she'd be at home 35 like she used to be. I don't think a woman's place is in the home or anything like that, but I do think a career should be fitted round the children, not the other way round, and in my opinion what the children think should come first' ● *Joyce Robins*

From Living Magazine

4 Now work with a partner again to ask and answer the five questions.

5 Say whether the following statements are true or false in your opinion and why.

   a Both Debbie and Peter have similar relationships with their sisters.
   b Neither Debbie nor Peter liked their mothers working at the beginning.
   c They both feel that the opportunity to work has been good for the mothers.
   d They were both given special jobs to do around the house.
   e Both their mothers started working at difficult times for their children.
   f Both Debbie and Peter admire their mothers for what they have done.
   g Debbie feels that other girls probably find it more difficult than she did when they first leave home.
   h Peter thinks the trial period at the beginning worked well.

When you have finished, compare your answers with another student's. Some could be either true or false depending on your argument.

6 Debbie uses several idiomatic expressions. Choose the best explanation for the six examples below:

   a I had **enough on my plate** *(line 10).*
     a enough things to deal with.   *b* enough food to eat.   *c* enough work to do.

   b without having Sarah **tagging along** *(line 11).*
     a watching.   *b* waiting.   *c* following.

   c she **shrugged us off** *(line 23)*
     a behaved violently towards us.   *b* made us angry.   *c* treated us as unimportant.

   d she wouldn't **nag** *(line 29)*
     a understand.   *b* complain.   *c* approve.

e to **fend for themselves** *(line 35)*
    a protect themselves. *b* look after themselves. *c* earn a living.

f **come down to earth** with a bump *(lines 35/36)*
    a face practical realities. *b* take a lower position. *c* have an accident.

7 Find words or phrases in the section about Peter Swift which mean the same as those below. Paragraph numbers are in brackets.

a experimental (2) ....
b exciting (2) ....
c over an extended period of time (2) ....
d cut (with a machine) (4) ....
e find time for doing something (4) ....
f scolded (spoken angrily to) (5) ....
g exchange (5) ....

Discussion points

● Peter says . . . *a career should be fitted round the children and not the other way round.* Do you agree? Why/why not?
– Of course, he's talking about a woman's career. What are the problems for a woman of giving up a successful career after the birth of a child?
– Do you think a man's career should be fitted round his children?

● Do you think Peter might change his mind about the subject when he reaches Debbie's age? Why/why not?

▶ Focus on grammar 2 · Reporting statements

TENSE CHANGES

1 Look at the examples below and then complete the tables which follow.

a I work here on Saturdays   → She said (that) she worked there on Saturdays.
b I'm going to London tomorrow. → He said (that) he was going to London the next day
c I've written a letter today. → He said (that) he'd written a letter that day
d I saw an old friend yesterday. → She said (that) she'd seen an old friend the day before
e I'd forgotten to tell you. → she said (that) she'd forgotten to tell me.
f I'll ring you later this week. → He said (that) he'd ring us later that week

Direct speech	Reported speech
a Present simple	
b Present continuous	
c	Past perfect
d Simple past	
e Past perfect	
f	would

Direct speech	Reported speech
now	then
today	
tomorrow	
yesterday	
this	
here	
ago	before

Note

● When the reporting verb is in the present tense, it isn't necessary to change the tense. *For example:*

    I'll send you a postcard. He says he'll send us a postcard.

● In spoken English, if the original words are still true, the tense is sometimes left unchanged. *For example:*

    He said he'll send us a postcard.

2 Present modal verbs normally change to **past** forms. *For example:*

    I may join you later.   He said he might join us later.
    I can't hear you.   She said she couldn't hear me.

Past modal verbs normally don't change. *For example:*

He might come.	She said he might come.
That could be our train.	He said that it could be our train.
You ought to lie down.	She said that I ought to lie down.

REPORTING VERBS

There are a number of other verbs, apart from 'said' which can be used in reported speech with a **that** clause.

Exercise 1 Put the sentences which follow into reported speech and choose one of the reporting verbs below for each one.

explained   admitted   complained   argued   promised

a 'You never lift a finger to help me!'   His wife . . .
b 'I'll give you a hand with your homework this evening.'   My father . . .
c 'I'm late because the bus broke down.'   I . . .
d 'I'm afraid I've had an accident with your car.'   My friend . . .
e 'John ought to go first because he's the youngest.'   The teacher . . .

Note ● When the verb **suggest** is used to report advice, it's normally followed by **should**.   *For example:*

'Ask in the Post Office for directions.'
He suggested that we should ask in the Post Office for directions.

3 The verb **tell** can be used to introduce a reported statement. It is followed by a personal object and a **that** clause.   *For example:*

He told us that the film was excellent.

Other common verbs like this are: **advise, warn, remind**.   *For example:*

They warned me that the road was icy'
You didn't remind me that the clocks change today.

4 The verb **tell** is also used to introduce indirect commands.   *For example:*

'Go to your room'	He told me to go to my room.
'Don't shout'.	He told me not to shout

Other common verbs which are used to introduce indirect commands, requests, advice etc, are:

advise   invite   recommend   forbid   warn   remind   ask

Exercise 2 Put the following sentences into reported speech and choose one of the reporting verbs above for each one:

a 'Could you shut the door, please?'   The interviewer . . .
b 'Don't forget to switch off the fire.'   My mother . . .
c 'Would you like to sit down and wait?'   The receptionist . . .
d 'I should lie down, if I were you.'   My friend . . .
e 'You mustn't tell anyone about this product.'   My boss . . .
f 'Don't move or I'll shoot!'   The gunman . . .
g 'Try to stay at the Imperial Hotel if you can.'   Some friends of mine . . .

Exercise 3 Complete the following sentences with either **to + infinitive** or a **that** clause.

a My neighbour invited me .... her garden.

b The mechanic warned him .... dangerous condition.

c They forbade the children .... in the road.

d Didn't I tell you .... my exam with Grade A?

e I told the children .... too much noise.

f Police warned drivers .... in the fog.

g I had to remind him .... the cat.

h The waiter recommended us .... the salmon.

i Why didn't you remind me .... closed on Satuday?

j The travel agent advised them .... because the weather then would be very hot indeed.

Exercise 4 Look at what Debbie says at the end of Text 2 (page 109). Change lines 30–38 into reported speech. Note that 'must have done' does not change.

► Focus on writing 1 · Informal letter

Writing Bank: page 220

> Imagine that an English friend is coming to stay with your family (or another family you know well). Write a letter to your friend describing the members of the family and their lifestyle.

Plan **First paragraph** Express pleasure that your friend is visiting.
Middle paragraphs Describe the members of the family. Mention jobs, hobbies, interests etc. Explain what a typical day in the life of the family is like (mealtimes, household tasks, entertainment, etc). Make suggestions about what your friend will be able to do and see during the visit.
Last paragraph Explain arrangements for meeting your friend and say how much you're looking forward to the visit.

Note Remember to mention the things that your friend may find quite different from English family life.

► Focus on listening 2 · Single parent family

Listen to the conversation between two old friends, Helen and Gay, who have just met.
For questions 1-8 tick (√) whether you think the statements are true or false.
For questions 9–12 fill in the missing information by writing short answers in the spaces.

	True	False
1 Gay has just separated from her husband.		
2 She has two children.		
3 She has several friends who help her look after the children.		
4 Her mother pays for some of the children's clothes.		
5 Gay lives in a friendly neighbourhood.		
6 She has to nurse her elderly father at his home.		
7 She thinks her ex-husband should do more to help her and the children.		
8 The children rarely see their father.		

9 The course Gay has been attending was for .... only.
10 It lasted for ....
11 It cost ....
12 One good thing about Gay's situation is that her children have become very ....

Discussion points
● Do children need two parents? Why/why not?
● What are some of the problems for a single parent?
● Are the problems greater when the children are younger or when they are older?
● Should parents stay together for the sake of the children?
● In what way can children of single parent families grow up to be more independent?

STUDY BOX 2

Phrasal verb **Get.** (2)   As for ironing, I'll do anything to **get out of** it. *(Text 1)*
        . . . she never seems to **get round to** ironing my shirts. *(Text 2)*

get off – leave (usually a public vehicle).   Ask the conductor when to **get off**.
get on – make progress.   He's **getting on** very well in his new job.
get on with – manage to work/live with.   How do you **get on with** the neighbours?
get out of – avoid (a duty).   See above.
get over – recover from (illness/difficulties etc).   I haven't **got over** the shock yet.
get round to – find time to do.   See above.
get through – make contact (usually by telephone).   I couldn't **get through** because the line was engaged.

▶ Focus on grammar 3 · Comparatives: The . . . the . . .

Look at these examples:

> The younger the child, the more sleep he needs.
> The more children there are, the less peace we'll have!

This is a very convenient and common construction in English. Explain the meaning of the two examples in other words, and see whether your sentence is longer.

Change the words in red type so that the sentences say the opposite.

Form

> **The** + comparative word . . .   **the** + comparative word
>   (more/less/-er)   (more/less/-er)

Notes

1 **The** can be followed by both adjectives and adverbs. *For example:*

> The more chocolates he ate, the fatter he became.   (Adjective)
> The more slowly we walk, the longer it will take to get there.   (Adverb)

2 Sometimes, if the meaning is clear, the subject and verb may be left out. What has been left out at the end of the sentence in the following example?

> The hotter the weather is, the better.

In the English saying **The more, the merrier**, both subjects and verbs are left out. The meaning is: The more people who come, the merrier we shall be.

When would you say **The sooner the better**, and what would you mean?

Exercise 1 Complete the following sentences with suitable comparative words:

a The more exercise you take, the .... you will become.

b The .... the car, the .... it is to hire.

c The .... you speak, the .... it is for me to understand.

d .... you study, ... chance you will have in the exam.

e .... I get to know him, ... I like him, I'm sorry to say.

f The more frightening the film, ...

g The sharper the knife, ...

h ...., the more homesick I felt.

Exercise 2 Write sentences to describe the relationship between:

a Money and Happiness   b Age and Wisdom

STUDY BOX 3

The use of articles 3.   I was in my second year at comprehensive school   *(Text 2)*

The following words are used **without** an article when they are used for their main purpose.
They are used **with** an article when they are used for some other reason.

NO ARTICLE	DEFINITE ARTICLE
He's gone **to bed.** (to sleep)	Stand on **the bed** to reach the shelf.
I'm still **at school/college/ university.** (studying)	I'm going to **the school** to interview the headmaster.
They took him **to hospital.** (for treatment)	Will you come to **the hospital** to see me?
He's **in prison.** (for punishment)	I called at **the prison** to deliver some food.
Also: church, dock, court	

► Focus on writing 2 · Directed writing

Writing Bank: page 234

Below are suggestions for four places of interest to visit in Wales taken from the tourist leaflet *Great Days Out on the Cambrian Coast*.

1 Read through the information to find answers to the following questions:

a Which mention(s) the surrounding scenery?
b Where would you be able to see farm animals?
c Where would you be able to buy something to eat?
d Where could you probably buy souvenirs of your visit?
e Which can cater for groups of schoolchildren?
f Which could you go to during the Christmas holidays?
g Which mention(s) parking for cars?

Cadwgan Place, Aberaeron, Dyfed, SA46 0ED.
Tel. (0545) 570142 or 570608
Aberaeron is on the A487 coast road between Cardigan and Aberystwyth, in Dyfed. The Aquarium is situated on the Quay.

The Aquarium displays a collection of fish and other marine life to be found off the West Coast of Wales. There are informative displays of fossils and preserved specimens, with entertaining video. Also an interesting gift and bookshop. Cafe, parking and toilets are all nearby. No special disabled facilities, but the Aquarium and shop are level. The beach is only minutes away. Contact Geoffrey D. Browne, Bronaeron, Lampeter Road, Aberaeron, Dyfed, SA46 0ED.

Opening times: We open on Good Friday and then everyday – including Sundays – until 29th September. April, May, Sept. 11.00 a.m. to 1.00 p.m. & 2.00 p.m. to 5.00 p.m. June, July, Aug. 10.00 a.m. to 5.00 p.m. Open evenings until 9.00 p.m. in August only.

Museum of the Woollen Industry

2 **Dre-fach, Felindre, Llandysul, Dyfed, SA44 5UP.**
Tel. (0559) 370453
Signposted. 4 miles east of Newcastle Emlyn off the A484 Carmarthen to Cardigan Road. Details and Route Map available.

The Museum, situated in the most important woollen manufacturing centre of Wales, contains an extensive collection of textile machinery and tools dating back to the eighteenth century along with an exhibition of photographs tracing the development of Wales' most important rural industry. There is a car park and a picnic area and the visitors can also follow a factory trail where the evolutionary stages in the development of the woollen industry may be seen.

Opening times: 10 a.m.-5 p.m. April to September, Monday - Saturday except Good Friday and May Day. October - March, Monday - Friday except Christmas Eve, Christmas Day, Boxing Day, New Years Eve. Evening visits for pre-arranged parties.

Talyllyn Railway

3 **Wharf Station, Tywyn, Gwynedd, LL36 9EY.**
Tel. (0654) 711297
Close to British Rail Station in Tywyn.

Situated on the Mid Wales Coast, and running inland into the Snowdonia National Park, the Talyllyn is an historic steam narrow gauge railway dating from 1866. From the railway, footpaths give access to waterfalls at Dolgoch and extensive forest walks at Nant Gwernol. There is also a Railway Museum at Tywyn. Allow two and a half hours for the return journey. Car parks, shop and refreshments available. Special arrangements for groups and schools.

Opening times: Daily Easter to September with limited services in October and Christmas Holidays. Timetables available locally, or from above address.

FELIN GERI

Felin Geri is not only one of the very few surviving watermills in the country, and a holder of one of only 11 European Architectural Heritage Awards given in Wales, but is also an all year round working mill, producing traditional stoneground flour.

4 **Cwm Cou, Newcastle Emlyn, Dyfed.**
Tel. (0239) 710810
1 mile out of Newcastle Emlyn on the B4333 road, the mill is fully sign posted.

*See all stages of turning grain into flour, exactly as it was milled over 100 years ago. *Look in on our bakery, producing a whole range of specialist lines. *Take-home or eat at the mill, fresh baked bread and pastries. *Enjoy home-made lunches and fresh cream teas. *Meet our animals, rare breed ginger and black and white pigs, goats, ducks, geese, 'Sam' the dog, plus cats in various colours. *Picnic by the river, wherever you choose; there's a mile of river bank. *Use the mill as a base to explore the Ceri Valley, the most perfect naturally wooded valley in Céredigion — we can plan your route. *Examine and perhaps understand some of our old farm equipment — and see the rare 19th century water powered Sawmill. *Plus wholemeal cookery demonstrations **WITH SAMPLING.**

Opening times: 7 days a week EASTER to OCTOBER 1st.

2 The White family is spending a week's holiday in a cottage in Wales. During their stay they would like to make one or two day trips to places which would have something of interest for the whole family.

Here are details of the members of the family and their interests. Using the information given, continue in about 50 words each of the four paragraphs, giving your reasons.

Colin White is very interested in historical buildings. His wife, **Carol**, loves cooking and is always experimenting with new recipes. They both enjoy walking in the countryside and reading.

Their children, **Simon** (8) and **Isabel** (6) love all kinds of animals and they're longing to see the sea-side.

May Carter (65) is Carol's mother. She can't walk very far these days but she's happy to sit and enjoy the scenery if it's attractive. She's fond of her grandchildren but she · doesn't like places where there are lots of noisy children about.

paragraph 1: The best choice for the whole family would be . . .
paragraph 2: Another good choice would be . . .

paragraph 3: They might not all enjoy . . .
paragraph 4: I wouldn't recommend them to visit . . .

▶ Exam practice A · Vocabulary

Choose the word or phrase which best completes each sentence.

1 He has very strong views .... the subject of private education.

   a in *b* on *c* of *d* at

2 I've sent the children outside to play. They were getting in my .... all the time.

   a place *b* hands *c* nerves *d* way

3 You should try to get a good night's sleep .... much work you have to do.

   a whatever *b* however *c* no matter *d* although

4 It's your .... to do the washing up. I did it yesterday!

   a share *b* time *c* part *d* turn

5 You really must .... an effort to study harder.

   a have *b* do *c* make *d* put

6 He managed to come first in the race .... having a heavy cold.

   a in spite *b* despite *c* even if *d* through

7 It's only a bruise and the pain will .... after a while.

   a wear off *b* wear out *c* clear up *d* clear off

8 My doctor says I should .... the amount of coffee I drink in a day.

   a reduce *b* cut *c* lower *d* drop

9 I don't think it's ....! She does exactly the same job as me but she earns more.

   a even *b* equal *c* kind *d* fair

10 The children have .... lots of new friends since we moved to this town.

    a formed *b* become *c* made *d* got

11 They are quite concerned .... the amount of television their children watch.

    a with *b* for *c* in *d* about

12 There is a(n) .... training period of 6 months before you start work.

    a initial *b* first *c* primary *d* beginning

13 I'll buy my ticket on the train if the guard will .... me go through the barrier.

    a allow *b* let *c* permit *d* agree

14 She didn't feel she could .... him to keep a secret.

    a rely *b* trust *c* depend *d* ensure

15 I was .... in a city, and as a result I could never be completely happy living in the country.

    a brought out *b* brought off *c* brought about *d* brought up

16 He loves animals so his job in the pet shop .... him very well.

    a fits *b* matches *c* suits *d* agrees

17 The .... in Scotland was so magnificent that most of the photographs I took were of lakes or mountains!

    a scenery *b* scene *c* land *d* territory

18 He was extremely disappointed not .... first prize.

    a getting *b* to get *c* receiving *d* received

19 The table rocks a bit because the floor isn't quite .... You'll need to put a wedge under one of the legs.

    a smooth *b* steady *c* straight *d* level

20 He seemed to be very interested .... the work I was doing.

    a in *b* at *c* of *d* about

21 Poor Jack! He not only had a car accident last month .... also lost his job.

    a and *b* yet *c* but *d* while

22 He works more .... than anyone else I know.

    a hardly *b* hard *c* steadily *d* steady

23 The factory is .... in a suburb of Manchester.

    a placed *b* situated *c* built *d* surrounded

24 The prize money was shared equally .... the two winners.

    a with *b* between *c* amongst *d* for

25 I can't afford to buy new clothes but fortunately I don't .... wearing old things really.

    a care *b* complain *c* mind *d* object

UNIT3B Looking after yourself

▶ Lead-in 1 · What is health?

Being healthy means different things to different people. What do you mean by health? The following quiz will help you to find out.

Work with one or two other people. First tick the 5 statements you most agree with. Then compare your results. There will probably be large differences so find out the reasons your partner(s) chose the statements they did and explain the reasons for your choices.

For me, being healthy is:	You	Other(s)
1 living to be very old.		
2 being able to run for a bus without getting out of breath.		
3 hardly ever taking any pills or medicines.		
4 being the ideal weight for my height.		
5 taking part in lots of games or sports.		
6 never suffering from anything more than a mild cold or stomach upset.		
7 feeling glad to be alive when I wake up in the morning.		
8 being able to touch my toes or run a mile in 10 minutes (a kilometre in about 6 minutes).		
9 having all the bits of my body in perfect working condition.		
10 eating the right foods.		
11 enjoying some form of relaxation or recreation.		
12 never smoking.		
13 hardly ever going to the doctor.		/
14 having a clear skin, bright eyes and shiny hair.		

From The Good Health Guide

Now read the following paragraphs on this page and the next.

Health is . . . being fit
Statements 2, 5, 8 or 11 suggest that, for you, health is something to do with being physically fit. But can you be fit and still be unhealthy? Or unfit and still be healthy?

When you are fit your muscles are so well trained that they can do more work without putting extra strain on the heart. Another benefit of fitness is that blood pressure is lower. This means it is easier for the heart to pump the blood around the body. Being fit is part of being healthy.

Health is . . . not being ill
If you ticked 3, 6, 9 or 13 you probably think of health as something to do with medicine. Perhaps you think that you can only be healthy with the help of doctors. Unfortunately doctors can do little to help us to be healthy. They usually only help when we are ill. When scientists try to measure how healthy we are as a nation, they look at the amount of disease and death that occurs. *Health itself is not measured.*

118

Health is ... living to an old age
If you ticked 1, 4, 10 or 12 you probably think being healthy means reducing your chances of dying young.
But is living to 100 really a good measure of health for *you*? Some people live to be very old but don't enjoy their life very much. Living to an old age is only one aspect of health.

Health is ... positive health
Statements 7, 10, 11 or 14 see health as something quite different from illness or medicine. Although this is quite an ancient idea, we have only recently begun to take it seriously. Positive health covers all the things we can do to prevent illness plus all the things we can do to become even more well.

Lead-in 2 · Changing times

There have been many changes in the world we live in in the last 50 years and some of these have had a direct effect on our patterns of eating.

Look at the changes described in paragraphs 1–4 below. Then read the results on the right. **These are not in the correct order**. Match the change to the result by writing 1, 2, 3 and 4 in the correct boxes.

Changing times

Compared with 50 years ago ...

1 We now have labour saving machinery to do much of our work for us. Cars and public transport mean we walk less. Central heating warms us so we don't have to keep active to keep warm.

2 Modern technology has progressed so far that we can now have almost any food we like at any time of the year, usually at a reasonable price. Canning, freezing and drying of foods has taken away our dependence on the reasons for our food supply.

3 Many of us now have fridges and freezers in which to store food. Convenience foods, in which most of the preparation and some of the cooking is done for us, are easily available.

4 We live busy lives. We may have to rush off to work or school in the mornings. During the week our family may seldom all meet up. And when we want to eat, we want to eat fast!

So now ...

☐ We have a much wider range of foods from which to choose what we will eat.

☐ Fewer of us eat breakfast – certainly not the large traditional cooked breakfasts. Proper family meals may be restricted to weekends. We eat many more sweets.

☐ We use less energy and therefore need to eat less.

☐ We don't have to spend so much time shopping and preparing and cooking meals.

Adapted from 'The Good Health Guide' (Open University), Harper & Row

Now answer these questions:

a How many examples of labour saving machinery in the home can you think of? Work with a partner to make a list.
b Choose **one** from your list which you think is the most useful. Say why.
c Find out from your partner if he/she eats any convenience foods. Which ones? Are they canned, frozen or dried?
d Sometimes convenience foods are a necessity. Can you think of any such times?

Text 1

1 Before reading the text, work with a partner and say whether you think each of the following statements is true or false.

a Not having the right balance in our diet can damage our health.

b If other members of our family get fat quite easily, we probably will too.

c If we like eating sweet things, it's probably a habit we learnt from our parents.

d Men are just as likely to get fatter as they grow older as women are.

e Most people don't eat enough protein. (Protein is the basic building material of the body and is found in meat, fish, milk, eggs etc.)

f It's useless for most people to take vitamin pills.

g The more calories we eat in food, the more energetic we will feel.

h We should try to reduce the amount of bread and potatoes we eat.

Now read Text 1 and see how correct you were. Underline the word, phrase or sentence which gives the answer to each question.

---

1 Eating well

The average person swallows about half-a-ton of food a year – not counting drink – and though the body is remarkably efficient at extracting just what it needs from this huge mixture, it can only cope up to a point. If you go on eating too much of some things and not enough of others, you'll eventually get out of condition and your health will suffer.

So think before you start eating. It may look good. It may taste good. Fine! But how much good is it really doing you?

What you eat and the way it affects your body depend very much on the kind of person you are. For one thing, the *genes* you inherit from your parents can determine how your body-chemistry (metabolism) copes with particular foods. The tendency to put on weight rather easily, for example, often runs in families – which means that they have to take particular care.

2 Everybody's different

And your parents may shape your future in another way. Your upbringing shapes some basic attitudes to food – like whether you have a sweet tooth, nibble between meals, take big mouthfuls or eat chips with everything. Eating habits, good or bad, tend to get passed on.

And then there's your *lifestyle*. How much you spend on food (time as well as money), how much exercise you get – these can alter the balance between food and fitness.

And finally, both your *age* and your *sex* may affect this balance. For example, you're more likely to put on weight as you get older, especially if you're a woman.

So, everybody's different and the important thing is to know yourself. Read on and see if you think you are striking the right balance.

3 The right balance

Your food should balance your body's need for –

NUTRIENTS (proteins, fats, carbohydrates, vitamins, minerals and water) – the raw materials needed to build and repair the body-machine.

ENERGY (calories) – to power the body-machine, all the thousands of different mechanisms that keep you alive and active.

DIETARY FIBRE (a complex mixture of natural plant substances) – the value of which we are just beginning to understand.

4 Enough nutrients

If you're eating a fairly varied diet, it is just about impossible to go short of proteins, vitamins or minerals. It is likely, too, that you have more than enough fats and carbohydrates.

Take *proteins* for instance. On average, we eat about *twice as much* protein as we need.

Vitamin pills aren't likely to help either. A varied diet with plenty of fresh fruit, vegetables and cereals along with some fish, eggs, meat and dairy products will contain more than enough vitamins. Unless you have some special medical reason, it is a waste of time and money to take vitamin pills.

As for *minerals*, there is no shortage in the average diet and it is useless to have more than you need.

5 Energy crisis

Just about everything you eat contains energy – measured as *calories*; the higher the number of calories, the more energy. But don't make the mistake of thinking that eating extra energy-rich foods will make you more energetic. The amount of energy in your daily diet should exactly balance the energy your body-machine burns up. If you eat more than you use, the extra energy is stored as body fat. And this is the big problem.

6 Why is fibre important?

Over hundreds of thousands of years, man's food came mainly from plants. He ate cereals (like wheat), pulses (like beans and peas), vegetables, fruit and nuts. So our ancestors were used to eating the sort of food that contains a lot of fibre.

In comparison with our ancestors, the sort of food we eat today contains very little fibre. Our main foods are meat, eggs and dairy products, which contain no fibre at all.

Lack of fibre seems to be connected with various disorders of the digestive system. Some experts also believe that lack of fibre may even lead to heart disease.

If you're worried about your weight, eating more fibre may actually help you to slim! Food with plenty of fibre like potatoes or bread can be satisfying without giving you too many calories.

From The Health Education Council

---

2 Now look at sections **1** and **2** again and find the words which mean the same as:

Section 1

a able to do a job well
b taking out
c very big
d manage successfully
e in the end
f receive
g decide

Section 2

h have an effect on
i training and caring for a child
j take small bites
k change
l achieving

Describing food 3 Most people have their own favourite dishes which they prefer to new and unfamiliar foods. A favourite dish may be raw or cooked, very ordinary or quite exotic, simple or complicated to prepare, cheap or expensive.

a Write down your favourite dish: ....

Compare your answer with your neighbours' and say why you like your favourite so much.

b How would you describe the tastes of the foods below? Write the foods under the different Taste headings. (You may want to put the same food under more than one heading sometimes.)

Foods

lemon juice	bananas	beer	vinegar
honey	anchovies	Indian vegetable curry	thick onion soup
butter	ice cream	grapefruit	almonds
peanuts	yoghurt	peaches in syrup	sausages
olives	British fish and chips	black coffee	crisps

Tastes

Spicy	Bitter	Salty	Sweet	Sour	Greasy	Creamy

c Now decide which kinds of food that you've eaten would fit the following descriptions:

Most attractive to look at ....

Simplest to make ....

Most difficult to make well ....

Most unpleasant ....

Most enjoyable foreign ....

Most unusual ....

Adapted from 'The Good Health Guide' (Open University), Harper & Row

When you've completed your list, compare it with your neighbour's. Explain why you chose the foods and describe the colour, taste, smell and cost. You may like to check the expressions on page 213 of the Functions Bank before you begin.

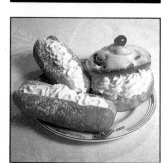

STUDY BOX 1

Verb + Preposition (2)   . . . taking part **in** lots of games or sports. (*Lead-in*)

accuse (somebody) **of**	believe **in**	discourage (somebody) **from**
(dis)agree **with** (somebody)	compare X **with** Y	distinguish **between**
about (something)	complain **to** (somebody)	look **for**
apologise **for**	**about** (something)	protect (somebody) **from**
apply **for**	concentrate **on**	provide (somebody/something) **with**
argue **with** (somebody)	congratulate (somebody) **on**	spend (time/money) **on**
about (something)	confuse X **with** Y	suffer **from**
	consist **of**	surround (somebody/something) **with**

Focus on listening 1 · Old wives' tales?

An old wives' tale is a traditional belief, or a piece of traditional advice, passed down from generation to generation.

Look at the 5 old wives' tales below and decide whether you think they are true, partly true, or false. Then read the questions which follow.

Now listen to the tape and answer the questions. Tick the correct box in **Part A**.

	True	Partly True	False
		✓	
			✓
	✓		

Part A
1 An apple a day keeps the doctor away.
2 You should always sleep with an open window.
3 If you get soaking wet you're more likely to catch a cold.
4 Feed a cold and starve a fever.
5 Carrots help you to see in the dark.

Part B Write short answers to the following questions.

1 What fruit contains more Vitamin C, according to the doctor?

....

2 Which two groups of people are most at risk of catching an infection?

....

3 How did the man in Norway get wet?

....

4 What advice does the doctor give to people with 'flu?

....

5 What other foods contain Vitamin A, according to the doctor?

....

Can you think of any other old wives' tales? Are they true or false?

Focus on grammar 1 · Expressing quantity

COUNTABLE AND UNCOUNTABLE NOUNS

a Uncountable nouns like **petrol** or **pride** cannot be used with an indefinite article **a/an** and cannot be made plural.

Put the following words in the correct place in the table below:

rice	apple	news	chair	furniture
spaghetti	snack	coin	information	journey
biscuit	plate	travel	weather	money
vitamin	crockery	music	programme	blood

Countable	Uncountable

b Some words can be either countable or uncountable depending on their meaning. Give different examples of the words below when they are used as i) countable and ii) uncountable.
For example:

box of chocolates – countable   a cake made of chocolate – uncountable

chocolate	wood	iron	exercise
time	hair	tin	skin

MUCH/MANY, A LOT OF ETC

a Many of the following words or phrases occur in Text 1. Put them in the correct column in the table below according to whether they are used only with countable nouns, only with uncountable nouns or with both types.

too much	no ... at all	hardly any	a large number of
too few	not enough	a lack of	a great many
a lot of	a large amount of	plenty of	
very many	very little	a great deal of	

Countable	Uncountable	Both

Exercise 1 *b* Now complete these sentences with the correct expression of quantity:

1 The quality of the material depends on .... you want to spend.

2 I'm afraid there's very .... I can do to help you.

3 There was .... applause .... after the performance and the conductor looked very uncomfortable.

4 I was worried about one child in the class who seemed to show a complete .... of interest in the subject.

5 We had to cancel the trip to Oxford because .... members wanted to go.

6 I saw a large .... of elephants by the lakeside on that early morning boat ride.

7 Make sure you put .... cheese in the omelette. I love it!

8 I know you spent a great .... money on the carpet but I still think it's rather ugly.

9 The trouble with me is that I take .... exercise apart from walking to the shops.

10 A great .... famous people are said to have stayed at this hotel.

AS ... AS
Look at these examples:

On average, we eat about twice as much protein as we need. (Text 1)
The club has only got half as many members as it had last year.
Your suitcase is about three times as heavy as mine!

Exercise 2   Now write sentences comparing the two items in each box below.

a
Population
Bristol: 426,000
Southampton: 213,000

b

£150
£30

c
Today's Temperatures
London 15°C
Athens 29°C

d
TRAINS
LONDON TO BRIGHTON
every 30 minutes
LONDON TO SWANSEA
every 1½ hours

e
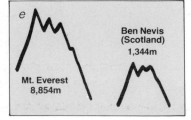
Ben Nevis
(Scotland)
1,344m
Mt. Everest
8,854m

f

BMW 135m.p.h.
Concorde 1,350m.p.h.

Communication activity

You are in a restaurant. A and B are customers and C is the waiter. You each have instructions on different pages. Read and remember your instructions and then turn back to this page.

A's instructions are on page 126; B's are on page 131; C's are on page 133.

The Laughing Cook Restaurant

MENU

STARTERS

Potato soup .50p   Tomato salad £1.50p   Spaghetti bolognaise £1.00

Smoked salmon £2.50p   Grilled sardines £2.00

MAIN COURSES

Cheese Omelette	*cooked with 3 large eggs and lots of tasty Cheddar cheese.*	£2.00
Caldeirada	*a delicious Portuguese seafood stew.*	£4.00
T-Bone Steak	*best quality, tender steak, cooked to perfection.*	£6.50
Moussaka	*the famous Greek dish, made with minced beef, aubergines, potatoes and covered with a creamy cheese sauce.*	£3.50
Paella	*an authentic Spanish recipe which includes chicken, prawns, mussels, green peppers, onions and rice.*	£4.50
Chilli con Carne	*a Mexican speciality – spicy beef and red kidney beans on a bed of rice.*	£3.50
Grilled Trout	*fresh from the River Wye, served with almonds.*	£5.00
Sweet and Sour Chicken	*A Chinese favourite – tender pieces of chicken fried in batter and covered with our famous sweet and sour sauce.*	£3.50

All dishes are served with a choice of fresh vegetables or salad.

DESSERTS

Fresh Strawberries	£2.00	Vanilla Ice Cream	.50p
Tinned Peaches	£1.00	Chocolate Cake	£1.50
Cheese and Biscuits	.75p	Apple Pie and Cream	£1.00

Your waiter will be happy to advise you on your choice of dish.

Focus on grammar 2 · Reported questions

Look at this example:

> I asked where the post office was.

What were the original words?
> 'Excuse me, where ....?'

Notes In reported questions
> a The **word order is different** from the original question. The verb follows the subject as in an ordinary statement.
> b The auxiliary verb **'do'** is not used.
> c There is **no question mark**.

QUESTIONS WITH QUESTION WORDS (When, Where, . . .)

Complete the following examples:

> 'How are your parents?'   She asked me how my parents ....
> 'Who did you go home with?'   They wanted to know who I ....

Exercise 1 Change the following into reported speech:

> a 'How much do you earn?'   He wanted to know ....
>
> b 'Where did you buy your watch?'   She asked ....
>
> c 'How many kilos have you lost?'   The doctor asked ....
>
> d 'When are you coming to stay with me?'   My aunt wanted to know ....
>
> e 'Why won't you marry me?'   Her boyfriend wanted to know ....
>
> f 'Who on earth gave you my address?'   I asked him ....

QUESTIONS WITHOUT QUESTION WORDS

These questions are reported with **if** or **whether**. Complete the following examples:

> 'Do you like jazz?'   I asked you if you ....
>
> 'Can I use the telephone, please?'   He asked if he ....

Exercise 2 Change the following into reported speech:

> a 'Have you got change of a £5 note?'   The man asked me ....
>
> b 'Have you seen Tim today?'   They wanted to know ....
>
> c 'Will you be at home this weekend?'   I asked if she ....
>
> d 'Does your wife speak any Portuguese?'   At the interview, they asked ....
>
> e 'Did you telephone me last night?'   She wanted to know ....
>
> f 'Can you lend me £1 till tomorrow?'   My friend asked ....

Exercise 3 Work in pairs. Student **A** – find out as much as you can about Student **B**'s family and childhood by asking direct questions. You will have **three** minutes!

Before you begin, spend a minute or two thinking about the questions you can ask. It may help to make a few notes: *For example:*

> Brothers and sisters?   ages?   where/born? etc.

When you have finished, report your questions and **B**'s answers to the class.
Then repeat the exercise with Student **B** asking the questions. (Try to think of some new ones!)

Sometimes we introduce a direct question with a short phrase. *For example:*

> 'Can you tell me who that man is?'
> 'Do you know if the bus has gone yet?'

In this case, the word order is the same as in a reported question and the tense remains the same.

Exercise 4 Work in pairs. Take it in turns to ask for the following information, using the phrases:

> Can/could you (possibly) tell me . . . I wonder if you could tell me . . . Do you (happen to) know . . .

Try to answer the questions too!

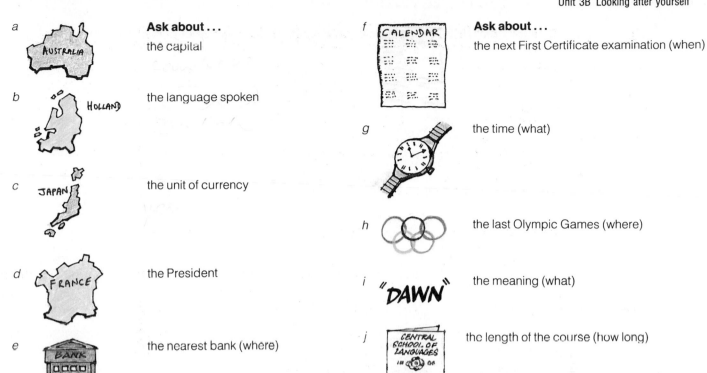

a AUSTRALIA

Ask about . . .

the capital

b HOLLAND

the language spoken

c JAPAN

the unit of currency

d FRANCE

the President

e BANK

the nearest bank (where)

f CALENDAR

Ask about . . .

the next First Certificate examination (when)

g

the time (what)

h

the last Olympic Games (where)

i "DAWN"

the meaning (what)

j CENTRAL SCHOOL OF LANGUAGES COURSES

the length of the course (how long)

Communication activity: role A

Before you begin, talk to B and decide whether you are:
1 boyfriend and girlfriend
or 2 business colleagues
or 3 friends who haven't met for a long time.

Now read on: you have invited B to dinner and you really want him/her to enjoy the meal. Unfortunately you're a bit short of money at the moment (you've only got £10 with you) but you don't want B to know this.

First, look at Language of Advice. Functions Bank (page 209). You being speaking.

▶ **Text 2**

1 Look at the list of eight words below. Six of them are names of minor injuries and two of them are types of dressings which can be put on injuries.
  a Underline the two words which are not minor injuries.
  b Write each word below the correct picture.

cut   bruise   plaster   bite   burn   bandage   graze   scald

a	*b*	*c* plaster	*d*
e	*f* bandage	*g*	*h*

2 Now read the following page from a health education booklet and answer questions 1 to 5.

Cuts, bruises bites & burns

Cuts

Bleeding can usually be stopped by applying pressure to the cut for 2 or 3 minutes. The cut can then be carefully inspected. If it has bled freely any germs will normally have been washed away by the blood.

Apply a plaster dressing firmly, bringing the edges of the cut together so that it knits quickly. Keep dry for 1 to 2 days.

If the cut is deep and the edges cannot be pulled together with a dressing consult the doctor or the practice nurse. A tetanus injection may be needed.

Grazes

Dirt will often enter a graze caused by falling on a hard or rough surface. It must be cleaned out carefully with an antiseptic solution.

After cleaning, leave the graze uncovered. Exposure to the air will cause a scab to form. This will gradually dry and fall off.

It is not a good idea to apply a dressing. This may stick to the graze or make it soggy and infected.

Bruises

Bruises are very common in children. They normally get better in 7 to 10 days. Parents sometimes worry that a bone may be broken. Children's bones are rubbery and rarely break, but if in doubt consult the doctor.

If a child gets up at once after a fall and moves about normally, it is unlikely that a bone has been broken. But the child may be stiff the next day because of the bruising which has occurred.

Severe bruising can be treated by:

Rest for 24 to 48 hours. In the case of a badly bruised leg, the limb should be raised. Lying in bed is the easiest way to do this.

A cold compress may ease a bad bruise if applied at once. This is made by soaking some material in water and applying it to the bruise.

Bruises on the head may cause anxiety. If the patient was not "knocked out" and can remember the accident it is unlikely that serious injury has resulted.

But if the patient was knocked unconscious and cannot remember what happened, he or she should be taken to a hospital casualty department.

Insect bites

These are common in the summer. They look like spots about 1/4 " across. They are very itchy and usually appear on exposed parts, e.g. arms and legs.

The itching can be relieved by calamine lotion.

Burns and scalds

Minor burns and scalds cause redness of the skin. Immediate treatment by pouring cold water over a burn is often helpful. If burns cause severe blistering or break the skin, the doctor should be consulted.

Sunburn should, if possible, be prevented by avoiding long exposure and covering exposed areas adequately. It may be treated by calamine lotion and soluble aspirin to relieve the pain.

From 'Minor Illnesses', Health Education Council

1 The purpose of the booklet is

a to tell us what to do until a doctor arrives.

b to explain what causes minor illnesses.

c to show that it is unnecessary to call a doctor.

d to help us to treat minor illnesses at home.

2 The one injury which we are told not to cover is

a a bruise.

b sunburn.

c a graze.

d an insect bite.

3 When treating a minor cut, we are first told to

a clean out the wound.

b press down on the wound.

c wash the blood away.

d close up the wound.

4 The injury which we are told how to avoid is

    a sunburn.   *c* scalds.
    b insect bites.   *d* cuts.

5 Patients with badly bruised legs are advised to go to bed so that

    a they can rest completely.   *c* they can soak their leg in water.
    b their injured leg can be lifted up.   *d* a cold compress can be applied.

Focus on listening 2

For questions 1 to 8 tick (√) the correct answers.

1 The course goes on for

    a one day.   *b* two days.   *c* one week.   *d* several weeks.

2 On the subject of bandages, the speaker tells his students

    a they should practise putting them on at   *c* they don't need to be able to use them
       home.   at all.
    b they must read about them in first aid   *d* they can do an extra course to learn
       books.   about them.

3 He realised that the situation in the restaurant was serious because

    a the man was lying across the table.   *c* the man's face had changed colour.
    b the man had fallen off his chair.   *d* the man hadn't eaten his food.

4 Which picture shows the position he put the man in?

    a   *b*   *c*   *d*

5 He shouted at the waiter because

    a the waiter didn't believe it was an   *c* he thought the waiter might be too
       emergency.   frightened to act.
    b the waiter was too far away to hear.   *d* he was angry with the waiter for
                                         walking away.

6 The man's problem was that

    a something had stuck in his throat.   *c* he had had a heart attack.
    b the food he had eaten had made him ill. *d* he had fainted.

7 The ambulance

    a was cancelled.   *c* took the man home.
    b came but wasn't needed.   *d* took the man to hospital.

8 Which is true? In First Aid

    a you must always act very quickly.   *c* you must stop and consider before you
    b you must realise when there's an   act.
       emergency.   *d* you must always call an ambulance.

STUDY BOX 2

Phrasal verb **Come.**   He was breathing and he was beginning to **come to.** *(Listening 2)*

come across – find or meet by chance.   I **came across** a very interesting book in the library.
                – be understood.   He didn't **come across** as a very serious person.
come off – succeed.   Do you think your plan will really **come off**?
come out – appear/bloom.   The garden looks lovely now the roses have **come out**.
come round – visit.   Can I **come round** and see you next week?
come round – regain consciousness.   When I **came round** after my operation, I couldn't think where I was.
come to – regain consciousness.   See above.
come up against – be faced with.   We've **come up against** a serious problem, I'm afraid.

Focus on grammar 3 · Expressing number

● Each, both, either, neither and all can be used with a noun (in the same way as a, the etc). They can also be used as pronouns, **in place of a noun**. *For example:*

> They looked at each house carefully. Each had its advantages.
> You can ask either waiter for service. Either will serve you.

● Every is never used on its own as a pronoun, but always with a noun. (Everyone/Everything are pronouns)

● None of is also used with a noun, but none is always a pronoun. *For example:*

> Every book on the shelf was a detective story.
> None of the books was by Agatha Christie.
> I looked at them all but none appeared very interesting.

The table below shows which words are used to refer to singular nouns (and may take singular verbs), and which refer to plural nouns (and may take plural verbs).

Singular	Plural
each every either neither none* all (with uncountable nouns)	both all (with countable nouns)

* 'None' sometimes takes a plural verb in informal speech when referring to countable nouns.

Notes a Each refers to **one** of a group of two or more.
Every refers to **one** of a group of three or more. It cannot refer to two.
The two words have a similar meaning and can sometimes be used interchangeably.
Each, however, suggests a distinct individual in a group, while every suggests any member of a group.
For example:

> Every actor must learn his words by heart.
> Each actor has a different method of learning his lines.

b Both refers to **two.**   Both my parents are still working.
All refers to **more than two**.   I'm lucky enough to have all four grandparents still.

c Either / Neither refer to **one of two**.   They're both good. You can have either of them.
I've got two brothers but neither lives nearby.
None refers to **one of several**.   There are three banks in town but none of them is open.

Exercise   Now use words from the table to complete the following sentences:

1 Near the junction there are shops on .... sides of the road.

2 .... professional musician has to practise regularly.

3 He painted several pictures during his time in Italy but .... of them has been found.

4 The Princess took the time to speak to .... child in the class individually.

5 Before you leave the plane, please make sure that you have .... your belongings with you.

6 .... of my parents has ever been abroad.

7 I've looked in the library and the canteen but there's no sign of her in .... place.

8 Not .... cooks can bake bread as well as you can.

9 He gave me the choice of two insurance policies but .... of them really suited me.

10 You can take .... the motorway or the A38. .... routes are equally fast.

Focus on writing · Directed writing

Writing Bank: page 234

Exercise is the key to fitness, the experts say.
Read what the two people below say about themselves and then look at the notes on five forms of exercise. Using the information given, continue in about 50 words each of the four paragraphs. Give reasons for your answers and use your own words as far as possible.
Look at Focus on grammar 3 before you begin and try to use some of the expressions in it.

Sue Adam, Age 24
'I used to belong to a sports club before I got married and had children. Looking after two little girls certainly keeps me busy these days but I'm not as fit as I'd like to be. Now my mother-in-law has offered to baby-sit for me on two afternoons a week, I'm planning to take up some form of regular exercise again. I'd prefer an activity I could do in the open air and one where I could develop a skill, especially a useful one. I couldn't afford to spend much, though, – we're a bit hard up at the moment!'

Chris Williams, Age 35
'As I'm a bachelor, my time's my own when I'm not working. Actually it gets a bit lonely at times and I wouldn't mind having the chance to meet people a bit more. I've got a good job as a salesman but that means I spend most of the day driving around so I'm pretty tired when I get home. I like to have my supper on a tray in front of the T.V. I watch and doze till 11.00 pm and then I take the dog for a short walk. I must admit I've been putting on weight a bit lately and I suppose I ought to take some exercise. Competitive sports don't appeal to me, though, and I'd prefer an activity which didn't need a lot of skill.'

Tennis
Good all-round exercise but not advisable for the very unfit! Your style and ability will improve with regular coaching but this doesn't come cheap unless you join a club.

Swimming
One of the most effective forms of exercise and easily available (both indoor and outdoor) in most cities. Join a club for the benefits of a structured training programme in general swimming, diving or life-saving.

Cycling

An excellent way to keep fit but also fun and free (as long as you own or can borrow a bicycle, that is!) Why not join your local cycling club and make friends? Choose quiet routes in cities and head for the open countryside whenever you can.

Jogging

Running freely and easily is one of the most natural and effective ways of exercising heart and lungs. You can jog when and where you want, even in the dark if you feel self-conscious! Be sure to start off gently and build up your effort gradually. See if there's a jogging club in your area – it's more enjoyable to jog in company.

Golf

A good way to get some fresh air but unless you run rather than walk between tees, better for relaxation than fitness. Joining the golf club may well improve your social life but remember that time spent in the bar or restaurant will not help your waistline!

1 In my opinion, the sport which would suit both Sue Adam and Chris Williams is ....

2 Other sports Sue Adam might consider are ....

3 Chris Williams could also choose ....

4 I wouldn't recommend Sue or Chris to take up ....

Communication activity: role B

Before you begin, talk to A and decide whether you are:

         1 boyfriend and girlfriend

or **2** business colleagues

or **3** friends who haven't met for a long time.

Now read on: A has invited you to dinner and you're sure you're going to enjoy yourself, especially as A is paying the bill! You especially like fish of all kinds. The only thing you can't eat is cheese which doesn't agree with you, but you'd prefer not to eat anything too fattening either.

First, have a look at the Language for Responding to Advice, and to Suggestions in the Functions Bank (page 210).

A will begin speaking.

Exam practice A · Vocabulary

Choose the word or phrase which best completes each sentence.

1 I'll try to get in touch with him but he's .... ever at home when I phone.

   a rarely *b* almost *c* hardly *d* occasionally

2 There'll be four of us going camping, not .... the dog!

   a counting *b* adding *c* involving *d* saying

3 The only sure way to lose weight, is to .... yourself!

   a diet *b* slim *c* exercise *d* starve

4 After climbing the stairs to the sixth floor, I was completely out of ....

   a wind *b* air *c* breath *d* gasp

5 Experts recommend a .... diet with plenty of fresh vegetables and fibre.

   a various   *b* varied   *c* wide   *d* changeable

6 He has a very serious .... towards his work.

   a attitude   *b* view   *c* opinion   *d* respect

7 She longed to visit the house in Scotland where she was .... as a child.

   a brought in   *b* brought up   *c* brought out   *d* brought about

8 You are unlikely to need vitamin pills .... you have some special medical reason.

   a if   *b* because   *c* while   *d* unless

9 Put your hand in cold water. That will help to .... the pain of the burn.

   a bear   *b* avoid   *c* relieve   *d* resist

10 .... carrots are said to be much better for you than cooked ones.

   a raw   *b* rare   *c* crude   *d* fresh

11 They were all badly .... by mosquitoes on their first night in the tent.

   a picked   *b* stung   *c* bitten   *d* scratched

12 He's certainly .... a lot of weight since I last saw him.

   a taken on   *b* put on   *c* put up   *d* taken up

13 I didn't feel too bad really. I only had a .... attack of flu.

   a weak   *b* small   *c* gentle   *d* mild

14 In comparison .... the Japanese, the British eat far more fatty foods.

   a from   *b* to   *c* with   *d* of

15 These trousers are far too big for me now and I've asked a tailor to .... them to fit me.

   a alter   *b* exchange   *c* make   *d* sew

16 He still suffers .... headaches as a result of the accident.

   a of   *b* by   *c* from   *d* for

17 Did you .... my passport while you were clearing out the desk, by any chance?

   a come round   *b* come across   *c* come to   *d* come up against

18 The doctor recommended me .... on a strict diet.

   a go   *b* going   *c* to go   *d* I should go

19 There wasn't .... news in his letter.

   a a great many   *b* hardly any   *c* a great deal of   *d* a large number of

20 It costs nearly twice as much to take the train .... it does to go by coach.

   a than   *b* for   *c* while   *d* as

21 We're not sure if we can hold the barbecue yet. It depends .... the weather.

    a of *b* from *c* for *d* on

22 Fortunately, the bank clerk .... press the alarm button before the robbers got away.

    a was able to *b* succeeded in *c* could *d* managed

23 Could you .... me to the railway station, please?

    a show *b* direct *c* lead *d* indicate

24 If you take the third turning .... your right, you'll see the station ahead of you.

    a on *b* in *c* at *d* by

25 I bought a large Chinese .... lampshade to put in my bedroom.

    a old *b* round *c* white *d* paper

Odd man out

In each of the following groups of words, there is one which does not fit. Work in pairs to choose the 'odd man out' in each group and say why it doesn't belong there.

Note: There may be more than one correct answer!

    1 chin jaw cheek thumb lip
    2 bandage thermometer plaster pill ribbon
    3 wrist ankle stomach elbow shoulder
    4 cut spot bruise sting scratch
    5 eggs milk cheese butter cream
    6 grill fry boil bake roast
    7 spaghetti rice meat chips bread
    8 butcher's grocer's fishmonger's ironmonger's baker's
    9 tennis golf judo cricket football
    10 Sydney Barcelona Munich Moscow Seoul

Communication activity: role C There are only 15 minutes left before you go off duty and you don't want to spend too long with these customers. The chef has told you that there's a lot of steak, moussaka and sardines left over and he'd like you to encourage customers to order these. The caldeirada has run out completely. **Mark these on your menu**, but don't show to your customers.

Let A and B discuss the menu for a few moments before you ask if you can take their order. In the meantime, have a look at the Language of Advice, Recommendation and Persuasion in the Functions Bank (page 209).

UNIT4B Narrow escapes

► **Lead-In** Newspapers often carry stories of disasters but occasionally they also feature stories of lucky escapes.

1 Look at the four headlines below and discuss with a partner what you think the story was about in each case.

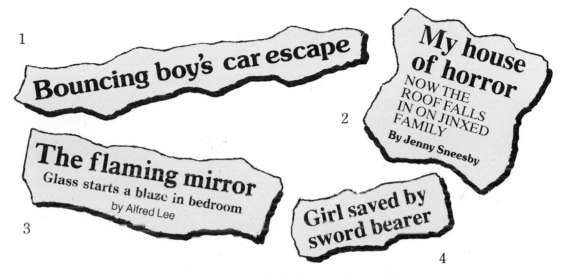

1 Bouncing boy's car escape

2 My house of horror
NOW THE ROOF FALLS IN ON JINXED FAMILY
By Jenny Sneesby

3 The flaming mirror
Glass starts a blaze in bedroom
by Alfred Lee

4 Girl saved by sword bearer

2 To find out if you were thinking along the right lines, match the extracts from the articles below to the headlines. There are three extracts for one of the headlines and two each for the rest.

a **Cause**
There were no electrical appliances or wires near the curtain. There was no radiator nearby. The Coxes were non-smokers. The bay windows were shut and no spark could have come from outside.
Firemen were mystified at first until they discovered the cause of the fire.
On the dressing table, 18 inches from the curtain, was

b Mr Robinson, of Greyfell Close, Stanmore, Middlesex, behaved "magnificently" when he heard Tracey Roke, aged 18, screaming for help outside his home late at night.

c A YOUNG mother has branded her council house "a disaster area" after a second major incident in three months wrecked her home.
An attic tank, containing 60 gallons of water, burst on Friday night, crashed through two floors and landed in the sitting room.

d "When I walked in on Friday night I couldn't believe it. The carpet was completely wet and the ceiling was coming down," said Teresa.
"We were very lucky no one was in at the time."

e Running back down the road she saw an incredible sight. Sam, sobbing but otherwise completely unhurt was limping to the side of the road. Nearby were several stationary vehicles which had narrowly missed him.

f The sun's rays had hit the magnifying mirror and were reflected on to the velvet curtain, causing it to smoulder and burst into flames.
Mrs Cox, of De Vere Road, Thrapston, Northamptonshire, said: "I hope the accident does not happen to anybody else. If we had not been at home, it would have been disastrous."

g He grabbed a ceremonial sword, ran outside and stopped the car in which she was trapped. He took the weeping girl into his home after noting the number of the car.

h In November, Teresa's solid fuel stove exploded, burning husband Joseph's hair and lips and setting fire to the furniture.

i WITH her four-year-old son Sam playing boisterously with a friend in the back of her Mercedes estate car, Mrs Linda Norton turned into the busy main road and began accelerating.
She was approaching 20 mph when suddenly she heard a loud noise. Glancing in the mirror, she saw the car's tailgate had swung open.
And to her horror she was just in time to catch sight of Sam falling out on to the

3 Now explain in your own words what each of the narrow escapes was.

4 Below are dictionary definitions of two of the words in the headlines. Can you explain why they are used?

to bounce – to spring back up again from the ground like a ball.
to be jinxed – to suffer from a lot of bad luck.

▶ **Text 1**

1 Read the text below fairly quickly in order to find the answer to these questions:

    a What was the cause of the emergency?
    b What happened to the plane during the emergency?
    c How did the story end?

JUMBO NIGHTMARE

The voice that came over the intercom of the British Airways Jumbo as it cruised at 38,000ft over southern Sumatra was cool, calm and collected.

"Good evening, ladies and gentlemen," it said, ... "This is your
5 captain speaking. We ... er ... have a small problem ... all four engines have stopped.

"We are doing our best to get them going again, and we trust you will not be given too much distress."

Then the stricken Boeing 747 plunged earthwards at up to 2,000
10 feet a minute as the pilot struggled desperately with the controls.

For captain Eric Moody, 24 years a pilot, it was the understatement of the year. The giant jet had just flown into a cloud of volcanic ash, putting all of its four Rolls-Royce engines out of action.

15 Even as the 41-year-old pilot was fighting his life-or-death battle in the cramped cockpit to regain control of the damaged airliner, and trying to reassure his 239 passengers at the same time, the plane's cabin was filling with ash and smoke.

"It was coming out of the air vents," said Mr Jerry Middleton,
20 who was on his way from Kuala Lumpur to Perth. "I looked out to see an engine apparently on fire, then all the engines stopped and we went into a steep dive. It seemed to go on for an eternity.

Everybody was terrified. By the time we pulled out everybody was almost on their knees praying.

"All the captain told us at first was that the aircraft had met mild 25 turbulence and that we were not to worry. But the oxygen masks dropped down and the emergency exit signs lit up and we knew it was more serious."

It was not until the plane had dropped 25,000ft that captain Moody was able to restart first one, then two, and finally all four 30 engines as they cleared the bottom of the dust cloud which had starved the engines of oxygen and blocked them with choking ash.

Back in Jakarta, where he managed to put the damaged jet down despite having its landing lights disabled in the dust storm, 35 Captain Moody shrugged off the hero's welcome with typical British cool. "When it was all over I felt we had done a good job," he said. "It was all due to training and following instructions."

The British Airways man in London was equally unemotional. Said Colin Barnes: "The crew did an absolutely splendid job in 40 very difficult circumstances."

A Boeing representative who examined the aircraft said: "It was the most seriously damaged 747 to have kept flying that I have seen."

From The Book of Narrow Escapes by Peter Mason

---

2 Now read the text again more carefully to answer these questions in your own words.

    a What did the captain **not** tell the passengers when he made his announcement?
    b What was the first sign the passengers had that there was something wrong?
    c What did one passenger see when he looked out of the window?
    d How did the passengers know there was a real emergency?
    e When were the passengers most afraid?
    f When was the captain able to regain control of the plane?
    g What made the landing difficult?
    h How did the captain explain his ability to handle the emergency so successfully?
    i What surprised the engineer who examined the plane afterwards?

3 Find words or phrases in the text which mean the same as:

Column 1   *a* communication system   ....

           b anxiety   ....

           c badly affected   ....

           d dived   ....

           e a statement which is true but not expressed strongly enough   ....

           f limited in space   ....

           g a very long time   ....

Column 2   *h* violent movement of the air   ....

           i prevented from having enough   ....

           j having been put out of action   ....

Language check   **4** Prepositions

Complete the following sentences with the correct prepositions. (Sometimes two words may be needed.) They all come from the Lead-in extracts or Text 1.

a I didn't know what to do .... first, but then I started shouting .... help.

b There was nearly a major fire .... Friday night when some children set fire .... a pile of rubbish in the street.

c That's the second accident he's had .... six months.

d I'd be grateful if you wouldn't make so much noise late .... night when other people are trying to sleep!

e Before you turn .... a main road, always stop and make sure the road is clear.

f When I looked .... my mirror, I saw a police car was following me.

g If you leave now you'll be just .... time to catch the 5.20.

h I'll call at the bank .... my way to work.

i She was struggling .... an enormous suitcase so I offered to help.

j When the 'No Smoking' signs lit ...., I knew we were going to land.

STUDY BOX 1

Phrasal verb **Go.**   It seemed to **go on** for an eternity. *(Text 1)*

go down with – become ill.   I hope I'm not **going down with** 'flu.
go in for – enter an exam/competition.   Are you **going in for** the race?
go off – explode.   We heard the bomb **go off.**
go off – go bad.   This milk smells as if it's **gone off.**
go on – continue.   How long does this concert **go on?**
go on – happen.   What exactly has been **going on?**
go over/through – examine.   The teacher **went through** our test papers.
go through – search.   **Go through** your pockets to see if you can find it.
go with – match/suit.   That tie doesn't **go with** your shirt.
go without – manage without.   You can't **go without** water for long.

▶ Focus on grammar 1 · Expressing time

In telling the story of the aeroplane's narrow escape, Text 1 uses a number of link words for time and other time expressions.

Exercise 1   Look back at Text 1 and see how many time expressions you can find. Add them to the table below.

BEFORE	SAME TIME	LATER	SEQUENCE
before previously	while during meanwhile	as soon as immediately once later after afterwards when	first(ly) second(ly) etc next/then last(ly)

Special points   *a* **While/during/meanwhile**   (Complete the second examples)
During is a preposition and is followed by a noun.   *For example:*

I managed to sleep during the flight.
You are not allowed to take photographs during ....

While is a conjunction and introduces a clause.   *For example:*

Did you learn any Spanish while you were living in Madrid?
He likes to sing while ....

Meanwhile is an adverb which means 'during the time between'.   *For example:*

The taxi will be here in five minutes. Meanwhile , I'll just phone Jim.
The rice will take a bit longer to cook. Meanwhile , could you ....

b **First(ly) v. At first**
First(ly), as an adverb, means 'before anything else'. It's often used when describing a sequence of actions.   *For example:*

First check in your mirror that the road is clear, and then pull out.
Before they booked a holiday, they first ....

At first means 'at the beginning'.   *For example:*

I made a lot of mistakes at first, but now my typing's quite accurate.
It .... at first, but later the sun came out.

c **Last(ly) v. At last**
Lastly, as an adverb, means 'after everything else' or 'finally'.   *For example:*

He gave me my final instructions and lastly wished me good luck.

At last means 'in the end' (after a long time).   *For example:*

I spent the whole evening waiting for the call and at last the phone rang.

It had been such a hard winter that we were relieved when .... at last

d **After v. Afterwards**
After is followed by a clause.   *For example:*

After we had watched the film we ....

or by a noun. *For example:* After the film, we ....

Afterwards means 'after that'.   *For example:*

We watched the film and afterwards we had a Chinese meal.

Exercise 2   Choose one of the following time expressions to put in each space below.

before   at last   first
meanwhile   during   after
afterwards   finally   while
              at first   then

I didn't enjoy the course (1) .... but (2) .... a few weeks, I began to find

it very interesting. We were given a lot of work to do (3) .... the holidays, so

(4) .... my friends were having a good time, I was busy studying! I was terribly

nervous (5) .... the examination in June. There were three separate sections:

(6) .... we had a shorthand test; (7) .... we had to type a letter and a

report, and (8) .... there was a paper on office practice. I felt absolutely exhausted

(9) .... !

   We had to wait six weeks for the results and (10) .... I took a temporary job as an

office clerk. When the envelope with the results arrived (11) .... I found I had been

given a distinction!

Tenses after time links   Look at the following sentences:

I'll see him tomorrow. I'll be able to ask him then.
I'll be able to ask him when I see him.

She's going to see her solicitor. She'll contact you after that.
She'll contact you after she's seen her solicitor.

When these words are used to introduce a clause of time, they
are followed by a verb in the **present** or **present perfect** tense,
not the future tense.

> before,
> as, while,
> after,
> when, once,
> as soon as,
> until,
> by the time.

Exercise 3   Complete the following sentences with a suitable word or phrase. Use the correct form of the
present or present perfect tense.

   a By the time he .... home, it'll be dark.

   b You'll have to get used to driving on the left when you .... England.

   c I intend to fly to America as soon as .... visa.

   d He won't stop worrying until he .... train.

   e Once they .... their hotel, there'll be an evening free for sightseeing.

   f I'm hoping to hear the news on my car radio while I .... work.

   g Make sure you get a good night's sleep before you ....

   h After you .... the film, you'll want to buy the book!

▶ Communication activity 1

This is an old puzzle. Work in pairs or small groups to solve it.
You will need to use the words which mark sequence from Focus on grammar 1 to work
out the answer and explain your solution.

A man lives in a remote house with his
only possessions – a fox, a chicken and a
bag of grain. One night the nearby river
overflows and the house is surrounded
by water. There is a rowing boat with
enough room for the man and either the
fox, or the chicken, or the grain. If he
takes the grain, the fox will eat the
chicken. If he takes the fox, the chicken
will eat the grain.

How does the man carry them all safely
to land?

▶ Focus on listening 1 · A survival kit

You are going to hear a short talk about making a Survival Kit. As you listen, complete the table below, and answer questions 2 and 3.

1

Item	Purpose	Special notes
1 .... (a)	to hold your kit	
2 fishing line **3** .... (c) }	to catch fish	Use only .... (b)
4 a razor blade	to gut fish	
5 plastic bag	to .... (d) to cover wounds to trap fish	Make sure .... (e)
6 .... (f)	to give light to make a waterproof seal	
7 balloon	to carry water to help start a fire	Don't .... (g) or it will burst.
8 needle	to sew, to .... (h) to make a compass	
9 matches	to light a fire	Make them .... with wax (i).
10 chalk	.... (j) to leave a trail	
11 .... (k)	to call for help	

2 Which item in the Survival Kit is the most important?   Item number   ....
3 Which item is carried separately from the rest?   Item number   ....

▶ Focus on writing 1 · Instructions

1 The drawings below show how you can make matches waterproof for a Survival Kit.

a The following instructions are out of order. Write the numbers 1 to 7 in the spaces provided to show the correct order. The first is done for you.

Drip the wax along the length of the match. ....

Lay the match in the wax. ....

Hold the candle over the base of your match box and let some wax drip into the base. ....

Light a candle. ...1...

Repeat the process for each match. ....

Lay the matches end to end so that . . . .

Place the head of a match in the wax and turn it carefully in order to . . . .

b Two of the instructions are unfinished. Decide with another student how they should end.

c Be careful not to . . .   Make sure you . . .   Once you . . .
Decide what sentences beginning with the above phrases you could add to the instructions, and where.

d Now write a paragraph of instructions to go with the drawings above.

Notes
● Start with a heading.
● Instead of the numbers you wrote above, use the words which show sequence from the Focus on grammar 1 section in this unit.

2 Write a similar set of instructions for making a solar still, using the information from the diagram below.
a Before you begin, make notes about the different steps which are necessary and decide which order they should come in.
b You may also find it useful to look at the Language of Location in the Functions Bank (page 212).

Fact Sheet Making a Solar Still

If you are ever lost in a desert area, you can collect an emergency supply of water by making a solar still. The still should be situated in a low area where there is no shade. It will only work in sunlight. You will need: A large piece of clear plastic, a container, a tool for digging, some stones.

STUDY BOX 2

Purpose clauses

for + -ing   You'll need matches **for** mak**ing** a fire.
                   You can use the plastic bag **for** cover**ing** wounds.
to   You use the chalk **to** mark trees.
in order to + infinitive   It's best to cover wounds **in order to** protect them from infection.
so as to   I've folded it very small **so as to** get it into the box.
so that + clause   You mark the trees **so that** you can leave a trail.

▶ Text 2 · Rescue from the rapids

Introduction   In 1983, a natural historian, Redmond O'Hanlon, and a poet, James Fenton, set out on a long river voyage into the interior of the Borneo jungle, hoping to find out whether the Borneo rhinoceros still existed. They travelled with three native trackers, Dana, the local chief, Leon and Inghai, in a canoe Dana had built.

In this extract from the book Redmond O'Hanlon wrote, the travellers are passing through dangerous rapids and the boat has stuck in shallow water, close to a waterfall. While Leon and Inghai clear a channel, Redmond and James are pulling on a rope attached to the boat to keep it straight. At this point, they are told to move a little to their right . . .

Read the text once, quickly, to answer these questions.

1 Why was James in serious danger?
2 Who rescued him?
3 What condition was James in afterwards?

It was only a stride or two. But the level of the river-bed suddenly dropped. James lost his footing, and, trying to save himself, let go of the rope. I stepped back and across to catch him, the rope bound round my left wrist,
5 snatching his left hand in my right. His legs thudded into mine, tangled and then swung free, into the current, weightless, as if a part of him had been knocked into outer space. His hat came off, hurtled past his shoes, spun round in the water, and disappeared over the edge
10 of the waterfall.

His fingers were very white and slippery. He bites his fingernails; and they could not dig into my palm. He simply looked surprised; his head seemed a long way from me. He was feeling underwater with his free arm,
15 impossibly trying to grip a boulder with his other hand, to get a hold on a smooth and slimy rock, a rock polished smooth for centuries by never-ending tons of rolling water.

His fingers bent straighter, slowly edging out of mine,
20 for hour upon hour, or so it felt, but it must have been seconds. His arm rigid, his fingertips squeezed out of my fist. He turned in the current, his arms and legs extended. Still turning, but much faster, he was sucked under; his right ankle and shoe were strangely visible
25 above the surface; he was lifted slightly, a bundle of clothes, of no particular shape, and then he was gone.

"Boat! Boat!" shouted Dana, dropping the rope, bounding down the rocks.

"Hold the boat! Hold the boat!" yelled Leon to me.

30 James's bald head, white and fragile as an owl's egg, was sweeping round in the whirlpool below, spinning, bobbing up and down in the foaming water, each circle of the current carrying him within inches of the black rocks at its edge.
35 Leon jumped into the boat, climbed on to the raised outboard-motor frame and then, with a loud cry, launched himself in a great curving leap into the centre of the whirlpool. He disappeared, surfaced, shook his head, spotted James, dived again, and caught him.
40 Holding on to him, Leon went once round the whirlpool until, reaching the exit current, he swam out downstream, edging, yard by yard, toward the bank.

Obeying Dana's every sign, I helped him to position the boat on to a strip of beach. James, when we walked
45 down to him, was sitting on a boulder. Leon sat beside him, an arm around his shoulders. "You be all right soon, my friend," said Leon "you be all right soon, my very best friend. Soon you be happy."

James, looking very sick, his white lips an open O in
50 his black beard, was gasping for air, his body shaking.

"You be okay," said Leon. "I not let you die my old friend."

Just then little Inghai appeared, beaming with pride, holding up one very wet hat.
55 "I save hat!" said Inghai, "Jams, Jams! I save hat!"

James looked up, smiled, and so stopped his terrible gasps for air. He really was going to be all right.

From 'Into the Heart of the Borneo' by Redmond O'Hanlon

Now read the text again to answer these questions.

4 James first got into difficulty because

   a the rope he was holding broke.
   b the clothes he was wearing were
        unsuitable.
   c he couldn't swim.
   d he lost his balance.

5 The writer reacted to the emergency by

   a grasping one of James's hands.
   b shouting for help.
   c handing James a rope.
   d hanging on to James's body.

6 James was swept away by the current because

   a he was too shocked to try to save
        himself.
   b he resisted his friend's efforts to save
        him.
   c there was nothing he could hold tightly
        to.
   d he tried to turn round in the water.

7 Leon went to James's rescue by

   a steering the boat towards him.
   b running along the bank to catch him.
   c jumping into the water near him.
   d throwing him something to hold on to.

8 During the emergency, the rope attached to the boat was held by

   a Dana.
   b the writer.
   c Dana and the writer.
   d nobody.

▶ Focus on grammar 2
Modal verbs 4: Certainty/probability/possibility

PRESENT/FUTURE

1 What do you think
   this picture shows . . .?

| Sure ↓ Less sure | **Affirmative**
 must

 can <br> may   + infinitive <br> might <br> could | **Negative**
 can't + infinitive

 Interrogative
 can <br> might + subject + infinitive <br> could |

142

Practice   Work in pairs. Suggest what these pictures show.

You'll find the answers on page 177.

Look at these examples:

a If that's the 6 o'clock news, my watch must be slow.
(The speaker is fairly **sure** that his watch is slow because it seems logical.)

b Food with plenty of fibre can be satisfying. (*Unit 3A*)
(This is **generally possible**, though perhaps not in all cases.)

c Eating more fibre may actually help you to slim. (*Unit 3A*)
(This is a **less certain** possibility.)

d Not having a car doesn't worry us. I suppose it might do later. (*Unit 2B*)
(Both 'might' and 'could' express an **even less certain** possibility than 'may'.)

e It can't be John at the door. He's still on holiday in Italy.
('can't' expresses **negative certainty** – the speaker is sure that something is **not** the case)

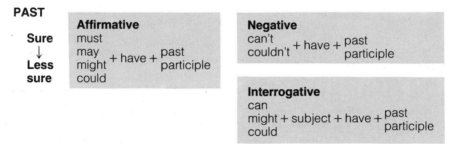

PAST

Sure ↓ Less sure	**Affirmative** must may might could + have + past participle	**Negative** can't couldn't + have + past participle
		Interrogative can might + subject + have + past participle could

2 Look at these examples:

a His fingers bent straighter . . . for hour upon hour, or so it felt, but it must have been seconds. (*Text 2*) (It's fairly **sure**)

b The Yankee Bandit may have earned a place in the Guinness Book of Records. (*Unit 4A*)
(This is a less certain possibility. 'Might have' and 'could have' also express this.)

c They could have stayed at home and bought a replacement car. (*Unit 3B*)
('Could have' and 'might have' are also used to talk about an event which was possible but did **not** happen.)

d I can't have made a mistake with the bill because I used a calculator.
('Can't have' and, less commonly, 'couldn't have' are used in negative sentences. The speaker is fairly sure that something was **not** the case.)

e What can have happened?

Exercise 1   Rewrite the following sentences using modal verbs from the table above. Be careful to use the correct past participle! You don't need to include all the information.

a There is a possibility that my mother 'phoned while we were out. My mother
....

b Perhaps Helen saw the film on TV last night. Helen ....

c The most likely reason for your stomach upset is that you ate too much at lunch. You ....

d I've just been reading quietly so I certainly didn't wake the baby. I ....

e I wonder where John is. Perhaps he forgot the appointment in his diary. John ....

f Oh no! Look at all the water on the floor. I suppose a pipe burst while we were away. A pipe
....

g It's possible that the cleaning lady threw your cheque book away by mistake. The cleaning lady
....

▶ Communication activity 2 · Brain-teasers

Work in pairs or small groups to solve the following puzzles.

A | Here is the last page from a statement which was made to the police. The rest of the statement has been lost. Can you tell *what had happened to the man?*

> I was very frightened of course. Nothing like this had ever happened to me in my life before. And I was all alone. I just sat in the car, and gripped the wheel tightly.
> The car came slowly to a stop. It seemed to take ages, but I could do nothing about it. It was very cold, and very dark. And I could see nothing outside.
> Speed was important of course. So I took off my raincoat – not easy inside a car. I knew I had to move fast.
> I wound the window down – I remembered you had to do that – and then I got out of the car. I used all my strength to move as quickly as possible.
> When I finally saw the city lights, they were a long way off. But I was so glad to see them that I almost cried. I went into the nearest police station, and made this report.

B | Although it was night and there was dense fog, Tom was able to give a warning to deaf Dan, who was in serious danger in a boat two miles off-shore. *How did he do it, without the use of any equipment?*

C | There's a place where the railway passes through a narrow tunnel. A single track runs through the tunnel but separates into two tracks again at each end of the tunnel.
One afternoon, a train went into the tunnel at one end, and another train went into the tunnel at the other end. Both trains entered the tunnel at top speed, and they didn't slow down or stop. But there was no crash, and both trains came out safely and went on their way. *How?*

D | A motorist was driving down a narrow country lane. His car lights were not working. There were no street lamps and no moonlight. Yet he still managed to avoid a man dressed all in black walking away from him down the centre of the road. *How?*

▶ Focus on listening 2

You will hear two people discussing an experience they had on holiday in Morocco. For questions 1–7, tick (√) one of the answers, *a, b, c,* or *d.* For question 8, you will have to mark a place on a map.

1 The two travellers got into difficulties because they

    a didn't read the map.
    b took the wrong road.
    c decided to take a short cut.
    d didn't notice the river on the map.

2 They ignored the shepherds who were warning them because

    a they didn't believe them.
    b they didn't notice them.
    c they couldn't understand them.
    d they couldn't hear them.

3 They decided to try to drive through the first river because

    a it didn't look dangerous.
    b it was an adventure for them.
    c they couldn't turn the car round.
    d they didn't want to turn back.

4 The situation became serious when

    a the car got stuck in the mud.
    b the engine stopped working.

    c the river carried the car downstream.
    d the car sank in the river.

5 They didn't expect to get any help because

    a they didn't think that anyone lived nearby.
    b they couldn't speak Arabic.

    c it was too dark for anyone to see them.
    d they thought the local people were unfriendly.

6 After the rescue there was a problem because

    a they didn't have any money.
    b they didn't have the right sort of money.

    c they didn't want to give any money.
    d they didn't know how much money to give.

7 They stopped on their way to Rabat in order to

    a rest for the night.
    b ask for directions.

    c repair the car.
    d empty the water from the car.

8 On the map below, mark the place where the car got stuck in the river with a cross (X).

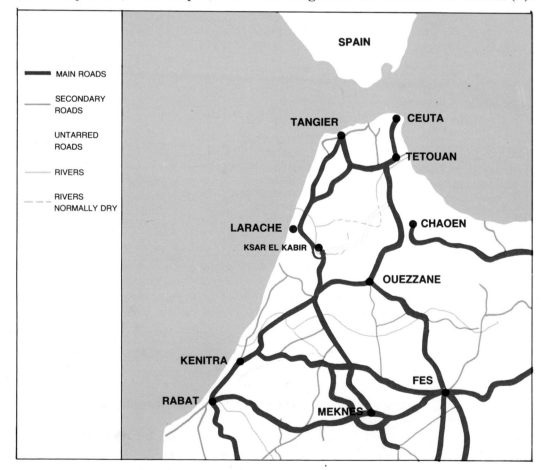

STUDY BOX 3

Prepositional phrases

on fire	**out of** danger	**at** last	**at** the same time
by accident	**in** difficulty(ies)	**at** once	**in** the end
in danger	**at** first	**at** times	

▶ Focus on grammar 3 · Question tags

Look at these examples from the conversation about the holiday in Morocco:

> The road had been pretty bad, hadn't it?
> It was marked yellow on the map, wasn't it?
> They were shepherds coming home, weren't they?

Question tags like these are often used in conversation to invite agreement.

Form   Question tags consist of an auxiliary verb and a personal pronoun. There are a few basic rules:

a If there is an auxiliary (do, be, have) or modal auxiliary verb in the main clause, this is repeated in the question tag. *For example:*

> He hasn't arrived yet, has he?
> (NB **Have** can also be used as an ordinary verb)
> You should be in bed by now, shouldn't you?

b If there is an ordinary verb in the main clause, 'do' is used in the question tag. *For example:*

> You know how to change a wheel, don't you? (Present)
> They went to Russia last year, didn't they? (Past)
> He had an accident last year, didn't he? (Past – **have** as an ordinary verb)

c Normally an affirmative statement has a negative question tag, and vice versa:

Statement		Question tag	
Affirmative	+	Negative	You're coming, aren't you?
Negative	+	Affirmative	He doesn't like jazz, does he?

Exercise 1   Match the two halves of the sentences below.

a You usually catch the 9 o'clock train,
b You can't speak Spanish,
c You haven't got change of £1,
d You'd better answer the telephone,
e You could always borrow the money,
f You won't tell anyone,
g You didn't wear that to the party,
h You're going to see him tomorrow,
i You hadn't been to an opera before,
j You've got some time to spare,

1 aren't you?
2 couldn't you?
3 had you?
4 will you?
5 can you?
6 don't you?
7 hadn't you?
8 haven't you?
9 have you?
10 did you?

Special points   *a* 'I am' is followed by the question tag 'aren't I?' *For example:*
> I'm lucky, aren't I?

b After an imperative, 'will you?' or 'would you?' are the most common forms. 'Will you?' is the only form possible after a negative imperative. *For example:*

> Pay attention, will you?   Shut the door, would you?   Don't be late, will you?

c Negative expressions like 'no', 'nothing', 'nowhere' and 'nobody' in the main clause are followed by an affirmative question tag. *For example:*

> He takes no interest in his work, does he?

d Somebody/someone, everybody/everyone and nobody/no-one are followed by 'they' in a question tag. *For example:*

> Nobody called for me, did they?   Everyone was very pleased, weren't they?

e Nothing/anything in the main clause is followed by 'it' in a question tag. *For example:*

> Nothing could be better, could it?   Anything could happen now, couldn't it?

Exercise 2   Add correct question tags to the following statements.

a We left at dawn, ...
b You've no idea at all what I'm talking about, ...
c You'd rather be staying at home, ...
d Don't tell anyone, ...
e There are some fantastic bargains, ...

f You shouldn't have made such a fuss, ...
g We had some really bad luck, ...
h Nobody heard what you said, ...
i Switch on the light, ...
j I'm managing quite well, ...

▶ Focus on writing 2 · Narrative

Writing Bank: page 229

Tell the story of a narrow escape that you have had. 120–180 words

Whether you are telling a story aloud or writing it in a letter, an article or an essay, the most important thing is to hold the listener's or reader's attention so that they want to know what happened next.

Notes

1 Plan:

Opening Paragraph: Introduce the story and try to catch the reader's attention with a statement which makes him/her want to read on. For example:
'When we set off on our camping holiday, we had no idea that it was going to turn into a nightmare.'
or 'I'll never forget 12th September,' 19.. It was the day . . .'

Middle Paragraph: Develop the story clearly, step by step, describing each main stage in a new paragraph.

Closing Paragraph(s): Give the story a definite ending and comment on the experience. You might say what you have learnt from it, for example.

2 Tenses:

A good narrative is likely to include a variety of past tenses – past simple, past continuous and past perfect. Look at these examples from Text 1 and discuss why they are used.

a '. . . as the pilot was fighting . . . to regain control of the airliner, . . . and trying to reassure his passengers at the same time, the plane's cabin was filling with ash and smoke.'

b 'It was coming out of the air vents,' said Mr J.M. 'I looked out to see an engine apparently on fire, then all the engines stopped.'

c 'All the captain told us at first was that the aircraft had met mild turbulence . . .'

d It was not until the plane had dropped 25,000 ft that Captain Moody was able to restart . . . the engines.

► Exam practice A · Vocabulary

Choose the word or phrase which best completes each sentence.

1 I don't know if I'll be able to help you but I'll .... my best.

    a make *b* give *c* do *d* work

2 We apologise to passengers for the delay in our journey. This is .... water on the tracks.

    a from *b* for *c* according to *d* due to

3 The bank doesn't open for another half an hour so .... I'll do a bit of shopping.

    a previously *b* during *c* afterwards *d* meanwhile

4 If you'd like a fresh fruit juice, I can .... an orange.

    a press *b* squeeze *c* squash *d* smash

5 He .... of the lead for a moment and the dog ran off.

    a dropped *b* released *c* let go *d* took hold

6 Don't make him laugh while he's eating or he'll ....

    a gasp *b* sneeze *c* choke *d* swallow

7 You must .... the instructions on the packet carefully if you want the cake to be a success.

    a follow *b* do *c* keep *d* repeat

8 It's dangerous to swim in this part of the river because of the strong ....

    a stream *b* current *c* tide *d* flood

9 You .... have been delighted when you won the competition.

    a can *b* must *c* may *d* could

10 Be careful as you walk. I've just polished the floor and it's rather ....

    a smooth *b* slippery *c* sticky *d* stiff

11 I'm afraid the computer is out of .... and we're waiting for the engineer to come.

    a action *b* work *c* use *d* duty

12 He'd rather look for a different job than move to another city, ... ?

    a doesn't he *b* hadn't he *c* isn't he *d* wouldn't he

13 This is the third cold I've had .... six months!

    a for *b* during *c* in *d* since

14 He looked a bit tired when I met him, but .... well.

    a otherwise *b* in addition *c* elsewhere *d* except

15 The car hit a lamppost, causing it .... over.

    a fall *b* falling *c* to fall *d* fallen

16 He .... have lost his way. He knows the city so well!

    a would *b* might *c* mustn't *d* can't

17 You must clean the cut thoroughly .... prevent any infection.

    a so that *b* for *c* in order *d* so as to

18 I enjoy living alone although I do get lonely .... times.

    a at *b* for *c* in *d* by

19 Look at that smoke. I think a house must be .... fire.

    a at *b* on *c* to *d* in

20 I went to a party last night and .... some friends came back for coffee.

    a after *b* at last *c* finally *d* afterwards

21 I don't feel very well. I'm afraid I may be .... flu.

    a going down with *b* going in for *c* going off with *d* going into

22 She took the child .... the hand and led her into the room.

    a with *b* on *c* by *d* from

23 If you blow up that balloon any more it will ....

    a break *b* burst *c* crack *d* spill

24 You .... to meet me at the station. I can easily walk.

    a don't need *b* mustn't *c* needn't *d* haven't got

25 He hates washing up so he usually tries to .... doing it.

    a get away with *b* get out of *c* get by *d* get over

UNIT 5B The market place

▶ Lead-in · Topic vocabulary

1 Who is the person who sells:

a meat
b bread
c fish
d fresh fruit and vegetables

e newspapers and magazines
f cigarettes and tobacco
g medicines, drugs and cosmetics
h dry and preserved goods, such as rice and coffee

2 Where do you go to:

a buy tickets for the theatre
b buy a railway ticket
c buy books
d buy petrol

e arrange a holiday
f buy writing paper and pens
g find a house to buy
h buy goods for the home or garden, such as tools

3 Where do you go to:

a have your hair cut
b have your shoes repaired

c have your clothes washed
d wash your clothes in a coin-operated machine

4 Some items are usually bought by a particular unit. Choose two items from the list below that you would usually buy by the . . .

a slice	chocolate	bandage
b bar	flowers	gloves
c bunch	cold meat	soap
d roll	wallpaper	grapes
e pair	sunglasses	cake

▶ Text 1 · Inside a supermarket

1 Choose words from the list to label the picture below.

carrier bag   check-out   till   trolley   bar-code   basket

2 Work with another student to guess the answers to the following questions without looking at the text.

a When was the world's first supermarket opened?
       1912   1932   1952

b Where was it opened?
       USA   Britain   Japan

c Supermarkets are designed so that shoppers
       ● can find what they want as quickly as possible.
       ● have to walk a long way to find what they want.
       ● can reach the check-out easily.

You will find the answers when you read the text, but first . . .

3 Look at the questions below. Half the class should look for the answers to the questions under A. The other half should look for the answers to the questions under B.

A

1 Why do you often find the largest items near the entrance of a supermarket?

2 What change has there been in the typical British breakfast since 1970?

3 What helps supermarkets to appear so especially clean?

4 What are *hot spots* in supermarkets?

5 What new development is being introduced in supermarkets? How will it work and how will it help the supermarkets?

B

1 Why do supermarkets prefer shoppers to use a trolley rather than a basket?

2 Supermarkets sell considerably less of one particular product than they did in 1970. What is it?

3 There are four products in particular which British shoppers are likely to plan to buy. What are they?

4 What was the *Piggly Wiggly* and what is interesting about it?

5 Why are supermarkets developing new trolleys which lock together?

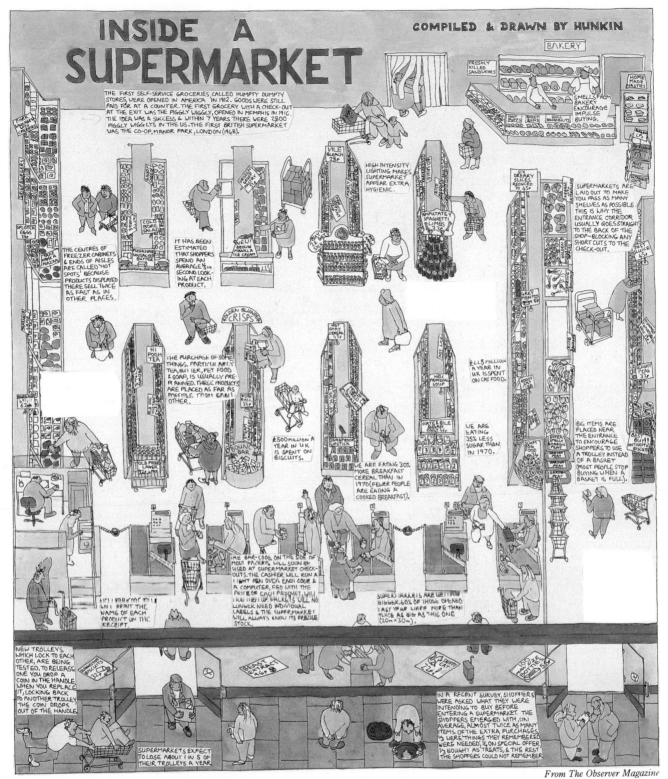

From The Observer Magazine

● When you have finished, work with a student who has answered a different group of questions.
● Ask questions and tell each other the answers in your own words.

Discussion points

4 a What four products would shoppers in your country be most likely to buy?
  b Why do you think that the sales of sugar have gone down so much since 1970?
  c Look at the text again. Would a supermarket in your country be different in any way?
    For example: lay-out; size; items sold.
  d What are the advantages of shopping in a supermarket?
  e What are the disadvantages?

▶ Focus on grammar 1 · The passive voice

Look at these sentences from Text 1 and answer the questions which follow.

£5 million a year is spent on biscuits.   (**Who** spends this amount?)
The first self-service groceries were opened in America in 1912.   (**Who** opened them?)

There are at least eight more examples of the passive voice in Text 1. Find as many as you can and underline them. When you have finished, compare your answers with another student's.

MAIN USES OF THE PASSIVE VOICE

a When the person doing the action (the agent) is not known, or when it is unnecessary to mention the agent. *For example:*

My car's been stolen!   Milk is often sold in cartons.

b To emphasise the action or event rather than the agent. *For example:*

Letters are collected from the boxes, taken to the sorting office, sorted and then sent to the correct part of the country.

c To avoid using **you** or **one** when making an impersonal statement. *For example:*

Taking photographs in the museum is forbidden   Children are not allowed in the bar.

Form a In the active voice, the normal order is Subject – Verb – Object. To make a sentence passive, the object must become the new subject and this must be followed by a passive form:

| **Active** | Subject | Verb | Object | *For example:* | Someone | has stolen | my car |

| **Passive** | New Subject | Passive form | *For example:* | My car | has been stolen |

b The passive is formed with the different tenses of the verb **to be** followed by a past participle.

Exercise 1 The passive voice can be used in most tenses and also with **going to** and modal verbs. Complete the following table with a partner so that you have a complete record of how the passive voice is formed.

Tense	Subject	Verb *to be*	Past participle
Present simple	Dinner	.......is........	served.
Present continuous	....	is being	built.
....	A stolen car	has been	found.
Past simple	The thief	was	....
Past continuous	The room	...was being...	painted.
....	The decision	had been	taken.
Future simple	Your offer	will be	....
Future perfect	....	will have been	posted.
OTHER STRUCTURES			
Going to	His car	....	serviced.
Modals (Present)	This machine	can ...be......	mended.
(Past)	....	shouldn't have been	opened.

Exercise 2 The passive voice is often used in signs and labels. There are some examples below but they've been jumbled up. Match the word or phrase in column **A** with the correct ending in column **B**.

A

1 Rooms
2 Shoplifters
3 This wine
4 This dictionary
5 No goods
6 Applications
7 Bags
8 This building

B

a must not be removed from the library.
b should be addressed to the Registrar.
c will be prosecuted.
d must not be left unattended.
e is protected by guard dogs.
f can be exchanged without a receipt.
g must be vacated by 12 p.m.
h is best served at room temperature.

When you have finished, compare your answers with another student's.

Exercise 3 · Look at the signs below and write suitable captions for them using the passive voice.

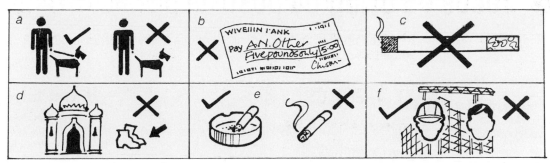

Exercise 4 · Put the verbs in brackets into a suitable passive form. Don't forget to make any necessary changes in word order. (The first five sentences come from texts in Unit 5A.)

a Every year, a forest the size of Wales (cut down) to make paper for use in Britain.
b Cycleways should (build) to make cycling safer.
c Vast amounts of money (spend) on nuclear power each year.
d Energy could (also/save) if more short journeys (make) by bicycle.
e Rubbish, with the hard bits removed, can (grind up), (mix) with sewage and (sell) as compost.
f Our team (only/beat) once so far this year.
g This painting (probably/paint) by Dali.
h She's only crying because some soap went into her eye while her hair (wash).
i A new guidebook to the cathedral (write) at the moment.
j Women (still/deny) the right to vote in some countries.
k This strike (not/forget) very quickly.
l It's not like him to be late. His train must (delay).
m The wine that (spill) on the carpet during the party has left an awful stain.
n The votes (count) by midnight?
o He noticed at once that the safe (break into).

▶ Focus on listening 1 · Chips with everything

You are going to hear a short talk about how computers are being used to help to make shopping easier.

The table below gives a summary of the information in the talk. Study it carefully before you begin and, while you listen, fill in the missing information.

System	Town	Equipment needed	Home delivery?	Cost
Over-60's Shopping Line	Gateshead	☎ ✓ ▣. ✓ ?	☐	
	Birmingham	☎ ☐ ▣. ☐ ? ☐	✓	
Shopping Link		☎ ☐ ▣. ☐ ? ☐	☐	£1.73 for each order
Comp-u-Card	Windsor	☎ ☐ ▣. ☐ ? ☐	☐	

Key: ☎ = telephone   ▣. = television   ? = no information

154

▶ Text 2 · Buying by post

Read the notices and the advertisements below in order to answer the questions which follow.

A FEW GOLDEN RULES

When you buy by post a little common sense can avoid a lot of trouble.

1 When you see something you like, check that the newspaper, magazine, or catalogue is up to date.

2 Read the advertisement carefully.

3 When you write off (and when you return goods) always include your name and address.

4 Keep a copy of your order and a note of the date it was sent.

5 Keep details of the advertisement – when it appeared, advertiser's address, the main points.

6 Never send cash through the post.

7 Send cheques, postal orders, etc., only if you're asked for payment in advance, and make sure you keep cheque stubs or counterfoils.

If you have to complain

● *'Postal Bargain' advertisements:*

write to the Advertising Manager of the newspaper or magazine if goods you've ordered haven't arrived within 28 days. Include the following information (tick them off on this checklist):

☐ date of advertisement

☐ date of your order

☐ details of goods ordered

☐ name and address to which goods should be sent

☐ amount paid (cheque, postal order)

☐ if you still have a receipt

☐ trader's full name and address

And anything else you think may be useful.
If the trader has gone bankrupt, you will be told. You must then send in a formal claim, together with some proof of payment.

From The Central Office of Information

BARGAINS from SAVE-A-LOT!

POST TODAY TO SAVE-A-LOT LTD, DEPT. M.,
42 WINDSOR GARDENS, LONDON NW3X 6TS

A

SWEATER DRYER
Keep the value and shape of your sweaters. With this incredible dryer you can retain shape without pulling or stretching delicate fibres. Easy to use at home – folds flat for travel or storage. Perfect for Jumpers Cardigans Baby clothes Fine woollens Synthetics etc. No home should be without one.
Only £7.95 incl. p&p

B
BRIGHT SUPER LAMP
The lamp that can be fixed almost anywhere – fit in seconds with contact stickers. Use as bedside lamp, in attics, sheds, garages. Completely safe. No wiring. Ideal for power cuts too. Super deluxe model. Do not confuse with inferior models.
Only £6.75 + 80p p&p

C
SOFT ICE PACK
RELIEF TO ALL THOSE ACHES
Now you can relieve those nagging aches and pains caused by bruising, headaches, toothaches etc – the old-fashioned way. Simply fill the bag with ice, and place over the area of your choice – feel and note the difference! Indispensable for home - car - office. A must in any first-aid box. Try relief the old-fashioned way!
£3.75 + 60p p&p

D
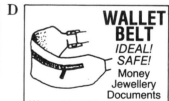
WALLET BELT
IDEAL! SAFE!
Money Jewellery Documents
Wear this strong "invisible" belt with the king-size double pockets and your worries are over. Protect yourself from loss, pickpockets and thieves. Order now while stocks last.
£4.50 + 65p p&p

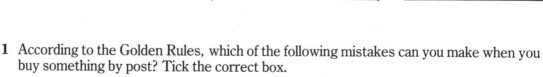

1 According to the Golden Rules, which of the following mistakes can you make when you buy something by post? Tick the correct box.

☐ *a* Order something old-fashioned.
☐ *b* Ordering something which is no longer available.
☐ *c* Not keeping a record of the advertiser's address.
☐ *d* Sending a cheque before you receive the goods.
☐ *e* Putting the wrong date on your cheque.
☐ *f* Not giving the newspaper or magazine your address.
☐ *g* Sending something back without giving your address.
☐ *h* Not keeping a record of your payment.
☐ *i* Not making a note of the date of your order.
☐ *j* Not keeping the receipt for your goods.

155

2 Look at the four 'small ads' and answer the following questions:

  a Which advertisement suggests that a particular product is very easy to install? **A B C D**

  b Which advertisement suggests that supplies of a particular product are limited? **A B C D**

  c Which advertisement suggests that using a particular product will help prevent damage to your clothes? **A B C D**

  d Which advertisement suggests that a product is copied by other manufacturers? **A B C D**

  e Which ad suggests that a product can give you peace of mind? **A B C D**

  f Which advertisements suggest that it is essential to have a particular product? **AB BC AC CD**

► Focus on writing · Formal letter

Writing Bank: page 222

Imagine that you ordered one of the items advertised on page 155 a month ago. It still hasn't arrived and you are beginning to get worried!

Following the instructions on the same page, write a formal letter of complaint. Before you start, check the notes on layout and style in the Focus on writing section of Unit 1B (page 98).

► Communication activity · Selling pets

Note Before you begin, check the Functions Bank (page 209) for the Language of Asking for and Giving Advice, and of Persuasion.

Instructions 1 Work in pairs. If numbers are uneven, two students may work together in one of the roles. Alternatively, one student may act as an observer, noting language used.

  2 Role A: You have one of the animals in List A. Your job is to persuade your partner(s) to buy it. Before you begin, tell your partner what the first letter following your animal is. Give him/her time to read through the role. Your partner will begin.

  3 Role B: Your partner will tell you which role you have from List B. You want to buy a pet and you go to your partner for advice on what animal to choose. Look through your role quickly and then be prepared to begin the conversation.

  4 After 5 minutes, change round so the buyer is now selling, and the seller is buying. You should have a new animal and, this time, Role B is the second letter after the animal.

List A							
snake	*a*	*b*	canary	*c*	*e*	goldfish	*f*	*d*
tortoise	*d*	*f*	white mouse	*e*	*a*	cat	*c*	*b*

List B

a You live in a small flat and you want a pet that's not too much trouble to look after.

b You live alone and would like a pet for protection.

c You want a pet that will keep you active.

d You are a teenager. You want a pet that you can have fun with.

e You are a filmstar. You want a pet as a mascot.

f You are an elderly person. You want a pet to keep you company.

Discussion points ● Were any of the sellers successful? If so, what techniques of persuasion did they use?
  ● If you were unsuccessful in selling your animal, how and why did the buyer reject your advice?

Text 3   Read these four short extracts and answer the following questions.

A

BEWARE SUPERMARKET SELLING
Much research has been done by supermarket chains to find out how to persuade shoppers to buy more. Supermarkets are arranged to take advantage of the impulses of the people shopping in them – for example by putting sweets at check-outs in racks at children's eye-level. In general, you are likely to spend less shopping if you leave the children behind, if you have eaten recently and if you shop infrequently.

B

USE YOUR OVEN SPARINGLY
Ovens are expensive to heat (particularly electric ovens), and can be costly to run for any length of time. Try to plan your cooking to have a full oven, so minimising the number of times it is used. An asbestos mat will let you cook things slowly on top of the cooker to avoid using the oven to heat one thing only.

C

DO YOU NEED A CAR AT ALL?
Your car could be costing you more than you think. The cost of just owning a car (ie tax, insurance, depreciation and loss of interest on capital) can be at least £15 a week for the cheapest car – before you have put any petrol into it or paid for servicing. Using public transport, taxis or minicabs, and hiring a self-drive car for trips further afield could save money. Think particularly carefully about running a second car – you might find that you can get by with one car by taking a few taxi rides each week (almost certainly saving money).

D

BUY IN BULK
Buying food in large packets and bulk quantities can knock up to 10% off your food bills. If you form a bulk-buying cooperative with friends and neighbours, you could afford to buy food in wholesale quantities and make even bigger savings.

From The Consumers' Association

1 The four extracts all
   a warn against going to certain shops.
   b recommend buying particular products.
   c suggest different ways of saving money.
   d explain the best way to do your shopping.

2 Extract A suggests that if you take your children to the supermarket
   a it will take you longer to do your shopping.
   b you will forget what you wanted to buy.
   c they will encourage you to buy more.
   d they will get in other shoppers' way.

3 Extract B recommends
   a cooking several things at once in the oven.
   b putting an asbestos mat in the oven.
   c only using the top of the cooker.
   d cooking food slowly in the oven.

4 Extract C warns about the high cost of
   a hiring a car.
   b owning two cars.
   c travelling by taxi.
   d replacing your car.

5 Extract D advises you
   a not to buy more food than you need.
   b not to ask shopkeepers for a discount.
   c to share your food with other people.
   d to buy food in large amounts.

STUDY BOX 1

Have something done   They choose when they want to **have** it **delivered**.
(*Listening 1*)

Have, used with an object and a past participle, 'means to cause something to be done'.

You might go to the dentist's surgery to **have** a tooth **pulled out**.

Why might you . . .   go to the shoe-mender's?   take your car to a garage?
                       go to the hairdresser's?   call a plumber?
                       go to an optician's?   employ a carpenter?

► Focus on listening 2 · The auctioneer

In this conversation you are going to hear Mr Ewing, an auctioneer, talking about his work.

Notes 'An auction' is a public sale where goods are sold to the person who offers the most money.
'A bid' is the money which is offered: I made a bid of £5 for the mirror.
'A lot' is an item, or a group of items, sold at an auction: I'm interested in Lot 59, the four dining chairs.
'An auctioneer' is the person who conducts the sale.

For questions 1–4 tick (√) which you think is the correct answer in each case – *a, b, c* or *d*.

1 Mr Ewing became an auctioneer when

   a he completed a training course in auction selling.
   b his family started up an auction business.
   c his firm gave him the chance to work in its auction room.
   d he failed his Polytechnic course in surveying.

2 One of the most usual ways of making a bid at an auction is to

   a wave your arms.
   b raise your voice.
   c make a secret signal.
   d lift your catalogue.

3 When auctioneers take a bid from someone who was only signalling to a friend, it's usually

   a a genuine mistake.
   b an arrangement which has been made in advance.
   c a way of entertaining the audience.
   d a way of selling unpopular goods.

4 Auction fever happens when people get very

   a excited.
   b frightened.
   c ill.
   d angry.

For questions 5–9 tick (√) whether you think the statements are true or false.

	True	False
5 Country house sales are always well-attended because the prices tend to be reasonable.		
6 When the painting was found it was in a very poor state.		
7 Mr Ewing was very surprised by the price the painting was sold for.		
8 The four-poster bed was found in several pieces.		
9 As a provincial auctioneer, Mr Ewing is only expected to give expert advice on a limited number of items.		

For questions 10–12 fill in the missing information in the spaces.

10 Mr Ewing is especially interested in ....

11 His problem is that he .... the items he would like to own.

12 His advice is not to be .... about going to an auction for the first time.

STUDY BOX 2

Prepositional phrases followed by a noun or a gerund.

according **to**	except **for**	**as** regards	in addition **to**	instead **of**
on account **of**	as far **as**	in spite **of**	apart **from**	by means **of**

▶ Focus on grammar 2 · Gerund and infinitive

1 Some verbs can be followed by either the gerund or infinitive with no difference, or only a small difference in meaning.

a **like, love, hate, prefer** *For example:*

Do you watch much TV?   Well, I like | watching | the breakfast show. | (= enjoy)
                                      | to watch | | **no difference**

I like to be early when I'm catching a train. (= prefer/choose)

After **would**, the infinitive is normally used.

Would you like to go for a walk?   I'd hate to miss the chance.
We'd love to hear from you.

b **begin, start** *For example:*

It's started | snowing.   **no difference**
             | to snow.

After the continuous form of a verb, only the infinitive is used. *For example:*

It's beginning to get dark.

2 Some verbs can be followed by either the gerund or infinitive, but with a difference of meaning.

a **remember/forget**

PAST action event ← | **remember** | I don't remember seeing you at the party. Were you there?
                    | **forget** | I'll never forget flying over the Alps for the first time.

| **remember** | FUTURE | Don't forget to feed the cat, will you?
| **forget** | →action event | Did you remember to post that letter while you were out?

b **regret**

PAST action event ← **regret**   He regrets stealing the money now.
     I'll always regret not going to university.

regret | **to say** **to inform (you)** **to tell (you)** | I regret to say I lost my temper with him.
We regret to inform you that your flight has been delayed.
Mr Brown regrets to tell you that he is unable to see you today.

c **try**

(You've lost your keys.) Try emptying your pockets. (possible action – see if it succeeds)

Try to remember when you last had them.
(action may not be possible – see if you can do it.)

d **need**

The windows need cleaning   (Passive meaning: need to be cleaned)
I need to call at the post office. (Active meaning: have to call)

e **stop**

When stop is followed by a gerund it means to finish an action.
Could you stop shouting?

When **stop** is followed by an infinitive, it means to interrupt one action **in order** to do something else.

We had to stop (walking, driving etc) to look at the map.

Exercise 1   Put the verb in brackets in the correct form, gerund or infinitive.

a You must remember (call) at the bank on your way home because we need (order) some traveller's cheques.

b Could you stop (type) for a moment? I need (concentrate) on this letter.

c I hope you haven't forgotten (telephone) the garage because the car badly needs (service).

d We could try (make) a dash for the car if it would only stop (rain) for a moment.

e I'm sure you won't regret (buy) the house, even though it needs (paint) and (decorate).

f I regret (say) that he's forgotten ever (promise) you a job.

g I don't remember (take) my wallet out of my bag, but I must have done when I stopped (buy) petrol.

h As I told you, he's rather deaf, so don't forget (try) (shout) if he doesn't answer the door at first.

Exercise 2 Gerund and infinitive revision

a I've considered (ask) him (raise) my salary, but I don't think he can afford (do) it.

b If the machine happens (stop) (work), just telephone and arrange for the service engineer (call).

c I can't help (think) that we shouldn't have agreed (lend) him our car.

d If you've finished (use) the typewriter, I'd like (borrow) it for a while, so that I can get used to (type) with that machine.

e He denied (take) the money and warned us (not/call) the police.

f I'm delighted (hear) that you are intending (visit) us and I look forward to (see) you when you come.

▶ Exam practice A · Vocabulary

Choose the word or phrase which best completes each sentence.

1 My washing machine has been so useful that I don't know how I managed to .... without it before.

   a get by   *b* get over   *c* get away   *d* get across

2 I'm afraid I can't give you your money back unless you have a(n) .... for the pullover.

   a bill   *b* invoice   *c* ticket   *d* receipt

3 They're going to .... central heating in the office.

   a include   *b* install   *c* connect   *d* conduct

4 There's a ...., of silk scarves in the shop window.

   a scene   *b* display   *c* sight   *d* view

5 It was a small class so the teacher was able to give us each a lot of .... attention.

   a single   *b* private   *c* individual   *d* lonely

6 The special offer in the magazine looked so good that I .... for it straight away.

   a wrote out   *b* wrote off   *c* wrote up   *d* wrote down

7 No, I'm afraid I don't know you. You must have confused me .... someone else.

   a with   *b* from   *c* for   *d* by

8 I was very worried about the examination and it was a great .... to hear that I had passed.

   a news   *b* relief   *c* reward   *d* escape

9 He wore thick gloves and a scarf to protect him .... the cold.

   a for   *b* by   *c* from   *d* at

10 I asked the assistant if he had any football boots in ....

a store   *b* shop   *c* stock   *d* sale

11 Those gloves are much too small for you. Don't try to put them on or you'll ....
them.

a extend   *b* spread   *c* stretch   *d* swell

12 I want to .... advantage of the sale at the shoeshop while it's on.

a make   *b* have   *c* get   *d* take

13 If the telephone number you want is engaged, ... the receiver and your money
will be returned.

a recall   *b* restore   *c* recover   *d* replace

14 If I'm late for work I take a short .... across the park to save time.

a cut   *b* way   *c* road   *d* direction

15 When I .... up the bill, it came to more money than I had with me.

a counted   *b* checked   *c* added   *d* calculated

16 The bank clerk asked me for some .... of my identity, such as a passport or
driver's licence.

a card   *b* signal   *c* notice   *d* proof

17 He was .... from prison last year after serving a 6 month sentence.

a rescued   *b* released   *c* reformed   *d* removed

18 When you have .... the goods, you can collect them from the store.

a paid for   *b* paid   *c* settled   *d* returned

19 He doesn't know anybody in London, apart .... his sister.

a from   *b* for   *c* than   *d* of

20 It doesn't say on the box what the contents ....

a is   *b* are   *c* has   *d* have

21 This society was .... in 1970 and the membership has been growing ever since.

a set off   *b* set out   *c* set in   *d* set up

22 I don't really enjoy going to the theatre .... myself. I'd rather have company.

a on   *b* with   *c* by   *d* for

23 We thoroughly enjoyed our holiday .... the poor weather.

a despite   *b* although   *c* even   *d* in spite

24 I wonder if I .... possibly borrow your pen for a moment.

a may   *b* should   *c* can   *d* could

25 I'll call you tonight at 10 o'clock .... I can find a telephone that works.

a unless   *b* suppose   *c* provided   *d* when

UNIT 6B Turning points

▶ Lead-in 1

Look at the photographs below. Each one shows an event which marks a turning point in a person's life.

1 Discuss what is happening in each picture and what changes the event will lead to.

2 Which of the four events is likely to be the most important turning point, in your opinion?

3 What other possible turning points in a person's life can you think of?

4 Have you ever experienced a particular turning point in your life? Describe it.

162

▶ # Lead-in 2

In the quotations *a–e* below five different people are talking about a particular experience. Read what they each say and decide what the experience was.

a It has changed my life considerably in that it has given me more scope and opportunity; it hasn't changed me myself, my outlook, my personality, one little bit.

b My friends did not react very well. The majority of them became embarrassed. Before, when we used to go out, everyone had the same sort of money in their pocket; so now I really don't have the same sort of friends.

c After the win you think 'That's it, I'll never do any work again, just finish'. It doesn't last very long, you've got to have something to do if your mind is active, you've got to make your mind active as well.

d Some of my relatives were jealous. My brother hasn't spoken to me since, although I gave his son £800. I've given up worrying about it now.

e I'm beginning to wish I had never won the money. I am fed up with all the begging letters, the proposals and all the friends I have suddenly found. All I want is a bit of peace and quiet and the only way I shall get it is to leave the country.

Now answer these questions:

1 Some people mention rather negative reactions. Which one is more positive?

2 Which person changed his mind about what he was going to do after the win?

3 Why do you think the friends mentioned in *b* felt embarrassed? Explain in your own words why that winner lost his friends?

4 Why do you think one winner's brother stopped speaking to him?

5 In *e*, what were the begging letters and proposals? Who were the winner's new friends, and why was she fed up with them?

6 How might a person's personality change as a result of winning a lot of money?

7 Imagine that a close friend of yours won £100,000. Would it make any difference to your friendship? What difficulties could it cause?

▶ # Focus on grammar 1 · Expressing wishes and regrets

I WISH.../IF ONLY...

1 When referring to the **present** or **future**, these expressions are followed by a **past tense**. *For example:*

I wish | I had a car!   (I haven't got a car)
      | he didn't have to go. (He **does** have to go)

If only | I knew the answer!   (I **don't** know the answer)
      | you weren't working tomorrow. (You **are** working then)

Note The correct form of the verb 'to be' after these expressions is **were**. *For example:*

If only | I were rich!
      | he weren't so lazy!

was is also possible, however, and is often heard in conversation.

Exercise 1 What would you say in these situations? Use **I wish** and **If only**.

a You planned to play tennis but it's pouring with rain.
b A friend has offered to lend you a car while you're in England but you can't drive.
c There's a party this evening but you've got an awful headache.
d You're staying in a Youth Hostel but the person in the bed next to you snores very loudly all night.
e You're only half-way through the last question on an examination paper and there's one minute to go before the end.
f You're out walking in New York and you're completely lost!

2 When referring to the **past**, **I wish** and **if only** are followed by a **past perfect** tense. *For example:*

I wish I hadn't won the money.
If only I had listened to your advice.

Exercise 2 Imagine you are the people in the pictures below. What would you say? Use **I wish** and **If only** and think of one positive and one negative statement for each situation.

3 Other expressions which are followed by a **past tense**:

would rather + object	I'd rather you didn't say anything about it.
as if/as though	You talk as though you knew a lot on the subject. (You don't!)
suppose/supposing	Suppose somebody saw/had seen you.
it's (about/high) **time**	It's high time we left

Exercise 3 Complete the following sentences.

a Your car is absolutely filthy! It's high time you ....

b It's stupid of you not to take out travel insurance for your holiday. Suppose ....

c I'm grown up now. Why do you still treat me as if ....

d Don't take her any more chocolates while she's in hospital. She'd rather you ....

STUDY BOX 1

Phrasal verb **Give.** I've **given up** worrying about it now. *(Lead-in 2)*

give away – give as a present. Father Curtin won £109,000 and **gave** it all **away**.
give away – reveal. The author refused to **give away** any secrets about the ending of his book.
give back – return. Please make sure you **give** me my pen **back**.
give in – hand in. This is the end of the test. Please **give in** your papers now.
give in – surrender. The government refuses to **give in** to terrorism.
give out – distribute. Children helped to **give out** presents to the old people.
give up – stop. My doctor has told me to **give up** eating cakes and sweets.
give up – surrender/abandon. I had to **give up** my flat when I got married.

► Text 1 · Just a normal day?

Read the text and answer these questions:
1 How did Mrs Barrett win £1 million?
2 When did she discover that she had won?
3 What is worrying her about her win?

newspaper comp 65
6pm Sat even 75 90
can she still play bingo

FRIDAY, Sept 28. Alice Maude Barrett, 67, got up at 7.30 a.m. as usual. She had her usual breakfast – a cup of tea and a
5 **bread roll.**
She browsed through her Mirror as usual. Then she did her washing. Not a lot of it to do – only her bits and
10 pieces.
She did it by hand. She only uses the machine once a fortnight to save on electricity.
15 She hung the washing out to dry in the yard behind her council maisonette. "Gives the sheets a nice airing."
20 Then she took Thumper the dog out for his walkies and popped into the Co-op as usual to do her shopping.
Most mornings she pops
25 into the Co-op. On this particular Friday she bought half a dozen eggs and half a pound of lard.
Back at her flat she
30 dusted around and made her bed and fried up sausages and chips for her dinner.

Then she and Thumper
35 had an afternoon snooze in the armchair until it was time for him to have another walk.
Home then to do the iron-
40 ing. Daughter Annie came round to bring her mum cabbages and carrots. Annie works on a farm.

Bingo
45 Then, as usual on a Friday, Alice Maude Barrett, who prefers to be called Maudie, washed and dressed and went to bingo, her
50 favourite thing next to watching snooker on TV.
Back home just after 10 p.m., watch telly for an hour and bed at 11.15.
55 That's how last Friday ended for Maudie.
Alice Maude Barrett will never again in her life have a normal, ordinary Friday.
60 On Saturday morning Alice Maude Barrett, aged 67, divorced, mother of five daughters, grandmother of ten great kids, stared at her
65 Mirror and it began to dawn

on her that she might, just might, have got the numbers right on her Who Dares Wins Win a £Million card.
70 She took a swallow of tea and rang Annie. Annie yawned and went back to sleep.
But by six on Saturday
75 evening there wasn't any doubt. Maudie was a millionaire.
Alice Maude Barret, lives in a council flat on £37.01 a
80 week social security.
The new millionaire came round to my place yesterday for a nice little talk and a cuppa to celebrate.
85 Tea is what she prefers. She is a very quiet person. Shy. A bit nervous. "Well you would be, wouldn't you?" she said. "You can't
90 take it in, can you?
"I'm only worried about one thing; how will I be able to go to bingo now?
"What'll they all think?
95 Suppose I won. I don't want to give up the bingo and all my friends."

From The Daily Mirror

Now answer these questions:

4 From the article we learn that Mrs Barrett normally led
a a very hard life.
b a very lonely life.
c a very unexciting life.
d a very unhappy life.

5 We understand that Mrs Barrett didn't have much money from the fact that
a she only did her washing twice a month.
b she had to worry about fuel bills.
c she had very little to eat.
d she couldn't afford to go out.

6 Mrs Barrett explained that she seemed nervous because it was difficult for her
    a to believe what had happened.   *c* to talk to people she didn't know well.
    b to decide how to spend the money.   *d* to agree to accept the money.

7 Mrs Barrett probably telephoned her daughter that Saturday morning
    a to tell her what vegetables to bring   *c* to ask her to help check the numbers
       that day.   on her card.
    b to let her know it was time to get up. *d* to tell her that her mother was a
                                          millionaire.

8 Bingo was important to Mrs Barrett because
    a it was her only chance to get out of the *c* she had no other entertainment.
       house.   *d* she enjoyed the company it provided.
    b it gave her the chance to win a million
       pounds.

Discussion points A

1 Judging from the information in the article, what do you think Mrs Barrett is likely to spend some of her money on?
2 Will Mrs Barrett be able to continue going to her bingo evenings? Why/why not?
3 Do you think she'll have a happier life as a result of her win? Why/Why not?

Discussion points B

1 Do this short exercise first, to remind you of the Conditional 2. Make complete sentences from these notes:
    a I/probably (feel) better/if I (take) more exercise.
    b If she (not have) a dog for company, she (be) quite lonely.
    c If you (win) £1,000, how/(spend)/money?
2 Look at the three questions below and decide on your answers. Do this alone. (5 minutes)

  ● If you won £100,000, how much of it would you:
    a spend   *b* invest   *c* give away

  ● Which charity organisations would you give part of your winnings to, if any? Choose from the following (or add your own ideas)

    A society which:
    a looks after orphans (children with no parents).   *e* fights pollution and protects the
    b prevents cruelty to animals.   *f* countryside.
    c helps blind people.   *g* helps old people.
    d is trying to find a cure for cancer.   ....

  ● Imagine that you have won £10,000 but you can only have it if you can say **exactly** how you would spend (and you must spend it all!)

    Make a list of things you would buy, with approximate costs.
3 Now discuss your answers with a partner. Give reasons for you decisions and make sure your partner explains his/her reasons.

The sequel to the story

Since Mrs Barrett's win, she has quietly moved out of her council maisonette to an ordinary-looking bungalow. Apart from investing money for her family, her only spending has been on a new bed and a remote-control colour television – which she has still not learnt how to work.
   'She has a solicitor and a tax expert at the bank to help her out with financial matters but for a lady of her age and background, she has shown tremendous common sense in the way she's adjusted to her new wealth,' says the man from the newspaper who looks after their big prize-winners.
   'It's not changed her at all and I'd be surprised if any of her neighbours even realise who she is. She's just like any other little old lady next door.'

Final footnote

Fourteen years ago Father James Curtin, a 65-year-old Catholic priest won £109,000 on the football pools and promptly gave it all away – the only thing he bought himself was a new mini. The rest went on church repairs and to various charities.
   'My life is no different,' says Father James, 'I was completely content then and I'm the same now. It was a wonderful feeling writing all those cheques. In fact, I'd recommend it for all people who win large amounts of money. It will make them feel better, believe me.'

by Mervyn Edgecombe in Woman Magazine

▶ Focus on Listening 1 · Is there life after redundancy?

1 Can you explain the words in bold type in the sentences below?

> 150 workers have been made **redundant** at a factory in Manchester.
> They will receive **golden handshakes** of between £200 and £2,000.
> (If not, check the explanations on page 177.)

2 You are going to hear about several people who were made redundant, but who started new careers. As you listen, complete the table below.

	Previous career	Length of time (years)	Redundancy pay	New career	Where?	Success? Yes/No/ Too early to say
A Brian Collins	1. Electrical Industry 2. Teaching Sailing	a.	b.	c.	Scotland	Yes
B William Rudd	Chemical company	d.	£70,000	e.	f.	g.
C Patricia and Rex Pole	h.	33	i.	j.	South coast	k.
D Graham Clarke	l.	m.	n.	Magician	Colchester	o.

▶ Communication activity · Turning points in history

1 Work with another student to answer the questions below. If you're not sure what an answer is, choose the answer you and your partner think is most likely.

1 Which of the following was invented first?
  a radio   *b* aeroplane   *c* submarine

2 The first dictionary appeared in
  a China in 1100 BC.   *b* France in 1697.   *c* England in 1755.

3 1961 was the year of
  a the first automatic digital computer.   *c* the first robot.
  b the first man in space.

4 Paper was first produced in the 1st century BC in
  a Egypt.   *b* China.   *c* Rome.

5 The first journey by hot air balloon took place over Paris in
  a 1783.   *b* 1867.   *c* 1903.

6 Which of the following great shipping canals was opened first?
  a Panama   *b* Suez   *c* Corinth

7 Television was invented in 1926 by
  a an Italian.   *b* an American.   *c* a Scotsman.

8 Which of the following was invented in China in 1000?
  a a wheel   *b* the watch   *c* gunpowder

9 Tobacco was first brought to Europe from
  a Mexico in 1490.   *b* America in 1553.   *c* Africa in 1840.

10 The first printed book was produced in 1456 in
  a Spain.   *b* Germany.   *c* England.

2 To see how well you've done, check the answers on page 177.

3 Which of the ten inventions or developments above was the most important turning point in your opinion, and which the least?

4 What other invention, discovery or achievement can you think of which was more important than any of those above?

▶ Focus on writing 1 · Exam practice

Writing Bank: pages 231, 227

1 Speech

> There is a plan to send a number of objects or photographs on board the next space mission. These will be intended to give an idea of life on Earth in the second half of the 20th century to any intelligent being from outer space who might find them.
>
> A competition has been held to find the most suitable 8 objects. Your list has been chosen for the final of the competition and now you must give a short speech to the judges, describing the objects on your list and explaining the reasons for your choices. Write what you would say. (120–180 words)

Notes

a Look back at the notes on this kind of writing in Unit 3A (page 35).

b Consider especially who you are speaking to and the occasion. It's very important that you explain your choices clearly and convincingly. Though it's a fairly formal occasion, don't be afraid to include an element of humour if you like.

c Remember that you will be addressing a group of people – the judges! Make it clear that this is spoken English. Include contractions (I'm, it's etc) and 'filler phrases' (Well, you see, as you know, etc).

d Start with a suitable introduction. *For example*:
'Good morning. I'm very pleased that my list has been chosen. I had a lot of fun making it and now I'd like to explain . . .'
and finish with a suitable conclusion. *For example*:
'Well, that concludes my list. I hope you agree with my reasons . . .'

2 Discussion

> Describe some ways in which television has made a difference to life. (120–180 words)

Notes

a It's very important to make a list of the main points beforehand.
Consider: – what people did before television was available.
            – what the main advantages of television are.
            – what the main disadvantages are.

b Include a balance of advantages and disadvantages even if you intend to argue that one outweighs the other in the end.

c Make sure you finish with a clear conclusion, giving your considered opinion as to whether television has had mainly a good, or a bad effect on our lives.

Useful language

Contrast links

Some people . . .	**while**	others . . .
	whereas	
On the one hand television . . .	**on the other hand** it . . .	

Summing up

| **In conclusion** **To sum up** **On balance** | I think/I feel . . . |

Look back, too, at the Conditional Link Words in Unit 5A (page 62).

► Focus on grammar 2 · Conditional 3

Form

| If | had(n't)
had(n't) been | + past participle | would(n't) have
would(n't) have been | + past participle |

For example:

> If I had (I'd) told you the truth, you wouldn't have believed me!
> I would (I'd) have taken you to the station if my car hadn't broken down.

The Conditional 3 refers to the past. The '**if**' event is therefore impossible since we cannot change the past.

If a result is **not sure**, we can express this element of doubt with **would probably**, **might**, and **could**.
For example:

> If you had driven that car, you | would probably | have had an accident.
> | might
> | could

Exercise 1   Put the verbs in the following sentences into the correct form to make Conditional 3 sentences.

a If Mrs Barrett (not buy) the Daily Mirror, she (not take part) in the competition.

b If she (forget) to check the numbers on her card, she (not win) a million pounds.

c She (not ring) her daughter if she (not be) so excited.

d If Annie (not be) so tired, she (not go) back to sleep.

e She (not be interviewed) if she (not become) a millionairess.

f If she (not win) so much money, she ....

Exercise 2   Using the information in each question below, write Conditional 3 sentences. (There may be more than one possibility.)

a The Incas of Peru had no paper. Their architects had to make models in clay for the builders to follow.

If the Incas ....

b The first photograph was taken in 1826. Napoleon, who died in 1821, never had his photograph taken.

If Napoleon ....

or If the camera ....

c Penicillin was discovered in 1928. It helped to save many lives in World War II.

Many lives ....

d The mariner's compass was invented in the 12th century. Christopher Columbus reached the West Indies in 1492.

Christopher Columbus ....

e Tobacco was imported to Europe in 1553.

If tobacco ....

MIXED CONDITIONALS
When we want to talk about the present result of a past event, we can use a mixed conditional.
For example:

> If I hadn't been invited, I wouldn't be here.
> I wouldn't be surprised if he had been delayed

Form

| If | had(n't)
had(n't) been | + past participle | would/could/might | + infinitive |

Exercise 3   The Suez Canal was opened in 1869. Before that, ships had to travel round Africa to reach India.

Complete the following sentences, putting the verbs into the correct form so that they describe the present result of a past action.

a If the Suez Canal hadn't been opened in 1869, ships (have to) travel ....

b If/Panama Canal (complete)/1914, ships/(sail)/South America/Pacific.

c Ships (go)/Peloponnese/Aegean Sea/if/Corinth Canal/(not build)/1893.

▶ # Text 2

Read the article below in order to answer the following questions:

1 What did David Cassidy do before he retired?
2 What made him decide to retire?
3 How did his life change afterwards?

What made David Cassidy retire at 25?

It was just after 11pm and David Cassidy was lying in the bath in a New York hotel when his world started to fall apart. Even though it's now ten years ago, that
5 moment is one he remembers all too vividly. He felt as though a lorryload of ice had been emptied into his bath tub.

He remembers it so clearly because it was a 'day that had begun in such
10 triumph. At that moment he was simply the biggest pop star in the world. There were millions of women who dreamed of him and he was worth around £20 million. But the night ended in disaster and
15 changed his life for ever.

His performance that evening was his hometown show – for an audience of 20,000 in New York's famous Madison Square Garden. And right from the start
20 he knew something wasn't quite right. David says "I was used to the audience getting hysterical but this time it was different. The entire building seemed to rumble with the emotions of that crowd. It
25 was the most terrifying experience of my life."

Afraid for David's safety when he tried to leave the building, security men arranged for him to be wrapped in a
30 blanket, dumped in the boot of an old car and driven to a cheap hotel in one of the poorer New York suburbs.

"The hotel was a real dive," David recalls. "It smelt disgusting and looked as
35 though it had never been cleaned. I ran myself a hot bath, got in, lay back and then it hit me ... I was in a state of complete shock. One moment I had been performing in front of 20,000 people who
40 all loved me – 30 minutes later I was completely alone, in a dirty bathroom, with no money, no clothes to wear except a sweaty jumpsuit, absolutely nothing. And for the first time in my life, I digested
45 my situation. I had plenty of time because

© Camera Press

I sat there, wrapped in a towel, for three hours, waiting to be collected. I thought, this is it, this is what I have been working so hard for. The kids who couldn't afford
50 to get into one of my concerts were far richer than me, because at least they were having plenty of fun. I was having no fun at all."

"I felt that I had to make a choice –
55 either my career had to go or I had to sacrifice my life to my work. That night in New York showed me that. Then soon after I was having dinner with John Lennon, who was just one of a handful of
60 people who had experienced that sort of adulation. And he talked about how he became an ordinary guy, a family man, a father, and stopped being a living legend."

65 "I owe quite a lot to that conversation – it's the main reason I'm here today and have never felt better."

When David retired almost ten years ago there was no great announcement –
70 he just disappeared. Suddenly there were no more records and, surprisingly for a man who had only months ago been so incredibly popular, no one seemed to care. Then came what David calls his
75 thawing out period "when I became human again."

He spent a considerable amount of time touring the world, seeing all the things he had missed when he'd been
80 surrounded by security men. He took care to disguise himself – wearing glasses, tucking his hair into a cap, and dressing untidily. It worked because for much of the time he travelled
85 unrecognised.

He didn't listen to the radio, he didn't buy one record, he avoided any club or bar where there might be any sort of music being played. He ignored his
90 guitar and he didn't sing a note.

"Looking back to those early days is like looking back to another life, as though I was someone else. It's as if I was an actor throwing an enormous party for
95 all those people. I was just lucky that I didn't choose drugs as a way out from those problems, otherwise I could easily have been on the casualty list like so many of my friends."

by Simon Kinnersley in Sunday Magazine

4 Find words or phrases in the text (lines 1–64 only) which mean the same as:

a great success (paragraph 2) ....
b uncontrollable with wild excitement (3) ....
c make a deep continuous sound (3) ....
d thrown down carelessly (4) ....
e awful place (5) ....
f it became clear to me (5) ....
g thought over (5) ....
h small group (6) ....
i enormous admiration (6) ....

Now choose the correct answer for the following questions:

1 His last performance was a disaster because

a the crowd was so noisy that no one could hear him.

b the critics didn't like his singing.

c the audience got dangerously out of control.

d he collapsed and had to be carried off.

2 He was unhappy with his life because

a he wasn't earning much money.

b he was treated badly by his employers.

c he wasn't enjoying his success.

d he was given poor accommodation.

3 John Lennon helped him by

a explaining the problems of being a pop star.

b allowing him to stay at his house for a while.

c giving him professional advice on his singing.

d describing how he had acted in a similar situation.

4 After his retirement, he dressed untidily because

a that was how he felt most comfortable.

b he didn't want anyone to know who he was.

c it was more practical to travel like that.

d he wanted people to think that he was poor.

5 Nowadays he feels

a grateful that he didn't have more serious problems.

b angry that he wasted so much money.

c sad that he gave up such a successful career.

d surprised that he has lost touch with his friends.

Discussion points

● David Cassidy says he was having no fun at all as a super star. What are the things which a pop singer, actor or actress has to give up when they become really famous?

● What do you think the end of the story was? Did David Cassidy continue to live a quiet life out of the public eye, or did he begin to miss the life he had led and try to make a comeback?

STUDY BOX 2

Phrasal verb **Take.**   You can't **take** it **in**, can you? *(Text 1)*

take after – resemble.   He **takes after** his father as far as his interest in sport is concerned.

take in – understand, absorb.   When I heard the news, I didn't **take** it **in** at first.
  – deceive.   Don't think you'll **take** me **in** with your stories!

take off – remove.   You look so hot – why don't you **take** your pullover **off**?
  – leave the ground.   The plane **took off** half an hour late.

take on – accept.   You mustn't **take on** more work than you can manage.

take over – assume control of.   While the Principal is away the Vice-Principal will **take over** his duties.

take to – develop a liking for.   I really **took to** Spanish food while I was in Spain.

take up – adopt as a pastime.   I feel much fitter since I've **taken up** jogging.
  – occupy space/time.   We'll have to sell the piano. It **takes up** too much room.

Footnote   Everything changed for a second time when David turned on his car radio a couple of years ago and heard a record by The Police. 'It was so exciting, it made me feel that I was 16 again. After years of being without music, I was suddenly in love with it again, I suppose I'd also become bored . . .'

As a result, David is now doing what he would have thought impossible only a couple of years ago – making a comeback as a pop singer. 'Some of my friends have said that I'm mad to get into it all over again for a second time. They tell me that I'm playing with fire and that the same thing could happen a second time – that I could have spent all that time and yet find myself back where I started.'

Frankly, this seems unlikely. After all, there's a whole bunch of new names now – and he's been away long enough to let those memories fade completely. Significantly, throughout our meeting at the Savoy Hotel in London, no one asked for his autograph.

▶ Focus on grammar 3 · Review of tenses

1 Put the verbs in brackets into a suitable tense.

   a Don't worry, I (give) Mr Brown your message as soon as he (come) in.

   b He (run) to the bus stop but when he (get) there, the bus (already/go).

   c Of course I trust you! Look, I (not/offer) to lend you the money if I (think) you (not/pay) me back.

   d Oh no! You (break) my best plate. Now you (have to) buy me a new one.

   e What time (this train/get) to Edinburgh?

   f It (say) in today's paper that a number of valuable paintings (steal) from the Tate Gallery.

   g I (tell) my boss yesterday that I (want) to give in my notice because I (find) a better job.

   h If you (not/stop) making that awful noise, I (call) the police.

   i We (go) to America this year for our holiday. We think it (be) a complete change because we (usually/tour) in Europe.

   j I hope you (not/wait) too long. I'm afraid the lift (break down) and I (must) walk down the stairs from the 24th floor!

   k While we (wait) to take off at Hong Kong airport, the pilot (announce) that we (fly) through a thunderstorm.

   l I (work) hard on my novel all day and when this page (finish), I (write) three whole chapters.

   m We (buy) tickets for the film in advance, but as the cinema is half empty, we (not/need/do) so.

   n It was extraordinary! In fact, if I (not/see) it with my own eyes, I (never/believe) it.

   o I'd rather you (not/smoke) if you (not mind). Cigarette smoke (always/make) me feel ill.

2 In the following conversation, put the verbs in brackets into a suitable tense (active or passive).

   A Hello Jim. I (not/see) you for ages! What (you/do)?

   B I (work) abroad, actually. I (have) a 6 month contract with the British Council to teach English in China. I only (get) back two days ago.

   A China! How marvellous. Where (you/live)?

   B Well, I (spend) four months in Beijing, and then I (go) to Shanghai and Xian.

   A And (you/manage) to see the Great Wall?

   B Oh yes, and I (climb) it too! I also (see) the Forbidden City, or the Palace Museum as it (call) nowadays. That's fantastic. And lots more.

   A And (you/take) many photographs?

   B Hundreds! Unfortunately some of them (not/come) out too well because the camera I (use) (not/have) a flash. I really wish I (take) better equipment.

   A Well, I hope you (show) them to me one day soon. If I (know) you (go) to China, I (ask) you to bring me some silk.

B I (invite) to go at very short notice, in fact. I'm afraid I (not/have) time to let anyone know.

A Don't worry, I (only/joke)! Look, what (you/do) on Saturday evening?

B This Saturday? My parents (come) in the afternoon but they (leave) by 6 o'clock.

A Well, why (you/not/come) to supper in the evening? Then you (be able to) show me your photographs and tell me all about your trip.

B Thank you, I'd like to. I (even/bring) a bottle of Chinese wine with me to go with the meal!

3 Put the verbs in brackets into a suitable tense (active or passive) or into an infinitive or -ing form.

After I (leave) college, I (find) it very difficult (get) a job. I (must/write) fifty or sixty letters of application but all the replies (say) the same thing: 'We are sorry (tell) you that the post you (apply) for (now/fill).' I only (have) one interview and they (tell) me that there (be) over 200 applications. Needless to say, I (not/get) the job!

In the end I (decide;/take) a part-time job as a waitress just (earn) enough money (pay) the rent. Then, while I (serve) meals one day, I overheard two customers (talk). One (explain) that his secretary (leave) at very short notice and that he (not/know) what (do). I (stop; serve) at once and (ask) the man if he (consider) me for the job because I (have) all the necessary qualifications. He (must/be) very surprised but he (agree/interview) me the next day. To cut a long story short, I (give) the job and I (work) as a secretary for a year now. I expect I (still/serve) meals in a cafe, if I (not/have) the courage to interrupt that conversation!

▶ Focus on listening 2 · A new direction

You are going to hear an interview with a man who left the Merchant Navy and became a nurse. Listen to the interview and answer the questions which follow.

For questions 1–10, tick (√) whether you think the statements are true or false.

	True	False
1 John decided to go into nursing while he was a patient in hospital.		
2 There was no job he could do when he left the Merchant Navy.		
3 You need certain qualifications before you can train to be a nurse.		
4 He has worked in several hospitals during his career.		
5 He did more than three years' training.		
6 He joined a special course for male nurses.		
7 The working hours for nurses have decreased slightly since John started.		
8 He earned far less as a trainee nurse than he had before.		
9 Most of the other students on his course were younger than him.		
10 While he was training, he had to live in the nurses' home.		

For questions 11–13 put a tick (√) next to the correct answer *a, b, c* or *d.*

11 John's training course reminded him of his life in the Merchant Navy because in both

  a there was very strict discipline.
  b there were frequent changes of scene.
  c there was a lot of travelling involved.
  d there was a lot of hard work and not much money.

12 He decided to become a nurse teacher because

  a he was bored with working on the wards.
  b he wanted to earn more money.
  c he wanted to develop his career.
  d he had always been interested in teaching.

13 Looking back on his life, John feels that

   a he should have left the Merchant Navy sooner.

   b he should have stayed on at school longer.

   c he regrets the bad things that happened.

   d he wouldn't want to change anything.

▶ Focus on writing 2 · Exam practice   *Writing Bank: pages 220, 229, 225*

1 Letter

> You had arranged to spend a holiday with an English friend and you know he/she has made a lot of preparations for your visit. Very recently, however, you have been offered an extremely good job and you have decided to accept even though this will mean your missing your holiday. Write to your friend and explain the situation.
> (120–180 words)

Notes   *a* Look back at the notes on this type of writing in Unit 2A (page 29).

        b Make a plan of your paragraphs before you start. Include a short introduction, separate paragraphs to explain the situation and apologise, to give details of your new job, to suggest another time when you can see each other. Finish with a short closing sentence.

Useful language

> **Result Links**
>
> **so . . .**
>
> **as a result . . .**
>
> **This means . . .**

2 Narrative

> Tell the story of either an event which marked a turning point in your life or an event which was a turning point in history.
> (120–180 words)

Notes   *a* Make a plan of your paragraphs before you start.

        b Look back at the notes on this kind of writing in Unit 4B (page 147) and at the Language for Expressing Time in the same unit (page 137).

        c You are likely to need to use the past simple and past continuous tenses and the past perfect. Check these in Units 2A and 1B if necessary.

3 Description

> Write a description of a person who has had an important influence on your life.
> (120–180 words)

Notes   *a* This question calls for a description of a person's character and relationship with you, rather than a detailed physical description. If you would like to include some information about appearance, however, look at the Functions Bank page 214.

        b Make a plan of paragraphs before you start.

▶Exam practice A · Vocabulary

Choose the word or phrase which best completes each sentence.

1 We've arranged .... our furniture to be sent by sea.

   a that   *b* from   *c* with   *d* for

2 I don't know how he'll .... to the news when you tell him.

   a act   *b* answer   *c* react   *d* behave

3 The trouble is that we're just not used .... work so hard.

   a to have to   *b* have to   *c* to having to   *d* having to

4 There are only two things you can do: .... you save up the money or you borrow it.

   a if   *b* or   *c* either   *d* whether

5 Make sure you .... that present carefully or it may get damaged in the post.

   a enclose   *b* close   *c* fold   *d* wrap

6 He'd really like to see the match on Saturday but he just can't .... a ticket.

   a pay   *b* afford   *c* spend   *d* spare

7 We were given a lot of information at the beginning of the course but I'm afraid I didn't .... very well.

   a take it up   *b* take it in   *c* take it on   *d* take it over

8 The third attempt to reach the top of the mountain ended .... failure.

   a in   *b* by   *c* to   *d* up

9 Despite what the critics said about the play, the .... in the theatre last night seemed to enjoy it.

   a viewers   *b* spectators   *c* audience   *d* sightseers

10 A very important battle took .... here in the 14th century.

   a part   *b* charge   *c* hold   *d* place

11 If it ...., I'd have gone for a walk.

   a didn't rain   *b* wouldn't have rained   *c* hadn't rained   *d* wasn't raining

12 The chairman usually says a few words to .... up before the meeting finishes.

   a sum   *b* close   *c* end   *d* follow

13 Oh dear, I don't feel very well. I think ....

   a I'll faint.   *b* I'm going to faint.   *c* I'm fainting.   *d* I've fainted.

14 I'm relying on you and I hope you won't let me ....

   a off   *b* out   *c* down   *d* in

15 I'd rather you .... anything about this to anyone, please.

   a don't say   *b* didn't say   *c* won't say   *d* hadn't said

16 A large number of people have stopped smoking .... recent years.

   a in   *b* for   *c* since   *d* from

17 Would you .... closing the door on your way out?

   a please   *b* kindly   *c* care   *d* mind

18 The first thing I learnt as a waitress was how to .... the table for dinner.

   a lay   *b* set up   *c* spread   *d* put out

19 The examiner smiled at me so .... that I didn't feel quite so nervous.

   a friendly   *b* kindly   *c* lovely   *d* well

20 As far as .... there's only one solution to the problem.

   a I think   *b* I see   *c* I'm sure   *d* I'm concerned

21 Could you .... me to post this letter? I'm sure to forget otherwise.

   a advise   *b* remind   *c* warn   *d* remember

22 His political views are completely opposite .... mine.

   a from   *b* to   *c* of   *d* than

23 I've .... trying to lose weight because it never seems to work.

   a given in   *b* given out   *c* given up   *d* given back

24 Nobody's accusing you .... the watch.

   a from stealing   *b* with stealing   *c* to steal   *d* of stealing

25 I'd like to congratulate you .... your recent engagement.

   a on   *b* for   *c* about   *d* of

Answer to puzzle on page 142
Martha is an orang-utan.

Answers to puzzle on page 143

1 A pig going round the corner of a barn.
2 A bear climbing a tree. (The top 'paw' is an ear.)
3 A snake going upstairs.
4 A Mexican riding a bicycle.
5 A giraffe going past a window.
6 A Boy Scout frying an egg.

redundancy: A worker becomes redundant when he or she is no longer needed by a firm.
golden handshake: A large amount of money given to somebody when they leave a firm, when they retire or when they are made redundant.

Unit 6B Communication activity (page 167)

Answers

1 *c* Built in about 1620 by a Dutchman. (radio – 1901; aeroplane – 1903)
2 *a* Produced almost 2000 years before the great French and English works.
3 *b* The Russian, Yuri Gagarin, made a complete circuit of the Earth in Vostok 1 before landing safely. (automatic digital computer – 1944; robot – 1928)
4 *b* Paper, made from wood ash and cloth pulp, was one of the great technological achievements of the Han Dynasty.
5 *a* The two Montgolfier brothers built and flew their balloon 8 km across Paris. (1903 was the year of the first aeroplane flight.)
6 *b* 1869. (Corinth – 1893; Panama – 1914)
7 *c* John Logie Baird.
8 *c* (the wheel – 4000 BC in Mesopotamia; the watch – 1502 in Germany)
9 *b*
10 *b* A Latin bible produced by Johannes Gutenberg in Mainz.

Exam practice B

▶ Use of English · Units 1A/1B

1a Fill each of the numbered blanks in the following passage.
Use only **one** word in each space.

When you take out travel insurance, you usually just accept the little form
.............(1) the clerk pushes ....(2) the counter. You fill it all ....(3),
make out your cheque and, ...(4) return, you receive a thin sheet of paper with
very small print. But nobody ever expects that anything could really ....(5)
wrong. It always ....(6) to someone else. Well, my family is ....(7)
someone else!

   I ....(8) never forget the 'phone call from my daughter who was
.............(9) holiday abroad. It began: "Mummy, something terrible ....(10)
happened to me today." Her hotel room ....(11) been burgled and all her
luggage stolen. Fortunately, she was insured and she reported the matter
.............(12) the police at the time. The insurance company, however, wanted not
only the police report, ...(13) also receipts for everything stolen
.............(14) they would recognise her claim. ....(15) nearly all her clothes
were from a chain store, we had no receipts. Other items stolen had ....(16)
gifts – a camera from her grandparents two years ....(17), a necklace from her
boyfriend. It ....(18) us nearly three months of writing letters ....(19)
get any offer from the company at all.

   A fight like this teaches you one very important lesson – before you take out
insurance, first ....(20) the small print!

From an article by Mela Brown in The Sunday Times

1b Fill each of the numbered blanks in the following passage.
Use only **one** word in each space.

The traditional reason ....(1) exploration – to boldly go where no man has gone
.............(2) – has become a little ....(3) of date now. Corners of the world
.............(4) have not been explored are rare indeed. They do ....(5),
however, and – from polar ....(6) to tropical rainforest, from 8,000 m.
.............(7) in the Himalayas to submarine caves in the Caribbean – the attempts to
discover ....(8) continue.

   The increasing interest ....(9) exploration is reflected in the growth of
companies which specialise ....(10) holiday-length expeditions to the foothills of
the Himalayas, Africa and South America. Such tours ....(11) unlikely to involve

real danger but they offer sufficient challenge to allow the traveller some of
............(12) achievement of full-scale exploration.

The line dividing exploration ....(13) vacation is difficult to draw now.
Expeditions may range ....(14) packaged adventures along well-known routes
to a demanding assault on some remote mountain face ....(15) survival relies
............(16) good training, technical skill, judgement and good luck. As one climbing
enthusiast put it: "Some people ....(17) get full satisfaction from simply
admiring a mountain ....(18) a safe distance. ....(19) might only be
satisfied by actually ....(20) the mountain".

From 'Supplies and demands of the wild' by Ronald Faux in The Times

2 Finish each of the following sentences in such a way that it means exactly the same as
the sentence printed before it.

Example: I haven't enjoyed myself so much for years.

Answer: It's years ...*since I've enjoyed myself so much*...........................

a He's an enthusiastic football player.
He's very keen ...

b It's going to cost more to travel by coach next year.
The cost ...

c We all enjoyed the walk even though it rained heavily.
In spite ...

d A shop near here used to sell fresh fish. It's closed down now.
There used to be ...

e The train left at 6 o'clock and we arrived just after that.
When we ...

f Remember to take some extra money with you. It could be useful.
It's worth ...

g The remark was so unexpected that she didn't know what to say.
It was such ...

h That woman's dog bit the postman the other day.
That's the woman ...

i It wasn't easy to persuade her to come.
There was some difficulty ...

j You use a saw to cut wood.
A saw is a ...

3 Complete the following sentences with one appropriate word for a form of travel.

Example: The train .....*journey*... from London to Glasgow lasts five hours.

Note: Do not use 'journey' again.

a The package holiday in Mexico included a number of optional .... to ancient
Aztec sites.

b We took a Mediterranean .... for our holiday last summer and I must say that the ship was very luxurious!

c Our .... was delayed because of fog and the airline provided all the passengers with lunch.

d If you're going to South America by sea, make sure you take enough to read on the

....

e Air .... doesn't appeal to me because I prefer to see the countries on the way.

4 Fill each of the blanks with a word formed from the word given in capital letters.

Example: They had a ...*disagreement*.... about politics and   **AGREE**
now they hardly speak to each other.

a I'm afraid I have a .... to make. The watch I bought here   **COMPLAIN**
keeps stopping.

b Would you mind explaining your .... from work yesterday?   **ABSENT**

c I wrote to the company to ask about the delay in delivery, but I didn't   **RESPOND**
receive any ....

d It says on the packet that two tablets will bring .... from pain   **RELIEVE**
in minutes.

e He's acting as the Prime Minister's .... at the State Funeral.   **REPRESENT**

f The shop will only make exchanges if you've got a .... for the   **RECEIVE**
goods bought.

g I don't know why you're so afraid of spiders. They're completely   **HARM**
....

h The excitement of the competition was .... by the presence   **HIGH**
of TV cameras.

i I've given the problem a lot of thought and I think I may have found a   **SOLVE**
....

j They decided to surprise their father by going to the port to meet   **EMBARK**
him as he .... from his ship.

5 Make all the changes necessary to produce, from the following eight sets of words and phrases, eight sentences which together make a complete letter. Note carefully from the example what kind of alterations need to be made.

Example: I/wonder/why you/not/reply/last letter.

Answer: I was wondering why you had not replied to my last letter.

Dear Sir,

I write/complain/holiday/arrange/your company.

a ...

My wife and I book/two-week cruise/the 'Orient Maiden'/July this year.

b . . .

The brochure describe it/holiday/lifetime/we decide/spend all our savings/it.

c . . .

We expect/luxury ship/first class service but/cabins/dirty/waiters/rude.

d . . .

The ship suppose/call/Naples and Athens but/captain say/impossible because/bad weather.

e . . .

There be nothing at all/do/ship except/watch/old films/cinema.

f . . .

We/seriously dissatisfied/cruise/want/money back.

g . . .

If not/hear from you/next seven days/contact/solicitor.

h . . .

Yours faithfully,
Harold Smithson

▶ Use of English · Units 2A/2B

1a Fill each of the numbered blanks in the following passage.
Use only **one** word in each space.

When Michelle was . . . . (1) school her friends and teachers would never
. . . . (2) guessed how she'd turn out. . . . . (3) only daughter of a postman,
she . . . . (4) up in a small village near Lyons in France. When she won a place
. . . . (5) Bordeaux university to . . . . (6) Humanities, her parents were
delighted that she was . . . . (7) to have the educational opportunities they had
. . . . (8). They hoped she . . . . (9) be a school teacher. . . . . (10)
things didn't happen quite as they . . . . (11) wished. When she finished her
studies, Michelle . . . . (12) her driving test, bought an old car and . . . . (13)
fascinated with engines. She decided to . . . . (14) a course in car maintenance
which . . . . (15) thirteen weeks. . . . . (16) the end of the course, she
. . . . (17) told that of all the students she had . . . . (18) the most progress.
She now works in a local garage . . . . (19) a mechanic and, in a few years, would
like to open a garage of her . . . . (20).

From 'Equal at Work?' by Anna Coote

1b Fill each of the numbered blanks in the following passage.
Use only **one** word in each space.

(Julia lives with her children and her old mother and father in a village in Lesotho, a
mountainous country in southern Africa. Her husband works in the mines of South
Africa.)

The land around their village is rocky and the soil is poor. Julia and her husband worked
hard in their fields but they could not . . . . (1) enough food to . . . . (2) their
family or buy the things . . . . (3) needed. Julia's husband was forced to look

............(4) work in South Africa. There was no work for him in Lesotho because there were so ....(5) factories and businesses. Many families in Lesotho are in the same ....(6). ....(7) a man has a lot of land or animals, he has ....(8) choice but to leave his wife and children and get a job ....(9) from home.

Julia's husband ....(10) to get home and see his family about once a year but the children are ....(11) up fast and they hardly ....(12) their father. Their mother has to ....(13) all the family decisions. She is the ....(14) who keeps them ....(15) order, makes sure they do not go hungry and ....(16) them when they are sick or unhappy. Julia's parents help ....(17) looking after the youngest children and ....(18) some of the housework but they are ....(19) weak to work in the fields now. So Julia has to plough, sow, weed and harvest the ....(20) by herself, while she waits anxiously for the next envelope containing money from her husband.

From 'Family Life' by Olivia Bennett

2 Finish each of the following sentences in such a way that it means exactly the same as the sentence printed before it.

Example: As far as I'm concerned, Saturday would be the best day.
Answer: From my point of view, Saturday would be the best day.

a The water was so cold that I couldn't swim in it.
The water was too...

b I like travelling by train more than going by air.
I'd rather...

c 'He went home five minutes ago and took his papers with him,' his secretary said.
His secretary told me...

d If you work carefully, you won't make so many mistakes.
The...

e No-one in the world drives as badly as you do!
You're...

f 'Don't touch the plate — it's hot,' the waiter said.
The waiter warned...

g There is room for five passengers in our car.
Our car is big...

h He said he was sorry that he had kept me waiting.
He apologised...

i It's often quicker by underground than by bus.
The bus often takes...

3 Complete the following sentences with an expression formed from the word *put*.
Example Could you ....put out.... your cigarette, Madam? We're about to land.

a As there's a train strike, we'll just have to .... the meeting .... until next week.

b Hold the line, please, I'm trying to .... you .... to the number you want.

c We offered to .... him .... for the night but he'd already arranged to stay at a hotel.

d He's .... quite a bit of weight since I saw him. In fact, he looks quite fat!

e There was such a horrible smell in the dining room that it .... me .... eating there.

4 Fill each of the blanks with a word formed from the word given in capital letters.

Example They finally reached ..*agreement*.. on the price of the house.　　　　**AGREE**

a I have a very good working .... with my boss.　　　　**RELATION**

b He asked what my .... salary was.　　　　**MONTH**

c I wish you wouldn't ask me .... questions.　　　　**END**

d The only .... she'd ever committed was for parking.　　　　**OFFEND**

e I asked the .... if she could help me find a book.　　　　**LIBRARY**

f They went upstairs so .... that they woke the baby.　　　　**NOISE**

g I don't undertand the .... between the two words.　　　　**DISTINGUISH**

h The .... men began loading our furniture into the van.　　　　**REMOVE**

i The postal service is rather .... round here so I'm afraid my letter may take ages to reach you.　　　　**RELY**

j I have found all the staff extremely .... and I'd be grateful if you would thank them for me.　　　　**HELP**

5 Make all the changes and additions necessary to produce, from the following sets of words and phrases, sentences which together make a complete letter. Note carefully from the example what kind of alterations need to be made.

Example: I/wonder/why you/not/reply/last letter.

Answer: I was wondering why you hadn't replied to my last letter.

Dear Mrs Thomas,

a I write/tell/rather worried/your son Peter/pupil/my class.

b Peter/be absent/school/several occasions/last three weeks.

c He/not give/reason/his absence and /refuse/apologise.

d He/intelligent boy and/always be/near top of class/up till now.

e Unfortunately/work/now begin/suffer and/marks/very poor.

f Unless/big improvement/attendance and work/he/unlikely/pass/exams.

g I think/good idea/if/meet/discuss/problem.

h I/grateful/if/telephone me/school/arrange/appointment/see me.

Yours sincerely,

Mary Welsh

▶ Use of English · Units 3A/3B

1*a* Fill each of the numbered blanks in the following passage.
Use only **one** word in each space.

I was born and brought …………(1) just outside Bristol and …………(2) the ages
of seven and fourteen, I spent far more of my waking hours on the ice rink
…………(3) I did at home.

When I was six, we went to Bournemouth on holiday and saw an ice show and
…………(4) then on I was hooked. …………(5) was on that same holiday that we
…………(6) a man who …………(7) us that an ice rink was …………(8) built in
Bristol. As soon …………(9) it was opened, I …………(10) skating lessons and I
never looked back.

Within a couple of years, I was skating …………(11) three hours before school,
…………(12) lunchtime and then …………(13) the evening again. …………(14)
the time I was nine, I was doing this at …………(15) three or four times a week.

Mum and Dad used to …………(16) it in turns to …………(17) me up at 5am
with a cup of tea. Fortunately I wasn't the …………(18) one in the family needing all
this attention because I had two older brothers …………(19) were already doing
their own thing. One was a musician and …………(20) were sportsmen.

From an article by Robin Cousins in The Sunday Express Magazine

1*b* Fill each of the numbered blanks in the following passage.
Use only **one** word in each space.

Most people can …………(1) minor repairs in the home – such …………(2)
mending a fuse or stitching …………(3) a button. Most car owners know how to
change a …………(4) if they have a puncture.

This booklet will help you to cope …………(5) minor illnesses at home. Helping
yourself will help the doctor …………(6) the same time. It explains simple
treatments …………(7) minor illnesses and accidents which …………(8) likely to
occur …………(9) time to time. In some cases there is …………(10) a doctor can
do …………(11) the patient cannot do just as …………(12).

This booklet will help you to know when you can treat yourself and ....(13) the doctor valuable time to help patients who are more ....(14) ill, and when you really need to ....(15) the doctor.

We hope you will find the booklet useful. ....(16) the back there is a list of simple medicines which ....(17) will be helpful to have ....(18) hand.

And remember, whenever you are really anxious or ill, advice can be ....(19) over the telephone. ....(20) you have to do is ring the practice number.

From 'Minor Illnesses', a Health Education Council booklet

2 Finish each of the following sentences in such a way that it means exactly the same as the sentence printed before it.

Example: We couldn't sleep because of the noise from the discotheque.
Answer: The noise from the discotheque *prevented us from sleeping*.

a She's never been to a circus before.
It's ...

b 'How long will the journey take?' he asked the guard.
He asked the guard how ...

c The accident made it impossible for him to work.
Since the accident he ...

d They expected twenty guests but forty arrived!
There were twice ...

e Both of my brothers are bachelors.
Neither ...

f That cat's owner feeds it on the finest salmon.
That's the cat ...

g He suggested that we should go to the theatre.
He said 'How ...

h When did you break your arm?
How long ...

i People gave a lot of money to the Earthquake Disaster Fund.
A great ...

3 Fill each blank with a phrase made from the word *get*.

Example: If you let me know what time you'll be ...*getting up*........., I'll have breakfast ready.

a She didn't like her mother-in-law very much at first, but now they
.... each other very well.

b I don't know why I feel so depressed. Perhaps it's just this wet weather which is
.... me ....

c I meant to write to you but I was so busy that I just didn't .... it.

d I don't know how she manages to .... on such a small salary.

e Don't lend Tim anything because you'll never .... it .... !

f The children hate helping with the washing up and they'll do anything to

.... it.

4 In each of the following sentences there is a blank with a word in red just before it. Fill each blank with a word that combines with the one given, making a new word that fits the sentence.

Example: Don't just stand there on the door ...., come in and meet everyone!

Answer: doorstep.

a He was leaning so far over the ship's rail that I thought he was going to fall

over.............

b We've only just moved into this neighbour............. and we don't know many people yet.

c While I was waiting at the airport, I heard an announcement over the loud............. saying that I should go to the Information Desk.

d He's determined to ask his land............. to reduce the rent he pays for his bed-sitter.

e Did you hear that broad............. from the Vienna Opera on the radio last night?

f This letter says the head............. are in Brussels so it must be a Belgian company.

g Go into that shop and ask the shop............. if you can use his telephone to call the police.

h I can see it's you in the front of the picture, but who's that in the back ....?

i The weather forecaster said the out............. for the rest of the week is for more snow.

j If he doesn't look where he's going, he'll fall head............. into a ditch!

5 Alan is talking to his elder brother. Complete the dialogue.

Alan: Will you lend me your camera for the weekend, John?

a John: ....

Alan: Because I'm going camping in Wales with some friends and I want to try to photograph some wild birds.

b John: ....

Alan: Since I saw a programme about birdwatching on television, if you must know. But what about the camera?

c John: ....

Alan: Yes, of course I do. There's no need to explain anything at all.

d John: ....

Alan: Yes, yes, I promise. You needn't worry at all. You'll let me have it then?

e John: ....

Alan: Thanks John! Actually I've already bought three rolls!

▶ Use of English · Units 4A/4B

1*a* Fill each of the numbered blanks in the following passage.
Use only **one** word in each space.

Contrary ....(1) popular belief, most burglaries take ....(2) during the
day. The quick dash you ....(3) to the shops before they close or to
.............(4) the children from school are ideal opportunities. Burglars know about
.............(5) things and what time they are likely to ....(6). The garage door
which you ....(7) open because you didn't have time to shut it before you
.............(8) away is as good as an invitation card.

Your best protection is to make ....(9) that when the burglar does come to
your house, he decides it is not ....(10) the risk of breaking ....(11).
Your precautions have to be good enough to put him ....(12).

For most people the first ....(13) to better security is to frighten
themselves ....(14) really believing that their house could ....(15)
burgled. And that, if it happened, ...(16) be pretty unpleasant. Anyone who
.............(17) suffered the experience can tell you that the shock of ....(18)
your familiar home vandalised is at ....(19) as painful as the actual financial
.............(20) you suffer. *From 'Safe as Houses – if the door's locked' by Richard Sleight in The Guardian*

1*b* Fill each of the numbered blanks in the following passage.
Use only **one** word in each space.

Larry Walters intended to ....(1) only a short trip when he took off from Long
Beach, California, ...(2) in a garden chair which was attached ....(3)
45 balloons filled ....(4) helium. Instead, the ropes ....(5) secured his
chair to the ground broke and he shot up to 16,000 feet. ....(6) startled airline
pilots eyed the strange flying machine, Larry began to ....(7) a little chilly. He
.............(8) at several of the balloons with an airgun he ....(9) taken with
him and began to descend. When the balloon ropes became entangled in a power line,
Larry was finally ....(10) to return to ....(11) after more than an hour.

Walters ....(12) rescued, uninjured, as his chair hung from the power lines.
"The part that was frightening was the last 300 feet, with the rooftops coming up so
fast", he ....(13) afterwards. "I was praying that I wouldn't ....(14) one
of those power lines and ....(15) killed. I fulfilled my dream but I wouldn't do

this again ....(16) anything."

    The U.S. Federal Aviation Administration is determined to see that he does not. An inspector said "We know that he ....(17) some part of the law. As ....(18) as we decide which part it is, some charge ....(19) be filed. If he ....(20) a pilot's licence, we'd suspend that, but he hasn't."

2 Finish each of the following sentences in such a way that it means exactly the same as the sentence printed before it.

Example: Someone stole all her belongings while she was on holiday.
Answer: She *had all her belongings stolen while she was on holiday.*

a We must get to the airport by 3 o'clock.
We've . . .

b It's possible that the robber hid his gun in a litter bin.
The robber . . .

c Don't cry. That won't help at all.
It's no . . .

d It's not necessary for you to make an appointment.
You . . .

e I threw away the receipt and so I couldn't get my money back.
Having . . .

f I only remembered it was my birthday when I got your card!
It wasn't until . . .

g The road ran between steep hills.
There were . . .

h There's a sale starting on Saturday. I'll look for a new coat then.
I'll look for a new coat as soon as . . .

i He folded the letter in order to get it through the letter box.
He folded the letter so . . .

3 Complete the following sentences with an expression formed from the word *break*.

Example: We couldn't afford to buy coal, so we had to break ....UP...... two old chairs to make firewood.

a Seven criminals broke .... of prison yesterday.

b After that awful argument, we decided to break .... our engagement.

c When she heard that her husband had been kidnapped, she broke .... in tears.

d When I opened the front door and saw the mess in the hall, I knew that someone had broken .... while I was out.

e I just hope my car doesn't break .... on the way to the airport.

f She's feeling a bit depressed because she's broken .... with her boyfriend.

g It really annoys me, the way he keeps trying to break .... while I'm having a conversation.

4 Complete the following sentences with an expression formed from the word *look*.

Example: Why are you ...*looking at*.... me so strangely? Is something the matter?

a .... ! There's a big hole in the road and you're driving straight towards it.

b Some important papers disappeared from the office last month and now the police are .... the matter.

c Can I use the telephone directory for a moment? I want to .... a number.

d Could you possibly .... my two cats while I'm on holiday?

e The doctor said he would .... again on Monday to see how I was.

f He's always .... his father and tried to follow his example in every way.

g Have you seen my pen? I've been .... it everywhere.

h I .... the local newspaper quite carefully this morning but I didn't see any mention of the burglary.

5 Tony has had his car stolen and has gone to the police station.
Complete the dialogue.

Tony: I want to report a stolen car.

a Sergeant: ....

Tony: From the multi-storey car park on Broad Street.

b Sergeant: ....

Tony: At about midday. I heard the Town Hall clock strike twelve as I was locking the car doors.

c Sergeant: ....

Tony: It was a dark blue Marina estate with a white stripe along the side. The registration was OYH 142R.

d Sergeant: ....

Tony: Oh dear, I hadn't thought about that. Yes, I'm afraid there was a leather briefcase behind the driver's seat with a rather expensive camera in it and a calculator.

e Sergeant: ....

Tony: Yes, it was stupid of me, I know. But I was in a hurry and I completely forgot that they were there. I'll remember to be more careful next time. Anyway, thank you Sergeant. I hope you're able to trace the car and I certainly hope my briefcase is still inside when you find it!

▶ Use of English · Units 5A/5B

1*a* Fill each of the numbered blanks in the following passage.
Use only **one** word in each space.

............(1) 19th March 1967, ...(2) oil tanker 'Torrey Canyon' ran aground
on Seven Stones Reef, off the ....(3) of Cornwall, England. Days later, the
wreck was blown ....(4) in an airstrike by the Royal Air Force. ....(5)
that time the cargo of 50,000 tonnes of oil ....(6) spilled into the sea, making a
gigantic oil slick. The oil killed at ....(7) 25,000 birds and damaged hundreds of
beaches. ....(8) 1975, the 'Showa Maru' ran aground near Singapore.
............(9) salvage ships could reach her she had lost 3,000 tonnes of oil – and that
was only a small ....(10) of the oil she was ....(11)! The 'Showa Maru'
is not one of the world's largest tankers. What ....(12) happen if the 'Globtik
Tokyo' broke ....(13)? There are lots of other ways that small ....(14)
of oil ....(15) get into the sea – from the engines of pleasure boats, for
............(16).

The search ....(17) oil can make our surroundings ....(18) pleasant
in other ways too. Construction yards and oil rigs can ....(19) a beautiful view.
The fuel for cars is made ....(20) the oil in refineries and unfortunately
refineries are difficult to hide!

From 'The War on Pollution' by Mike Lyth

1*b* Fill each of the numbered blanks in the following passage.
Use only **one** word in each space.

Each minute that ticks by is costing you more ....(1) you think. Just staying
............(2) home, trying to save on the weekly budget costs something. For
example, there is the roof ....(3) your head. ....(4) £15,000 mortgage
works out at 35 pence every minute of the day.

............(5) the time you've read this far, your central heating bill will
............(6) gone up by another 25 pence – that's the cost per minute of
............(7) a typical 3-bedroomed house warm for eight hours a day ....(8)
the eight cold months of the year. Of course, you could switch it ....(9) and go

and warm ....(10) by someone else's fire, ...(11) go to the public
library, but you'll still ....(12) to eat. The average £40 weekly shopping bill for
a family ....(13) four is eaten away at the rate ....(14) 4 pence a
minute.

Home entertainment also adds up. Just watching television for an average of four
hours a day ....(15) you 5 pence a minute after you've paid ....(16) the
licence. And ....(17) you're watching television you can't be ....(18)
the repair work and maintenance. Hiring an emergency plumber when things
.............(19) wrong is one of the most expensive ....(20) of spending money
at 33.3 pence a minute.

From The Sunday Express magazine

2   Finish each of the following sentences in such a way that it means exactly the same as
    the sentence printed before it.

    Example: It would be a good idea to stay in bed today.

    Answer: You'd *better stay in bed today.*

    a The roof will collapse if no-one mends it.
       Unless . . .

    b Smoking is both expensive and harmful to the health.
       Smoking is not . . .

    c I'm very pleased that I'm going to have a holiday soon.
       I'm looking . . .

    d The wind blew several trees down in the night.
       Several trees . . .

    e He asked to use our phone.
       'I wonder . . .

    f The reason for the delay was a signal box failure.
       There was a delay as . . .

    g My advice to you is to take your dog to the vet.
       If I . . .

    h My mother would rather play cards than knit.
       My mother prefers . . .

    i Has someone mended your cooker?
       Have you . . .

3   Complete the following sentences with an expression formed from the word *go*.

    Example: How much longer does this programme ....*go.* ...*on*... for?

    a The security guard .... my bag very carefully before he let me in.

    b I don't feel very well. I hope I'm not .... flu.

    c She .... lots of competitions but she hardly ever wins anything.

    d It said on the news that a bomb had .... at the airport.

    e I don't think that brown jacket .... your blue trousers very well, do you?

4 The word in capital letters at the end of the following sentences can be used to form a word that fits suitably in the blank space. Fill each blank in this way. (All the answers come from texts in Unit 5A.)

Example: The factory is to increase its ...*production*... of cars next year. **PRODUCE**

a There was no label on the bottle so I didn't know what the .... **CONTAIN** were.

b He was .... from applying because of his age. **COURAGE**

c The society is worried about the .... of the world's rain **DESTROY** forests.

d The .... of X-rays in 1895 was an important development in **DISCOVER** the history of medicine.

e I'm afraid I .... broke one of your glasses. **ACCIDENT**

f We have a delivery service for the .... of our **CONVENIENT** customers.

g There's a .... of styles for you to choose from **VARIOUS**

h .... of typewriters have dropped since the invention of the word **SELL** processor.

i There has been an enormous .... in air travel in recent years. **GROW**

5 In the following conversation, the parts numbered (1) to (8) have been left out. Complete them suitably.

A Good afternoon. Can I help you?

B Yes, I'd like to buy a winter coat.

A Of course. Do you know what (1) .... ?

B No, I'm afraid I'm not very sure about English sizes.

A That's alright. What (2) .... ?

B Pure wool, if possible.

A That will (3) ....

B Oh, I don't mind about the price. I'm more interested in the quality.

A How (4) .... ?

B It looks very nice, but is it the right size?

A Why not (5) .... ?

B That's a good idea. I'll just slip my jacket off first.

A Does (6) .... ?

B No, it's a bit tight round the arms.

A Here's (7) ....

B Thank you. Oh, that's much better. I'll take it.

A Would (8) .... ?

B No thanks. I think I'll put it on straight away. It's so cold out at the moment.

▶ Use of English · Units 6A/6B

1*a* Fill each of the numbered blanks in the following passage.
Use only **one** word in each space.

Seventy years ago no one ....(1) ever heard the word 'robot'. It ....(2) first used by a Czechoslovakian writer, Karel Capek ....(3) the 1920's. He wrote a play about a scientist ....(4) invents machines which he ....(5) robots, from the Czech word *robota*, meaning 'slave-like work'. He gave them this ....(6) because they were ....(7) to do very boring work. ....(8) the end of the play, the robots kill their human owners and take ....(9) the world.

There are many robots ....(10) existence now, but they are quite different ....(11) the robots of science fiction films and books. ....(12) of being frightening, super-intelligent metal people, real robots are just machines controlled ....(13) a computer to work ....(14) a set way. They are generally deaf, ...(15), blind, have no ....(16) of taste, smell or touch, have difficulty in ....(17) around, and have no intelligence of their ....(18). However, advances ....(19) microchip technology mean that robots are beginning to be made ....(20) a TV camera 'eye' or a microphone 'ear' which give them very limited ability to see or hear.

From 'Robotics' by Tony Potter and Ivor Guild

1*b* Fill each of the numbered blanks in the following passage.
Use only **one** word in each space.

If you stopped the first two hundred people you ....(1) in the street and gave them each ....(2) quarter of a million pounds, ...(3) effect would it have ....(4) their lives? Winning the football pools is a kind of natural social experiment in ....(5) a number of people are selected more or ....(6) at random, and are suddenly ....(7) thousands of pounds. How do pools winners ....(8) their money, and what do their reactions tell ....(9) about their lives and the ....(10) of people they are? Are they happier ....(11) a result of winning? What does it feel ....(12) to be a pools winner? It is these questions that this book sets ....(13) to answer.

At the outset, our research involved following up 191 people who had ....(14) between £160,000 and half a million pounds. The winners were located ....(15) searching through telephone ....(16) and calling

............(17) their former neighbours and old friends to establish forwarding

addresses. They ....(18) then approached for an interview and asked a whole

............(19) of questions ....(20) their way of life and the effects of the win.

From 'The Pools Winners' by Stephen Smith and Peter Razzell

2 Finish each of the following sentences in such a way that it means exactly the same as the sentence printed before it.

Example: Despite her hard work she didn't earn much money.
Answer: Although she worked hard she didn't earn much money.

a The last time I played tennis was ten years ago.
I...

b Would you like me to give you a lift?
I'll...

c He doesn't want you to buy him anything expensive.
He'd rather...

d You didn't understand because you weren't listening!
If...

e I regret leaving home when I was 18.
If only...

f She doesn't sing as well as she used to.
She used to...

g I'll have lunch between 12 o'clock and 1.
By 1.15 I...

h I'll give you a door key because I may not be in when you get home.
In case...

i What are you doing in my room, may I ask?
Do you mind...

3 Complete the following sentences with an expression formed from the word *take*.

Example: We had a wonderful view of the harbour as the plane ..took off.......

a I think she .... her mother more than me. They're both very ambitious.

b I......... .... knitting as a hobby because there was absolutely nothing to do in the evenings.

c Are you sure that you haven't .... more work than you can manage?

d He's a terrible liar. Don't let him .... you .... with one of his stories.

e While I'm in hospital my wife will .... the running of the company.

4 Complete each of the following sentences with the correct form of either *do* or *make*.

Example: I ...*make*... several journeys to London each month.

a That was a stupid mistake to ....

b We all .... a test at the end of the course last week.

c A new discovery has been .... which may lead to a cure for the common cold.

d I'm not very good at cooking but I'll .... my best to help.

e He's .... me a lot of favours in the past so I can't very well refuse his request now.

f Some museums are thinking of .... a small charge for entrance.

g I was only allowed to watch television if I had .... my homework.

h He .... me such a good offer for my car that I had to accept it.

i .... sure that the road is clear before you pull out.

j This medicine seems to be .... me good.

5 Make all the changes and additions necessary to produce from the following sets of words and phrases, sentences which together make a complete letter.

Dear Mechtild,

   I/delighted/receive/letter/arrive/this morning.

a . . .

   It be/so long/we/last met/I be sure/you/forget me.

b . . .

   I/hardly believe/you/marry/six years and/two children.

c . . .

   If/any photographs/family/I love/see them.

d . . .

   I/still single/but good news/be/I/get married/February.

e . . .

   It/be/wonderful/you/come/wedding!

f . . .

   I/send/invitation/as soon as/know/date/place.

g . . .

   I/look forward/hear/you again.

h . . .

            Love Sue

Exam practice C

▶ Interview No 1

Section 1:
Picture
conversation

Look at the following photograph.

Now answer these questions.

1 The picture:
   a What can you see in the picture?
   b What is the two men's job?
   c Where do they seem to be working?
   d Would you be prepared to do their job? Why/Why not?
   e What do you think the two men might say if they were asked what they enjoyed about their job?

2 More general:
   f Have you ever been in a very high place? If so, how did you feel?
   g Do you think workers in a job like this should be paid extra because of the risk involved?
   h What other jobs can you think of where there is a similar risk?

Section 2:
Reading
passages

Read the following passages through carefully and be prepared to comment on them.

Consider, for example, whether you think the text was spoken or written, who the speaker/writer was, and what they are talking about.

Note

You may also like to read the passages aloud but this will not necessarily be required in the examination itself.

a 1 Be half-an-hour early. That's better than one minute late.
2 However you dress, look clean and smart. A shampoo in the morning is worth two 'O' Levels.
3 Try to relax and appear warm and pleasant. Remember the interviewer is choosing people he has to spend the next months or years of his life with.
4 Never answer questions just with Yes or No. What interviewers really want is to hear you talk.
5 Find out anything you can about the organisation – from friends, neighbours, local newspapers. Pieces of knowledge dropped into the conversation will impress proud employers more than anything.

b First, I had to sweep the floor, then I progressed to making the tea, then I became a mechanic. Like everyone of that age, I thought I knew it all. By the end of the first week I knew nothing. They cut me down to size, then built me up again. . . . The best possible start. I think your first job is vital. If nothing else, it shows you what you want to do – or don't want to do. It's the platform from which you make decisions . . .

Section 3:
Structured
activity

Work with one or two other students to discuss these questions.

1 Look at the **uniforms** shown below. What purpose do they serve, if any?

2 What other jobs can you think of which involve wearing a uniform? List as many as you can in 2–3 minutes.

3 Which of the uniforms you've listed would you be prepared to wear yourself? Which would you least like to have to wear?

4 Look at the uniforms below. Which do you think is most suitable for its job? Which is least suitable? How would you redesign it to be more suitable?

▶ Interview No 2

Section 1: Look at the following photograph, and answer the questions below.
Picture conversation

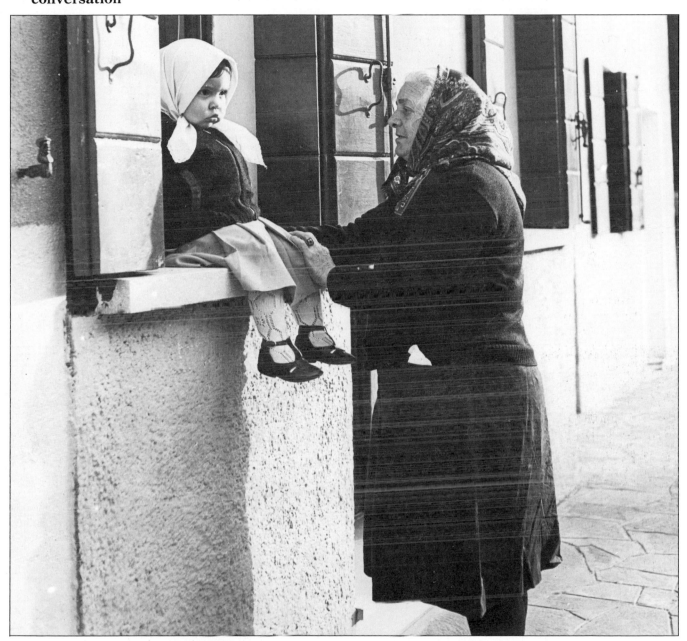

1 The picture:
   a What can you see in the picture?
   b What do you think the relationship between the two is?
   c What country might this be in?
   d Can you describe the appearance of the two people?
   e Do elderly women dress like this in your country?
   f Do they often live with their children's families?

2 More general:
   g Is it better for elderly people to be part of a family or to live independently?
   h What are the advantages and disadvantages for the family when an elderly relation lives with them?
   i Do children have a special relationship with their grandparents?

Section 2:
Reading
passages

Read each passage carefully and be prepared to comment on them.

Consider, for example, whether you think the text was written or spoken, and why; whether the passages have anything in common; who the speaker/writer may have been, etc.

Note

You may also like to read the passages aloud but this will not necessarily be required in the examination itself.

a My family is smaller than others in the village. My grandparents are dead and my father and eldest brother now live and work in England. They come home every two years. Only my mother, myself, my two sisters, my youngest brother and two uncles live at home now. This is why we only have one house. It's built of tin sheets. Many of the houses in the village are built of bamboo and thatch but they aren't as safe or as strong as ours in the heavy monsoon rains.

b **In the third of our Wednesday page series on the British family, Jane Morton looks at the life of the Chands from India.**

Karam Chand lived and worked in Britain alone for 10 years before his wife and five children could join him from the Punjab. Though he knew living in Wolverhampton would mean changes for them all, it never seriously occurred to him that they might have to revise their idea of family life.

Today, five years later, he is reluctantly accepting that the lifestyle he left behind in the simple but spacious family home in Jullundur does not work in a three-bedroom terrace cottage.

Section 3:
Structured
activity

1 Read the college report form below.

Leyhill College Report

Term	Summer
Name	
Course	Business Studies
Average Mark	42%
Test Result	30% (fail)
Attendance	90%

This student seems to have very little interest in the course, as the marks on the left show. Unless there is considerable improvement next year, there will be no hope of a pass in the final examination.

Course Tutor   L. G. Stanley

Date   11th July

2 Work in groups of three. Student A should turn to page 215. Student B should turn to page 218. Student C should turn to page 219.

▶ Interview No 3

Section 1: Look at the following photograph.
Picture conversation

Now answer these questions.

1 The picture:
  a What can you see in the picture?
  b What are the children doing, and why?
  c Can you describe the little girl in the middle?
  d How does she feel, and why?

2 More general:
  e Do you think it's good for children to go to classes like this?
  f What kind of exercise or physical training did you have as a child?
  g What exercise do you take nowadays?
  h Do you think fitness is important? Why?
  i Is it better to take exercise alone or with other people?
  j Are there any dangers in exercising too much?

Section 2: Reading passages

Read each passage carefully, and be prepared to comment on them.

Consider, for example, what they are each about and what they have in common. Do you think they were spoken or written, and why? Who might the speaker or writer have been?

Do you agree with what the two passages say? Do you have any experience of the subject?

a A certain amount of stress is an essential part of everyday life. It helps keep you on your toes and out of danger. Every time you cross a busy road or have an argument or watch an exciting programme on television, your stress level goes up for a while. But if anxiety or pressure of work continue for many months or years, your heart may suffer. But you can help yourself by learning how to relax and trying to take things easy.

b Have you ever found that colours affect your mood? Do you feel more cheerful when you're wearing that bright red shirt, for example? Well, now there's scientific evidence to prove that colours can cause us to have particular feelings. A Swiss psychologist has done research which shows that blue makes us feel peaceful and contented, while dark blue leads to a feeling of insecurity. Red makes us feel powerful and energetic, it seems, and yellow makes us confident and ambitious.

Note

You may also like to read the passages aloud, but this will not necessarily be required in the examination.

Section 3: Structured activity

Work with one or two other students.

The questions below come from an article on health in a Sunday newspaper.

Discuss whether the 'healthy' answer should be yes or no in each case, and give reasons for your opinions.

Discuss whether your own diet is healthy or not, and what you could do to improve it.

YOU ARE WHAT YOU EAT
(Put a circle round Yes or No to the following 11 questions.)

1 Do you have two or more helpings of protein foods every day (eg meat, fish, cheese or eggs)?
YES / NO

2 Do you drink at least half a pint of milk daily (including that in tea/coffee)?
YES / NO

3 Do you eat liver or kidney regularly (eg once a fortnight)?
YES / NO

4 Do you eat fatty fish (eg sardines, smoked mackerel, kippers) regularly (eg once a fortnight)?
YES / NO

5 Do you have, on average, at least one helping of fresh fruit or fruit juice daily?
YES / NO

6 Do you eat at least one helping of green vegetables or salad daily?
YES / NO

7 Do you eat two or more helpings of bread, breakfast cereals, rice or pasta daily?
YES / NO

8 If you do eat bread or cereal products, are they usually wholegrain (eg wholemeal bread, high fibre breakfast cereals, brown rice etc)?
YES / NO

9 Do you add sugar to tea or coffee?
YES / NO

10 Do you usually add salt to your food at table?
YES / NO

11 Do you eat the fat on meat?
YES / NO

Functions Bank references

Expressing Opinions p 208   Agreeing/Disagreeing p 208   Asking for/Giving Advice p 209   Expressing Likes & Dislikes p 208.

▶ Interview No 4

Section 1:
Picture
conversation

Look at the following photograph.

Now answer these questions.

1 The picture:
  a What is happening in this picture?
  b Can you describe what the men are wearing?
  c What equipment are they using, and what else is there likely to be outside the picture?
  d What kind of place does it seem to be?
  e How could the fire have started?

2 More general:
  f Would you like to do this job? Why/why not?
  g Do firemen in your country dress differently in any way?
  h Have you ever seen a building on fire? What happened?
  i How can fires in the home start?

Section 2:
Reading
passages

Read each passage carefully and be prepared to comment on them

Consider, for example, whether you think the text was spoken or written, who the speaker/writer was, and what they are talking about.

Note

You may also like to read the passages aloud but this will not necessarily be required in the examination itself.

a **Looking after the fireworks**

Never smoke when handling the fireworks or at any time during the display. Unpack the fireworks carefully, away from open fires and flammable materials, and keep them separate from their packaging. Remember that they can easily break or tear. Keep them in a metal or wooden box, which must be kept closed.

Lighting the fireworks

Read the instructions on each firework carefully. Always light them at arm's length. Make sure that all aerial fireworks, such as rockets, are directed away from spectators. They should never be fired over the heads of spectators.

b Now, what should you do if the oil does catch fire? Well, first of all, leave the chip pan where it is. Don't try to move it! Turn off the heat if you can safely. Then soak a teatowel in water and throw it over the top of the pan. If there's a lid which fits the pan, you could use that instead. Whatever you do, though, don't use water on the fire! Once you've covered the pan, leave it to cool for at least 30 minutes. Is everyone clear on that?

Section 3:
Structured
activity

The picture below shows a number of dangers which could lead to a fire or some other accident. Work with two partners to make a list of as many of these dangers as you can (there are 11 in all). Discuss how a fire or accident could be caused in each case and then write a list of instructions to help people avoid the most important dangers.

▶ Interview No 5

Section 1: Look at the following photograph.
**Picture
conversation**

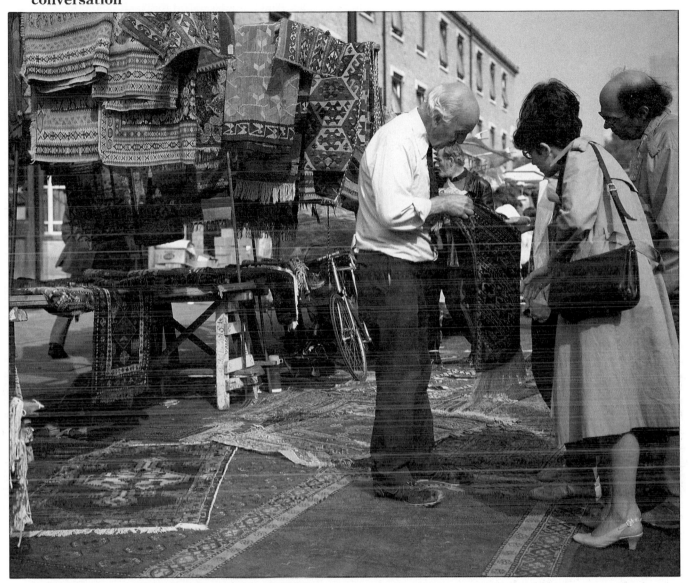

Now answer these questions.

1 The picture:
   a What kind of place is this?
   b Describe what you can see in the picture.
   c What are the man and woman wearing?
   d What could the man be saying?

2 More general:
   e Do you prefer shopping in supermarkets, small local shops or markets?
   f If you have a favourite shop, what do you like about it especially?
   g Do you prefer it when prices are fixed or do you enjoy bargaining?
   h Would you ever buy second-hand furniture?
   i Do advertisements have any influence on you when you are shopping?

Note: For the second group of questions, make sure to answer in as much detail as possible, giving your reasons and examples from your personal experience.

Section 2:
Reading
passages

Read each passage through carefully and be prepared to comment on them.

Consider, for example, whether you think the text was spoken or written, who the speaker/writer was, and what they are talking about.

a Day after day, all that awful washing up. Life's just too short to put up with it any longer. Leave it to a dishwasher. It doesn't just wash up dishes. It washes pots and pans, glasses and cups and other kitchen tools. And it doesn't stop there. It also does the drying up, which is where it really shines. Not just content with that, the Hoover Crystaljet goes further. It has seven different washing programmes, including a special economy programme that uses less electricity.

b Allow me to show you our new model, Madam. I think you'll agree that there's nothing quite like it on the market for the price. Beautiful isn't she? Neat and easy to park, but look how much space there is inside! There's room for four passengers with plenty of legroom. She's very economical too. You'll get forty to the gallon easily and yet you'd be surprised at how lively she is to drive. Would you like to take her for a trial run?

Note You may like to read the passages aloud but this will not necessarily be required in the examination itself.

Section 3:
Structured
activity

1 Study the information below:

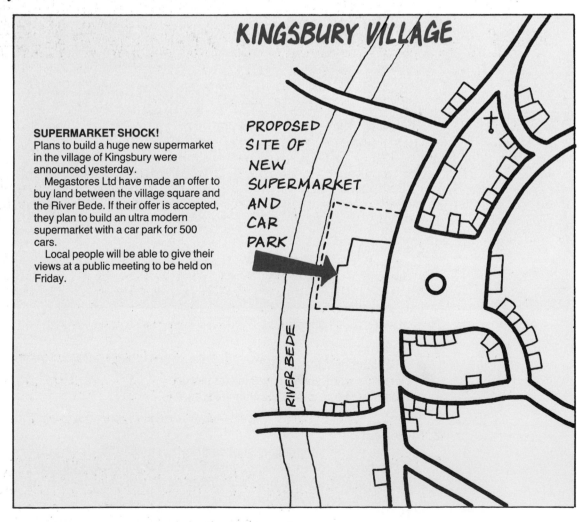

SUPERMARKET SHOCK!
Plans to build a huge new supermarket in the village of Kingsbury were announced yesterday.

Megastores Ltd have made an offer to buy land between the village square and the River Bede. If their offer is accepted, they plan to build an ultra modern supermarket with a car park for 500 cars.

Local people will be able to give their views at a public meeting to be held on Friday.

2 Work in groups of three. Student A should turn to page 216. Student B should turn to page 218. Student C should turn to page 219.

▶ Interview No 6

Section 1:
Picture
conversation

Look at the two photographs below.

 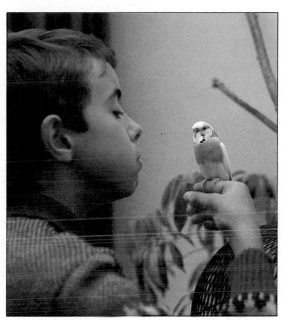

© Barnaby's

Now answer these questions.

1 The picture:
  a Describe each picture.
  b What can you guess about the two people's lives?
  c What parts do you think their pets play in their lives?
  d What pets are suitable for an old person to have? Which are unsuitable?
  e What can children learn by keeping pets? Are there any dangers to the children or the pets?

2 More general:
  f Did you have a pet as a child?
  g Are pets popular in your country?
  h Have you heard of people keeping unusual pets?
  i What animals do you prefer personally?
  j Are there any pets you would definitely not want to keep?

Section 2:
Reading
passages

Read the following passages through carefully and be prepared to comment on them. Consider, for example, whether you think the text was spoken or written, who the speaker/writer was, and what they are talking about.

Note

You may also like to read the passage aloud but this will not necessarily be required in the examination itself.

  a Another of my patients, Ben, is two years old and he sleeps on his owners' bed. Ben's sleeping arrangements are not that unusual, but the difference is that Ben doesn't allow his owners to sleep with him! Each night when he sees them getting ready for bed, he jumps on to it and watches them. If they even look at him, he growls fiercely and when they reach for the covers, he bites them. In spite of Ben's terrible behaviour, his owners still adore him and they have a practical solution to the problem – they're moving to the spare room.

b Dealing with animals in a television studio can sometimes be a problem. I was once involved in a Christmas programme which featured donkeys. They didn't like the smooth floor of the studio at all. They took two paces on it, lay down and didn't get up again until a pathway of hardboard was laid for their use. Sensible donkeys! They didn't slip, but once they realised the danger their motto was 'safety first' – lie down until it's safe to rise.

Section 3: Structured activity

You and your friend(s) have decided to pay a short visit to Bristol Zoo at lunchtime one day. You will be coming from different directions and entering by two different entrances.

You will only have about an hour to spend at the zoo so study the plan and the key and discuss:

● the best **place** to meet.
● the best **route** to take so that you can each see the animals you're most interested in, even if you can't see absolutely everything in the time. You'd also like to buy something to drink while you're there.

Notes **A** is very interested in seeing the elephants.
B wants to see the famous white tigers.
C likes birds of all kinds.

You'd all like to see the Nocturnal House which has strange 'night time' animals.

(Don't be afraid to discuss any difficulties you have with understanding the plan or with vocabulary. It's not a test of map-reading or vocabulary! Your discussion is what counts.)

You may find it useful to look at page 210 in the Functions Bank (Making Suggestions).

BRISTOL ZOO GARDENS

Guide

1	BIG CATS	17	TAPIRS
2	GREAT APES	18	ZEBRAS
3	REPTILES	19	BIRDS OF PREY & OWLS
4	WORLD OF WATER	20	MONKEY TEMPLE
5	CAMELS	21	PENGUINS
6	NOCTURNAL HOUSE	22	SLOTHS
7	MONKEYS	23	AVIARY
8	PLANT HOUSE	24	MEERKATS
9	MARMOSETS	25	ALPACAS
10	POLAR BEARS	26	AVIARY
11	KANGAROOS & STORKS	27	CHILDREN'S CORNER
12	OKAPI	28	BIRD HOUSE
13	PIGMY HIPPOPOTAMUS	29	WADING BIRD ENCLOSURE
14	ELEPHANTS	30	LEMURS & MARMOSETS
15	GIRAFFES	31	BLACK-AND-WHITE
16	FUR SEALS		COLOBUS MONKEYS & GIBBONS

＋ FIRST AID POST (when closed contact General Office in same building).
T Public Telephone.
L Ladies Toilets (Mother's room and disabled toilet at rear of Reptile House).
G Gentlemen's Toilets (disabled toilet near Rock Garden).
K Kiosk, Ices, Souvenirs, etc.
E Education Rooms and Lecture Hall.

Note: Bristol Zoo reserve the right to change exhibits at any time.

Functions Bank

▶ Expressing Likes, Dislikes and Preferences

a Likes

- I (really) | like / enjoy / love | ...ing   noun

- I'm (very) (really) | fond of / interested in / keen on | ...ing   noun

- I find ...ing) (really) | interesting / enjoyable / relaxing / fascinating / exciting etc.

b Dislikes

- I don't (really) like   ...ing   noun

- I (really) (absolutely) | hate / detest / can't bear / can't stand | ...ing   noun

- I'm not (very) (really) | fond of / interested in / keen on | ...ing   noun

- I find ...ing (a bit) (rather) | boring / dull / tiring etc.

c Preferences

- I prefer tennis / playing tennis **to** badminton. / playing badminton.

- I'd (I would) rather dance **than** jog.

▶ Asking for Opinions

What do you think of ... (the weather/the new Prime Minister/my hat)
How do you feel about ... (this suggestion/the idea of moving/going out for dinner)
What's your opinion of ... (yesterday's match/the news/the strike)

▶ Expressing Opinions

I think ... / I believe ...   +   STATEMENT

In my opinion, ... / In my view, ...   +   STATEMENT

It seems to me that ... / From my point of view, I think ... / As far as I'm concerned ... / If you ask me, ... (informal)   +   STATEMENT

▶ Agreeing

● Strongly

Yes, you're | quite / absolutely | right.

Yes, that's | quite / absolutely | right/true.

Yes, I | quite / absolutely | agree with you.

Yes, I couldn't agree with you more!

● **Reluctantly**

Well, perhaps.   Well, I suppose you may/could be right.

▶ **Disagreeing**

● **Gently**

Do you really think so?   I'm not sure you're right (about that)?
Are you sure that's right (about that)?   I agree up to a point, but don't you think . . .

● **More strongly**

But surely | that can't be right!   No, I'm | sorry but | I disagree with you | (there).
           | you don't really think . . . | afraid | I think you're wrong | (about that).
                                                           | | I can't agree with you |

● **Very forcefully**

But that's | absolute | nonsense!   You can't be serious!
           | complete | rubbish!   You must be joking!
           | total

▶ **Interrupting**

Sorry to interrupt (you) but . . .   I'd like to make a point . . .

May I | interrupt (you) | for a second . . .   Hold on a moment!
Can I | break in

▶ **Asking for Advice**

I've got a small problem . . .   Could you | give me some advice?
I'm not sure what to do . . .   Can you | offer me some advice?
I don't know much about . . .   I was wondering if you could | advise me?
You know a lot about . . .
You know more than me about . . .
You're the expert!

I'd like | your advice, | if you don't mind.   What would you do | in my place/position?
I'd appreciate | some advice, | if you were me?
I'd welcome

▶ **Giving Advice and Recommendations, and Persuading**

Why don't you . . .   How about . . .
You could . . .   What about . . .   + noun or
                                                 Have you thought of . . .   gerund

You (really) ought to . . .
          should . . .

I should . . . if I were you.
If I were you, I'd . . .

● **More formal**

I'd recommend you to . . .
My advice to you is to . .

● **Stronger**

The best thing you can do is to . . .
What you really ought to do is . .
need is . . .
I strongly advise you to . . .

Take my advice. You won't regret it!

▶ **Accepting Advice**

Yes, What | a good idea.
That's

Yes, I think I'll | take | your advice.
follow

▶ **Rejecting Advice**

Thank you | for the | advice.
Thanks | recommendation.

but (I think) I'd | rather . . . | (all the same).
better . . .
prefer to . . .

▶ **Making Suggestions**

Let's
Shall we | + infinitive
Why don't we

How about | + ing
What about

I think that | we should | + infinitive
it would be a good idea to

I suggest that we + infinitive

We'd better (not) | + infinitive
We could

▶ **Responding to Suggestions**

● **Positively**

That's a (very) good idea.
What a good idea!
That sounds (like) a (very) good idea (to me).
I think that's a very good suggestion (myself).

● **Negatively**

I don't think that's a very good idea (myself).
That doesn't sound (like) a very good idea (to me).

▶ **Asking for and Giving Permission**

● Can | I (possibly)
Could | he | come in?
May | she etc

● Is it alright if I | come in?
Would it be possible for me to

● Do | you mind if I | come in?
Would | came in?

Yes, (of course) you | can | (come in).
may

Yes, of course.
No, (I'm afraid) you can't

No, not at all. | Yes, (I'm afraid) | I do.
not in the least. | I would.

▶ **Making a Request**

Please shut the door

Could | you shut the door please?
Would |

Would you mind shutting the door (please)?

I wonder if you could | shut the door?
Do you think you could |

I wonder if you'd mind shutting the door?

▶ **Expressing Need and Use**

I'll need a camera | because . . .
| to . . .

I'll | need | to | have | a camera with me | because . . .
| have | | take | | to . . .

I can't | do | without a camera because . . .
I couldn't | manage |

A camera | is | (absolutely) | essential | for + gerund
Scissors | are | (very) | useful |
| will be | (really) | handy |
| would be | (extremely) |

If I | have | a camera | I can . . .
| take | | I'll be able to . . .
| had | | I could . . .
| took | | I'd be able to . . .

A camera | will | enable | me to . . .
| would | allow |

▶ **Asking For, and Giving Directions**

Excuse me, could you | tell me the way | to the station, please?
| direct me |
| tell me where the station is please?

No, I'm afraid I'm a stranger here myself!
Yes, of course . . .

 It's straight ahead.

 It's on the left/right.

 Go straight ahead | until you | get to . . .
Carry on | | come to . . .
Keep going | | see . . .

 Turn (sharp) left/right (at the junction/crossroads).

 Take the first/second etc turning on your left/right.

 Fork | left/right.
Branch |

 Go past the park.

Go across the crossroads.

 Go round the roundabout.

Go to the | end / top / bottom | of this | road. / hill.

You can't miss it!

► **Describing Location**

● **In 2 dimensions**

X is in the middle (of the page).
A is at the top.
B is at the bottom.
C is on the left.
D is on the right.
X is between C and D.
C and D are on either side of X.
E is above X.
X is below E.
F is in the top left-hand corner.
G is in the bottom right-hand corner.

A is in the north (of the island).
B is in the south.
C is in the east.
D is in the west.
E is to the west of the island.
F is to the north of B.

● **In 3 dimensions**

There is a garden in front of the house.
There is a tree behind the house.
There is a windmill beyond the house.
There is a pond next to/beside the house.
There are ducks on the pond.
There is a cloud above the house (higher than).
The house is below the cloud (lower than).
There is a bird over the tree (directly above).
The tree is under the bird (directly below).

► **Describing Shape**

● **In 2 dimensions**

NOUN	ADJECTIVE
A square	It's square in shape.
A rectangle	It's rectangular in shape.
A circle	It's circular in shape.
A triangle	It's triangular in shape.
An oval	It's oval in shape.
A semi-circle	It's semi-circular in shape.

COMPOUND ADJECTIVES	
	It's U-shaped.
	It's star-shaped.
	It's diamond-shaped.
	It's heart-shaped.

● In 3 dimensions

A cube	It's cubic in shape.
A cylinder	It's cylindrical in shape.
A cone	It's conical in shape.
A sphere	It's spherical in shape.

It's dome-shaped.
It's wedge-shaped.
It's pear-shaped.

● Other adjectives describing shape

straight

curved

diagonal

parallel

horizontal

vertical

rounded

pointed

sloping (of a path, garden, roof etc)

▶ Describing Sensory Perception

● Look, seem, appear + adjective

She | looks / seems / appears | tired.

Look + like + noun (resemble)

He looks like a detective.

● Taste, smell + adjective

This soup | tastes / smells | absolutely delicious.

It tastes | deliciously / slightly / rather / very / extremely / too / horribly | sweet. / creamy. / salty. / bitter.

Taste, smell + of
(have a particular taste)

This cake tastes of honey.
My hands smell of petrol.

Taste, smell + like (remind one of . . .)

This wine tastes like vinegar!
It smells like cocoa. What is it?

● Feel, sound + adjective

This material feels beautifully smooth.
Your music sounds rather loud.

Feel, sound + like + noun

This material feels like silk.
It sounds like Japanese music. Is it?

● **Colour**

It's | a | pretty | pale | green | colour.
They're | | lovely | bright | yellow |
| | horrible | dark | |

It's | pinkish | in colour.
| reddish-brown |

▶ **Describing people**

● **Hair**

He | 's got | short | straight (a) | blonde | hair.
She | | shoulder-length | curly (b) | fair |
	long	wavy (c)	red
			brown
			dark

He's bald.

| A | B | C |

● **Figure**

He's | fairly | thin.   He | 's | tall.
She | quite | slim.   She | | short.
| very | plump. | | medium height.
| extremely | fat.
| | well-built.

● **Complexion**

He's | got a | pale | complexion.
She | | fair |
| | dark |

● **Distinguishing features**

He's | got | a fringe. (a)   He's got a | beard. | (d)
She | | freckles. (b) | moustache. |
| | a scar. (c)

| A | B | C | D |

Communication Activities

**Interview No 2
Structured
activity
(page 199)**

Student A

You are on a Business Studies course at college which your parent, B, encouraged you to take. Unfortunately, you are not at all interested in the subject and, although you try, you are not doing very well.

The truth is that you love music and you are a very good musician (decide which instrument). What you really want to do is to become a professional musician. You have told your grandparent, C, but you haven't dared to tell your parent yet!

You have just shown your college report to your parent. *Wait for him/her to comment.*

**Unit 6A
Communication
activity 2
(page 84)   Student B**

**Interview No 5
Structured
activity
(page 205)**

Student A

You run a small grocery store in Kingsbury. If the supermarket is opened, you can expect to lose a lot of business because you won't be able to match its wide range of goods or its low prices.

Points to make: ● shops like yours will close down
                   ● increase in unemployment
                   ● loss of friendly, personal service
                   ● loss of old village atmosphere
Add any other points you can think of.

Unit 2A
Communication
activity
(page 23)

THE STRESS LEAGUE

Rating is from 10 to zero. The higher the rate, the greater the pressure.

Miner	8.3	Manager (commerce)	5.8
Police	7.7	Professional footballer	5.8
Journalist	7.5	Salesman, shop assistant	5.7
Pilot (civil)	7.5	Bus driver	5.4
Dentist	7.3	Farmer	4.8
Actor	7.2	Soldier	4.7
Politician	7.0	Engineer	4.3
Doctor	6.8	Hairdresser	4.3
Film producer	6.5	Secretary	4.3
Nurse	6.5	Architect	4.0
Fireman	6.3	Postman	4.0
Pop musician	6.3	Museum worker	2.8
Teacher	6.2	Librarian	2.0

Unit 1B
Communication
activity
(page 93)

How did you score?

1 *a* 1 *b* 3 *c* 0.   The ideal age is 29.

2 *a* 3 *b* 0 *c* 1.   Long-term emotional stability is essential. Distant fiancées can cause big problems.

3 *a* 0 *b* 0 *c* 3.   You have to be genuinely sociable if high seas are going to make your neighbours spill their puddings in your lap – or worse!

4 *a* 3 *b* 0 *c* 1.   A personality test. People who push forward are more likely to succeed.

5 *a* 3 *b* 1 *c* 0.   A test of honesty and respect for other people's property.

6 *a* 3 *b* 1 *c* 0.   A test of honesty again.

7 *a* 0 *b* 1 *c* 3.   Testing how practical and economical you can be.

8 *a* 0 *b* 3 *c* 1.   Smoking was forbidden on John's trip. Musicians were very popular.

9 *a* 1 *b* 0 *c* 3.   Peacemakers are like gold on a long voyage.

10 *a* 1 *b* 0 *c* 3.   It's important to have a long-term goal in mind.

11 *a* 0 *b* 0 *c* 3.   You must be able to take a joke against yourself.

12 *a* 0 *b* 1 *c* 3.   A loyalty test.

13 Score one point for each year. People who have already made a constant effort over studies are likely to do so in other areas.

14 Subtract one point for each day. Weaklings with more than a fortnight's illness should drop out here!

If you scored 40 or more, you can start getting ready tomorrow. You're an ideal candidate for a long and difficult voyage, living with others in limited space.

If you managed 20 or more, you have some of the qualities needed in a long-distance traveller, but don't start packing yet! You'll need to change some of those bad habits!

If you scored less than 20, you should look for a nice steady job with a pension. Wear warm clothes in case you catch a cold on the way to the office, and stay away from travellers of all sorts!

Interview No 2
Structured
activity
(page 199)

Student B

Your son/daughter, A, is at college on a Business Studies course. You are very keen that he/she does well because you want him/her to have a good career in business (as you did).

You don't think A has been working hard enough lately, and he/she seems to waste a lot of time playing some musical instrument. You think it's time to tell A just how important his/her studies are.

A has just shown you his/her college report for the term. *You speak first.*

Unit 2B
Communication
activity
(page 108)

Student A

Interview No 5
Structured
activity
(page 205)

Student B

You are a member of the Historic Kingsbury Society. You are afraid the new supermarket would spoil the character of the village.

Points to make: ● modern architecture unsuitable in village
● village square will be spoiled
● view of river will be spoiled by car park
● traffic problems from delivery lorries and shoppers' cars
Add any other points you can think of.

**Unit 2B
Communication
activity
(page 108)**

Student B

**Interview No 2
Structured
activity
(page 199)**

Student C

You are very fond of your grandchild, A, and you think B (his/her parent) is often too strict with him/her.

You know that A is not happy at college, doing a Business Studies course, and is not getting on very well. A has told you that he/she wants to be a professional musician, though he/she hasn't dared to tell B yet! You think that A should probably be allowed to make a career in music if that is what he/she really wants.

A has just shown his/her parent the college report for the term. *Wait for B to start.*

**Interview No 5
Structured
activity
(page 205)**

Student C

You represent Megastores Ltd and your company very much wants to build the supermarket. Kingsbury is rather old-fashioned and you expect some people to object, but you don't think they realise how many benefits there will be.

Points to make:
● cheaper prices and special offers
● very wide range of goods
● free off-street car parking
● more people visiting village, so more life and trade
● employment for 25 young people
● beautiful architect-designed building

Add any other points you can think of.

Writing Bank

Letters: Informal/Formal
Informal letters

23 Oxford Rd — Write your address (but **not** your name) on separate lines in the top right-hand corner.
Cheltenham
Gloucs. GL50 4QZ

4th August 19— Write the date below your address.

Write the first line next to the margin. Always use a name. Never begin *Dear Friend*.

Dear Gill,

Thank you for your postcard from New York. I really envy you going to all those exciting places!

There's no chance of a holiday for me this year, I'm afraid. I'm saving up to buy a car. The driving lessons are going well, and my test is booked for next month. Wish me luck!

I haven't seen you for ages and I'd love to hear all your news. Why don't you come down and stay one weekend?

Let me know if/when you'll be free.

Looking forward to hearing from you.

Love Hazel

Use separate paragraphs to:
– begin your letter
– deal with different topics

End your letter with an informal greeting: e.g. *Yours, Best wishes,* or *Love.*

220

Notes and useful language

Beginnings

It is usual to begin by referring to a letter you've received, or by making some other polite introductory comment:

Thank you for/Many thanks for *your (recent) letter/postcard.*
It was good/nice to hear from you recently.
I'm sorry I haven't *written/been in touch for such a long time.*
It's ages since *I've heard from you.* ***I hope*** *you're well./you and your family are well.*

Endings

It is usual to end with a polite remark, written on a separate line:

I look forward to/Looking forward to hearing from/seeing you.
See you soon./Write soon./Hope to hear from you soon.
Once again, thank you for *all your help.*
Give my regards/love to …

Apologies

Say what you are apologizing for and give reasons to explain your behaviour. Try to suggest a way of putting things right, if possible.

I'm writing to apologize for *missing your party last week* ***but I'm afraid*** *I was in bed with 'flu.*
I'm really sorry that I *forgot to send you a birthday card* ***but*** *I was so busy with my new job.*

If you let me know *where you bought it/how much it cost,* ***I'll gladly*** *pay for it/replace it.*
Please let me know *how much the bill is* ***and I'll gladly*** *pay it.*

Invitations – accepting/rejecting

Say what the event is and give clear details of the date, time and place. It may be helpful to give other informaation such as how to get there, who else is coming and what (if anything) to bring. It is usual, too, to ask for confirmation:

I'm/We're having a party on *Friday 19th* ***and I/we hope you'll be able to come.***
Would you like to *come/go to see 'Room With a View' with me at the weekend?*
I was wondering if you'd like to *go to the theatre/come on holiday with us?*
Could you let me/us know if *you can come/you'd like to join us?*

Thank you very much for your invitation. I'd love to come.
Thank you for asking me/inviting me to … but I'm afraid I won't be able to come/join you because …

Requests

In some cases, you may want to introduce your request immediately. In others, you may prefer to begin your letter with some brief news before going on to make the request. Either way, explain exactly what the request is, with reasons, and emphasize how grateful you would be for the help you are asking for:

I'm writing to ask for your help/you (if you could do me) a favour.
I wonder if/I was wondering if you could help me/do me a favour.
I hope you don't mind me asking but could you (possibly) …?
I'd be very/really/terribly grateful if you could …

Thank you/Congratulations/Good luck

When thanking someone for something, it is usual to say as much as possible about how useful/enjoyable/helpful it was. When offering congratulations for some success, you usually mention how well-deserved it is. When wishing someone good luck, try to reassure them or offer some friendly advice:

I'm writing to thank you for *your hospitality/the wonderful present.*
It was so kind of you to *invite me to stay with you.*
I really appreciated *all your help/advice.*

Congratulations on *passing your exams/your excellent exam results!*
You really deserved to succeed *after all your hard work!*

I wish you good luck/Good luck in/with *your exams/your driving test/your interview.*
Don't worry, I'm sure you'll do well/pass.
Do *be on time,* ***won't you, and don't forget to*** …

News/information

I thought you might be interested to hear about/know that …
This is just to let you know that …
By the way, have you heard about/did you know that …?

Formal letters

23 Oxford Road

Cheltenham

GL50 4QZ

4th August 19—

Write your address on separate lines in the top right-hand corner. Do **not** write your name.

Write the date below your address.

Write the name and address of the person or company you are writing to on the left-hand side, below the date.

The Manager

Goldspar Office Equipment

54 Old Market

Malvern

WR12 2PO

Write *Dear* ... next to the left-hand margin, followed by a comma.

Dear Sir or Madam,

I recently ordered a filing cabinet from your company and I am writing to say that I am not satisfied with the one which has just been delivered.

There are several reasons for this. In the first place, the cabinet is grey in colour rather than cream as I ordered. Secondly, the lock doesn't work. Thirdly, there is a large dent on the top, which was probably caused during delivery.

I must ask you to replace the filing cabinet with one which is the correct colour and in perfect condition. I would be grateful if you would telephone me on 06845 721399 as soon as possible in order to make the necessary arrangements.

Yours faithfully,

Hazel Smith

HAZEL SMITH (Ms)

Use separate paragraphs to:
– say why you are writing
– give details or extra information
– conclude your letter

End with *Yours faithfully,* if you began with *Dear Sir* or *Dear Madam*. End with *Yours sincerely,* if you began with a name.

Print your name clearly after your signature.

222

Notes and useful language

Beginnings/organisation

Write *Dear* + the person's name, if you know it (*Dear Mr Smith*). If not, begin *Dear Sir* (for a man), *Dear Madam* (for a woman), or *Dear Sir or Madam* (if it could be either). Don't use a title like *Dear Manager*.

In the first paragraph, clearly state your reason for writing. Use the middle paragraphs to explain the details, beginning a new paragraph for each main point. In the final paragraph, sum up and/or say what action you want to be taken.

Endings

Don't forget! If you began with a person's name, e.g. *Dear Mrs Blake*, you **must** end with *Yours sincerely*, **not** *Yours faithfully*. These endings are followed by a comma.

Job applications

First make it clear which job you are applying for, and mention where you saw the advertisement, and when. Give all the necessary information about yourself (including age, qualifications, past employment and other experience). Say why you are particularly interested in the job, and what you have to offer. Use a new paragraph for each main topic. It may also be useful to mention when you would be available for an interview:

I was interested in the advertisement in *(newpaper/magazine)* **on** *(date)* ***and I would like to apply for the post/position of*** *(job title).*
I am 21 years of age and I have a *Diploma in Business Administration.*
My reason for applying is that *I am interested in tourism and I would like to be able to use my foreign languages.*
I would be happy/able to attend an interview *at any time which is convenient to you.*

Apologies

Explain why you are apologizing and what the reasons were for your behaviour. If possible, offer to make up in some way (e.g. by paying for the damage) and/or promise that the problem won't happen again:

I am writing to apologize for *the things I said at our last meeting/losing my temper.*
I would like to say how sorry I am *about the trouble I have caused/that you were disturbed.*
The reason I missed the meeting was that *my car broke down.*
Please let me know how much it cost and I will gladly replace it.
I assure you that this will never happen again.

Complaints

State the subject of your complaint clearly in the first paragraph. Use the following paragraphs to give all the necessary details (including dates and times, the people involved, the inconvenience you've been caused, etc). Try to be clear and factual rather than emotional. Use the final paragraph to say what action you want to be taken now:

I am writing to complain about *a holiday I booked with your company.*
I am writing to say that I am not satisfied with *the standard of service at your restaurant.*
I must insist that you *refund the cost of the bill.*
I must ask you to …

Enquiries

In the first paragraph, explain what information you need. If you are responding to an advertisement, mention where you saw this. Use extra paragraphs to mention any specific questions you would like answers to:

I am writing to enquire about …
I was interested in your advertisement in 'The Daily News' and I would like to have further information about …
I would be grateful if you could send me full details of …
Could you send me *your brochure/catalogue.*
I look forward to hearing from you/receiving the information.

Opinions

Introduce the topic and give details of any letter, article, book or TV programme you are responding to. Develop your argument in separate paragraphs and sum up in the final one:

I strongly disagree with/I completely agree with *Mr Smith's letter, which appeared yesterday.*
I was interested to read the article on *immigration in Monday's* ***edition of your newspaper but*** *I don't think it gave all the facts.*
I was interested/fascinated/amused/delighted to see/hear/read …
I was horrified/shocked/disgusted to …
In my opinion *there is far too much violence in television dramas these days.*
In conclusion I feel/I believe …

Practice

Informal letters

1 An English friend of yours is planning to spend a week touring your country and has asked for your advice on what to see and do. Write a letter giving your friend practical information which you think will be helpful.

2 You recently stayed with an English penfriend and his or her family. Write a letter thanking them for their hospitality.

3 An English friend of yours is going to take an important examination soon. Write a letter wishing your friend good luck and offering any advice you can.

4 You are going away for a week and you are hoping a friend of yours will be willing to call round to feed your pet(s) and water your plants. Write a letter to your friend explaining the problem and asking for his/her help.

5 You promised to visit an English friend while on a visit to the town where he/she lives, but you were unable to do so. Write a letter apologizing and explaining the reasons.

Formal letters

1 You recently had a party at your house and your next-door neighbour rang up in the middle to complain about the noise. Write a letter of apology.

2 You have seen an advertisement for a company which specializes in bicycling holidays. Write a letter requesting more information and asking for some answers to specific questions.

3 You belong to a film club which shows a lot of English and American films but you are not happy with the type of film that has been shown recently. Write a letter to the Club Secretary explaining your views and making a few suggestions for the future.

4 You had a very bad meal at a restaurant recently. Write a letter complaining about the food and the service.

5 An English travel company is advertising for host families for English students on study visits to your country. Write a letter of application, describing your family and home.

Descriptions

> Write a description of a favourite member of your family.
> Describe a town or city anywhere in the world which you
> particularly like.

INTRODUCTION
sets the scene

My cousin, Christopher, is the son of my father's brother. He's three years younger than me and we didn't know each other very well as children because he and his family lived on the other side of the country at that time. Since then, he's married and moved closer so we meet quite often and I've got to know him much better.

different tenses to fill in the background

appearance/ clothes

There's nothing very remarkable about Chris's appearance. He's of average height and medium build, and he's got curly, mousy hair and a fair complexion. As he's quite short-sighted like me, he wears glasses. The clothes he likes are mostly casual: jeans or shorts and a tee-shirt. I don't think I've ever seen him in a suit!

character

He's a very active person who loves the outdoor life. He's extremely practical and he can build or repair almost anything, no matter how complicated it is. Another characteristic he has is that he's very outgoing. If you go to a show with him and members of the audience are invited onto the stage, Chris will be the first to volunteer. The thing I appreciate most about him, however, is his sense of humour. If I'm depressed, he can always cheer me up with a joke or a funny story.

Vary the sentence structure

CONCLUSION
sums up your feelings

They say you can choose your friends but not your relations. In Chris's case, I feel I'm very lucky because he's not only my cousin but also one of my best friends.

Notes and useful language

Structure

Descriptions need to be structured, like other tyes of writing, so that they have an introduction, a middle and an end. In the introduction, you should briefly set the scene, perhaps by saying why you have chosen the person or place you're going to describe. After that you should deal with the different main aspects of the subject in separate paragraphs. Use the final paragraph to sum up your feelings about the subject, if possible in a humorous or memorable way.

Personalization

Some topics give you more opportunity for personal comment than others. In general, though, including your reactions and feelings and an occasional touch of humour will make your description more interesting and enjoyable for the reader.

Tenses

You may be asked to write a description in the present, in the past or to make a comparison between the past and the present. Think carefully about the tenses you use: *He rides a bicycle* (present habit), *He's learning to play the violin* (happening now), *We've been friends for years* (links past and present), *It was raining* (sets the scene), *She frowned when she saw me* (past action).

Sentence structure

One problem which arises with this kind of writing is that you can find yourself beginning all your sentences in the same way: *He looks ...*, *He's got ...*, *He wears ....* This makes the description rather boring to read, so try to vary the sentence structure: *His eyes are ...*, *The first thing you notice is ...*, *Another characteristic is ....*

Vocabulary

Descriptions give you a golden opportunity to show off your vocabulary. Don't waste it! Avoid using a narrow range of adjectives like *big/small*, *good*, *nice* – think about better, more precise ones.

Describing people

Possible aspects: your relationship with the person/how you met, their appearance and style of clothing, their character, and your personal feelings about them.

Appearance (see Functions Bank, page 214):
  S/he looks/seems/appears ...
  S/he's got short, curly hair and a fringe.
  S/he's short with a pale complexion.

Clothes (see page 51):
  S/he usually wears jeans.

Order of adjectives (see Study Box, page 42):
  a brand-new white woollen sweater.

Describing places/events

Possible aspects: your interest in the place/event, your impressions when you first went there, main characteristics, location, atmosphere, sights, sounds, people, summing up/comparison with later visit.

Location (see Functions Bank, page 212):
  in the middle, at the top/bottom, on the left/right
  in the north, to the north of ...
  in front of, behind, beyond, above, over, below, under

Describing objects

Possible aspects: structure, shape, colour, material, use.

Shape (see Functions Bank, page 212):
  It is shaped like a circle/It's circular in shape/
  It's star-shaped.
  straight, curved, horizontal, diagonal, vertical, pointed, sloping

Sensory perception (see Functions Bank, page 213):
  It looks/seems/appears ... + adjective
  It tastes/smells/feels/sounds ... + adjective
  It feels/sounds like ... + noun
  It's a pretty pale pink colour.

Describing processes/instructions

Sequence markers:
  First ..., Next/After that .../Finally ...
  When/Once you have (done) that ...
  Before/After doing/you (do) ...

Purpose clauses (see Study Box, page 140):
  for + -ing
  to/in order to/so as to + infinitive
  so that + clause

Practice

1 Describe your ideal house and its location, giving reasons for your choices.

2 Write a description of a person who has had an important influence on your life.

3 Describe a party you've attended recently.

4 Describe a favourite meal or dish. What ingredients are needed and how is it prepared?

5 Write a description of your bedroom, its furniture and contents

Important note: In the First Certificate exam you must write between 120 and 180 words. The model given on page 225 is longer, in order to illustrate the various useful points.

Discussions

> There's no need to write letters any more. Telephoning is a better way of communicating with people. Do you agree?

OPENING introducing topic and argument

It's certainly quicker to telephone than to write a letter but it may not always be the best way to communicate. The right form of communication to use depends, like so many other things in life, on the circumstances.

qualifying the statement

points in favour of telephoning

Telephoning is ideal if you want immediate action. You wouldn't want to write to the plumber if you had water pouring through your ceiling, for example! It's also the obvious choice if you need a quick answer to a question like "What time is the next train to Oxford?" or "Did I leave my wallet in your shop?" Many problems can be solved more easily and decisions taken more quickly if you can discuss them with someone on the phone rather than wait for a reply to a letter. Finally, few people would disagree that telephoning is a pleasant way to keep in touch with friends and family.

giving specific examples

Introduce opposite point of view

points against telephoning/in favour of writing

On the other hand, there can be a number of disadvantages to telephoning. In the first place, some problems are too complicated to explain on the phone, especially if they involve facts and figures, and it may be clearer if you set them out in a letter. Secondly, it might be important to have a record of what you say, especially if it's a booking or a complaint. Last but not least, telephoning, especially long-distance, can be terribly expensive.

listing reasons

further support for letter writing

The nice thing about receiving letters is that you can keep them and re-read them. Who wouldn't rather have a six-page letter full of news from a friend abroad than a two-minute telephone call on a bad line?

CONCLUSION expressing personal view and summing up

To sum up, letter writing is far from dead, in my view. Each form of communication has its advantages and disadvantages: the important thing to recognize is which is more appropriate for what you want to say, and to whom.

balancing the argument

Notes

Topics

Typical discussion topics include statements which you are asked to agree or disagree with (e.g. *There's too much violence on television*) and invitations to discuss aspects of a subject (e.g. *What are the advantages and disadvantages of air travel?*)

Approach

Generally, the important thing is to consider the various aspects of the topic before giving a balanced opinion. Occasionally, you may be asked directly for a personal opinion (e.g. *What's the best way to bring up children?*);

but even here you would need to consider some different views so that you can contrast them with your own.

Structure

The structure of a discursive composition should be clear and logical. In the first paragraph, introduce the topic and your argument. In the next, deal with one aspect of the topic. Give supporting evidence in following paragraphs if necessary. After that, consider the opposite point of view. In the final paragraph, sum up your argument and give a balanced personal opinion.

Useful language

Introducing the topic

Many people believe/feel that …
It is said …
People's opinions on … differ widely.

Supporting your argument

One of the main advantages of … is that …
In the first place,/Firstly,/To begin with, …
Secondly,/Thirdly,/Finally,/Last, but not least, …

Adding further reasons

In addition,/What is more,/Furthermore,
(see Addition Links, page 67)

Expressing an opposite point of view

On the other hand, there are (also) a number of disadvantages.

Linking sentences

Although …,/However,/In spite of this, Despite
(see Concession links, page 67)
while/whereas (see Contrast links, page 168)

Expressing opinions

In my view/opinion,/It seems to me that …
(see Functions bank, page 208)

Summing up

In conclusion,/To sum up,/On balance,
(see Summing up, page 168)

Practice

1 What do you think the advantages and disadvantages of living in the country may be?

2 What, in your opinion, is the best way to learn a language?

3 It has been said that childhood is the happiest time of one's life. Do you agree?

4 What do you think of the idea, expressed in some countries, that women should be paid a wage for the work they do in the home?

5 'The most important quality in a partner is a sense of humour'. Do you agree?

Important note: In the First Certificate exam you must write between 120 and 180 words. The model given on page 227 is longer, in order to illustrate the various useful points.

Narratives

Describe a journey you made when everything went wrong.

OPENING
to catch the reader's attention

You don't necessarily expect everything to go smoothly when you're travelling. There's always likely to be the odd delay or small problem to deal with. Just occasionally, though, it seems that everything that can go wrong does go wrong, and then you begin to wish you'd stayed at home.

past continuous to set the scene

I had spent a week staying with friends in Eastern Europe and I was now beginning my journey home. Having got to the station in good time to catch the train, I went to the ticket office to buy a ticket. Imagine my dismay when the ticket clerk explained that the train had been cancelled and that there wasn't another one that day. Luckily there was a bus I could catch, but it didn't leave for two hours so I spent the intervening time walking the streets of the town, getting hotter and stickier by the minute.

events in clear sequence

When I finally boarded the bus, all the seats had been taken, so I had to stand for the first hour of the journey.

background

perfect participle for events before the main events

sequence links

new paragraph for each main stage

By the time we arrived, I was exhausted and longing for a shower, so I looked for a taxi and showed the driver the name of the hotel my friends had recommended. You've guessed it! He didn't recognize the hotel and wasn't interested in finding out where it was. Instead, I took a tram but, believe it or not, the tram broke down before we reached my stop. Fortunately, I had a map so I walked the last kilometre before practically collapsing in the hotel.

Things seemed to go better after that. I was relaxing in my room when an American girl I'd met at Reception knocked on my door and said, "Hi, I've got a lot of food left over from my journey and I can't possibly eat it all. I was wondering if you'd like to come and share it?" She was very friendly and we had great fun picnicking and chatting about our adventures. My flight was leaving the next morning so, after an hour or so, I said goodbye to her and returned to my room to pack my bags and look out my travel documents. It was only then that I discovered I had lost the return half of my airline ticket!

past perfect for events before the main events

direct speech for variety and interest

ENDING
to explain the final result or to surprise or amuse the reader

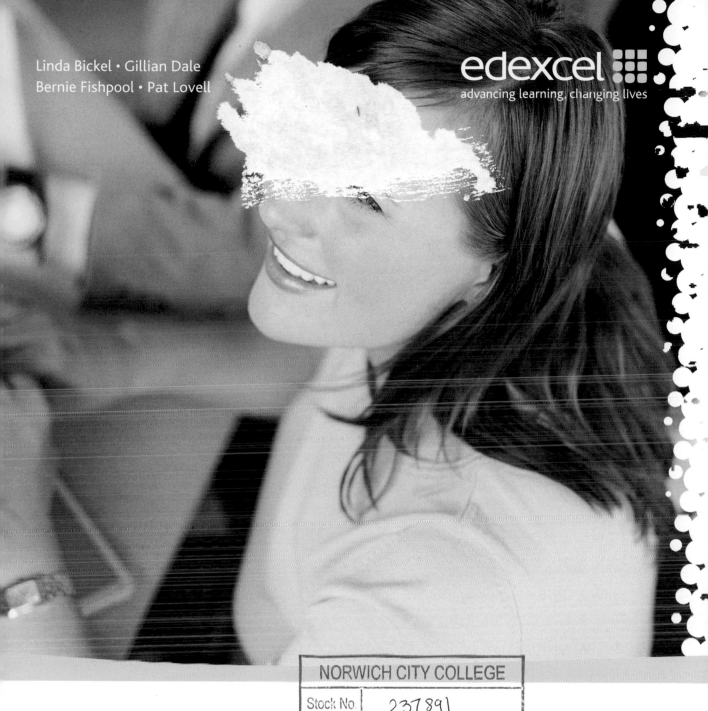

Linda Bickel • Gillian Dale
Bernie Fishpool • Pat Lovell

edexcel
advancing learning, changing lives

Edexcel Diploma

Business, Administration and Finance

Level 1 Foundation Diploma

Published by
Pearson Education
Edinburgh Gate
Harlow
Essex
CM20 2JE

© Pearson Education Ltd 2009

The right of Linda Bickel, Gillian Dale, Bernie Fishpool and Pat Lovell to be identified as authors of this Work has been asserted by them in accordance with the Copyright, Designs and Patents Act, 1988.

ISBN: 978-1-84690-510-0

Designed and typeset by Steve Moulds, DSM Partnership
Illustrations by Oxford Designers and Illustrators
Picture research by Thelma Gilbert
Cover photo © Plainpicture Ltd: Rauschen
Index by Indexing Specialists (UK) Ltd.
Printed and bound in Great Britain at Scotprint, Haddington

Acknowledgements

The publisher would like to thank the following for their kind permission to reproduce their photographs:

(key: b-bottom; c-centre; l-left; r-right; t-top)

Alamy Images: Ace Stock 92; Ali Arman 50; Avatra Images 27; Greg Balfour-Evans 41; Mark J. Barrett 11; Mike Goldwater 150; Imagestate 48; Darren Jenkins 152; mediablitzimages 144; Network Photographers 91; Martin Norris 73; Purple Marbles 151; Adrian Sherratt 160; TNT Magazine 101; Zak Waters 116; Janine Wiedel 25; David Young-Wolff 164; **Corbis:** 31, 32, 42; **DK Images:** 17b, 65; **Early Learning Centre**: 123; **Getty Images:** 18, 35, 38, 76; **iStockphoto:** 9, 45, 79, 115, 149; **PA Photos:** 168; **Pearson Education Ltd:** 37; Gareth Boden 146; istock 112; Punchstock 176; **Rex Features:** 19, 68, 86, 118, 162, 171, 175; **Science & Society Picture Library:** 17t; **Roger Scruton**: 22, 84, 108, 121

All other images © Pearson Education Ltd

Every effort has been made to trace the copyright holders and we apologise in advance for any unintentional omissions. We would be pleased to insert the appropriate acknowledgement in any subsequent edition of this publication.